PARE LORENTZ AND THE DOCUMENTARY FILM

PARE LORENTZ

AND THE DOCUMENTARY FILM

by Robert L. Snyder

University of Oklahoma Press : Norman

Library of Congress Catalog Card Number: 68–10301

Copyright 1968 by the University of Oklahoma Press, Publishing Division of the University. Composed and printed at Norman, Oklahoma, U.S.A., by the University of Oklahoma Press. First edition.

TO PARE LORENTZ, WHO HAD THE IMAGINATION TO CONCEIVE THE IDEA OF FILMS OF MERIT AND THE TALENT AND DETERMINATION TO MAKE FILMS OF MERIT

PREFACE

On January 28, 1963, Pare Lorentz received a gold medal from Secretary of Agriculture Orville Freeman as part of the centennial activities of the department. The award was made specifically for his production *The River*, and is only one of a series of honors that have come to Mr. Lorentz for his film work for the government.

Lorentz's films *The Plow That Broke the Plains*, *The River*, and *The Fight for Life* are classics of documentary film making. These films and those produced by the United States Film Service under his supervision were the only ones ever made by the government of the United States during peacetime that were intended to be seen by the general public on commercial screens. The idea was Lorentz's.

Although many books have been written on motion pictures and documentary films, there is no book dealing exclusively with Lorentz's work. Much of the information reported here is being printed in book form for the first time.

Lorentz's work has been presented in a recent series of television programs by the National Education Television (NET) network. Three of the films—*The Plow That Broke the Plains*, *The River*, and *Power and the Land*—are available from the Department of Agriculture.

This book is not a complete chronicle of Lorentz's service with the government. When Congress refused to appropriate funds for the continuance of the Film Service in 1940, he resigned. Following the outbreak of the Second World War, he accepted a commission in the Air Corps and formed a special technical service unit to produce training films for transient pilots of the major air ferry routes around the world. Floyd Crosby and Lloyd Nosler, from his old crew, joined him. They received decorations for their work. In 1946 Lorentz became Chief of Motion Pictures, Music, and Theatre in the Occupied Areas of Germany, under the Civil Affairs Division of the War Department. At this time he produced *The Nuremberg Trials* for the high commissioner of Germany, General Lucius Clay. Since then he has headed his own motion picture consultant firm in New York City.

The production of Lorentz's films raised questions about the government's use of media to inform the public about national problems and concerns. How is the government to inform the public when the commercial media do not? Why should the government be denied use of the most effective media? (It can publish books, pamphlets, and so on.) If the government does produce films, how can they be kept from the public when they are produced with public funds? These questions are still unanswered today.

I am especially indebted to Pare Lorentz for granting me access to his personal files, for responding to a barrage of questions over a number of years, and for graciously providing materials that became available later or had been overlooked.

I wish also to thank Arch Mercey, Floyd Crosby, Virgil Thomson, Frances Flaherty, Joris Ivens, King Vidor, Tom Parkinson, Joe Sullivan, Douglas Moore, and Oliver Griswold for taking the time to answer questions and provide information that gives this book much of its value; Herold Kooser of Iowa State University, Ames, Iowa, for granting me the opportunity to see a number of the films; Mrs. Eileen Bowser for making available the facilities of the Museum of Modern Art Film Library; John Kuiper of the Motion Picture Section of the Library of Congress for guidance in organizing the material; Pearl Andrews for typing the manuscript; and especially Irene, Barry, Wendy, Robbie, and Richie for waiting patiently until the book was finished.

ROBERT L. SNYDER

January 15, 1968
Oshkosh, Wisconsin

CONTENTS

ILLUSTRATIONS

PARE LORENTZ AND THE DOCUMENTARY FILM

I

THE ROOTS OF THE FILMS OF MERIT

In 1948, the World Union of Documentary, meeting in Czechoslovakia, defined documentary film as follows:

> ... all methods of recording on celluloid any aspect of reality interpreted either by factual shooting or by sincere and justifiable reconstruction, so as to appeal either to reason or emotion, for the purpose of stimulating the desire for, and the widening of human knowledge and understanding, and of truthfully posing problems and their solutions in the spheres of economics, culture, and human relations.[1]

This definition was subscribed to by fourteen nations attending the meeting. Ten years earlier, Pare Lorentz, in an interview with William Pinkerton, described a documentary film as "a factual film which is dramatic."[2]

The motion picture usually given credit for being the first documentary film by an American is *Nanook of the North* (1920). This recording of the life of an Eskimo was produced, directed, and photographed by Robert Flaherty in the frozen wastes of northern Canada with a native Eskimo as its star. The film was quite different from what Hollywood was offering at the time:

> It had no plot in the dramatic sense, nor was it fictional in the literary sense. It was a photographic description of the real life of eskimos in their own haunts, made without artificial properties or professional actors. Its fidelity alone made it fresh, honest, and far more moving than any studio-enacted film could have been.[3]

Following the success of this film, Flaherty was called to

[1] Paul Rotha, *Documentary Film*, 30–31.
[2] William Pinkerton, Associated Press news release, Washington, October 13, 1938. From the personal files of Pare Lorentz.
[3] Lewis Jacobs, *The Rise of the American Film*, 369.

Hollywood by Paramount Pictures and sent to the South Seas to direct a documentary film of life in the islands of the Pacific. This marked the beginning of a series of three trips to the South Seas by Flaherty, each trip for a different Hollywood studio. On the last two trips, Flaherty was accompanied by outstanding Hollywood directors, with whom he was supposed to co-operate. All three experiences were unsatisfactory and, in the last two instances, unhappy for Flaherty.[4] Flaherty left the United States for England, where he was able to solicit financial support for the production of three films: *Industrial Britain* (1931), *Man of Aran* (1934), and *Elephant Boy* (1937).

While Flaherty was producing his first film in the South Seas, three Europeans were producing significant documentary films on the European continent. The French Alberto Cavalcanti, in *Rien que les heures* (1926), and the German Walter Ruttman, in *Berlin* (1927), presented impressions of city life. Joris Ivens produced and directed two documentary films in the Netherlands: *The Bridge* (1927) and *Rain* (1929).

In the late twenties, documentary films were being produced also in Soviet Russia. These productions tended to fall into two separate schools or traditions. One school of filming was influenced by the experiments begun by Dziga Vertov in the technique called the "Kino-Eye"; this school has been called the "News-Reel Tradition" by Paul Rotha.[5] Of perhaps even greater importance in Soviet Russia was the development of what Rotha described as the "Propagandist Tradition,"[6] including the films of Pudovkin and Eisenstein.

The Propagandist Tradition became important also in the development of motion pictures in Great Britain, according to Rotha, who was active in the production of films there.[7] The Empire Marketing Board was created in 1928 for the purpose of

----

[4] *Ibid.*, 369–70. For a detailed account of Flaherty's career, see Richard Griffith, *The World of Robert Flaherty*, and Arthur Calder-Marshall, *The Innocent Eye* (New York, Harcourt, Brace & World, Inc., 1963).

[5] *Op. cit.*, 88.

[6] *Ibid.*, 92.

[7] *Ibid.*, 96.

[8] *Ibid.*

4

promoting "all the major researches across the world which affect the production or preservation or transport of the British Empire's food supplies."[8] Included among the forty-five departments of the board was the Film Unit, headed originally by John Grierson and Walter Creighton. In addition to producing one outstanding film —*Drifters* (1929)—this period was significant for encouraging the atmosphere of freedom and experimentation that developed in the Film Unit under Grierson's supervision and encouragement and for the productions of later years that resulted from this encouragement.

Much of the experimentation was necessitated by the limited funds provided for the production of the films. Ways had to be found to produce quality films on budgets below those of commercial producers. A parallel situation was to face Pare Lorentz throughout the period in which he produced films for the government of the United States.

The Film Unit under Grierson not only attracted and developed outstanding new cinematic talent but drew to itself at least one established name in the field—Robert Flaherty, who joined the unit to direct *Industrial Britain* (1931) with Grierson.

Economic difficulties arising out of the depression caused the British government to eliminate the Empire Marketing Board, the Film Unit, and the film library. But this was not the end of documentary production within the British government. In 1933 a new sponsor, the General Post Office, was found to support the work of the Film Unit and take over its film library.[9] The Film Unit and its library were selected to play a part in the public relations activities of the General Post Office because

> It was felt . . . with its pictures of life in Great Britain and in so many overseas parts of the Empire, [it] afforded the best possible setting for a special series of films depicting those postal, airmail, telegraphic and telephonic resources by which communications are maintained within the United Kingdom and the rest of the Empire.[10]

[9] *Ibid.*, 99.

[10] *Ibid.* This purpose of the Film Unit was set forth in the Preface to the *G.P.O. Film Library Catalogue*, 1933.

5

The films produced by and for the British government were an important contribution to the history of documentary films and motion pictures. Through them the possibility of using films for propaganda, for disseminating government information, and for shaping public opinion was shown to have value.[11]

Government production of documentary films was limited mainly to the Soviet Union, Great Britain, Germany, and Italy. The production of films to be distributed to the general public had not yet been tried by the federal government of the United States, although documentary productions had been known in this country since 1920.

Until 1935, when Pare Lorentz began shooting his first film for the Resettlement Administration (RA), the federal government had given little consideration to producing films for theatrical and commercial distribution.[12] The Creel Committee had produced such films for distribution during World War I.[13]

Motion picture production activity in the federal government began in the Department of Agriculture. In 1908, photographers in the department were convinced of the potential of motion pictures to communicate information. Either because they did not know what the secretary's reaction would be to such activity or because they knew all too well what he would say, they installed equipment for developing motion picture film in the Department of Agriculture laboratories without the secretary's knowledge. One of their first films had nothing to do with farming but was a record of flight by the Wright brothers that Department of Agriculture photographers shot for the Army Signal Corps.

These film experiments continued on this clandestine basis for many months, but it soon became apparent that if the work was to grow and obtain financial support Secretary James Wilson's support would have to be gained. The photographers knew this would

[11] For a full account of the British production record, see Rotha, *op. cit.*, 96–100, and Arts Enquiry, *The Factual Film* (London, Oxford University Press, 1949).

[12] Film Council of America, *Sixty Years of 16mm Film, 1923–1983*, 149.

[13] The official name of the Creel Committee was the Committee on Public Information. George Creel was appointed chairman on April 14, 1917.

not be a simple task because the secretary had once described motion pictures as "a work of the devil, a disreputable medium of expression."[14] They tackled the problem by deciding to shoot footage of the secretary when he would not know he was being photographed and to show the footage to him later. The secretary was scheduled to address a large meeting of farm boys, and the camera was set up in the room in such a way that he would not be likely to notice it. The crew carefully developed and printed the film. Wilson's first response to the invitation to see himself on film was one of surprise, but he agreed to come to the screening. He was delighted with the film, and his attitude changed from opposition to open support.[15] As a result, an office of the federal government for the first time decided to support motion picture production.

The production of government-sponsored motion pictures for release to the general public began three years after the Department of Agriculture started its experiments when the Department of Interior made a motion picture of the Pima Indian Reservation. A year later, in 1912, an agency of the government, the Civil Service Commission, asked a commercial producer, the Edison Company, to make a film.[16] This film, *Won through Merit*, described the operation of the government merit system at that time. According to Richard D. MacCann, "This is probably the earliest example in the federal government of a specific film planned for public relations purposes, but it stood alone and was not followed by any department program."[17]

After producing the Pima Indian Reservation film in 1911, the Department of Interior produced a series on the National Parks, other Indian reservations, and conservation subjects, its program

[14] Alfred Stefferud (ed.), *After a Hundred Years: The Yearbook of Agriculture, 1962*, 627.

[15] *Ibid.*

[16] Hartley Howe, "U.S. Film Service Presents," *U.S. Camera*, June–July, 1940. From the personal files of Pare Lorentz.

[17] Richard D. MacCann, "Documentary Film and Democratic Government: An Administrative History from Pare Lorentz to John Huston" (unpublished Ph.D. dissertation, Harvard University, 1951), 138.

being mainly one of public relations. The National Park films, for example, stressed the availability of recreation in the parks.

The next impetus given to the Agriculture film program came on September 12, 1913, when Secretary Wilson's successor, David Houston, appointed an interbureau committee to investigate the practicality of using films.[18] The committee reported that, "while the direct educational value of the motion picture could not be definitely predicted, the employment of films offered other advantages which warranted the Department in using them in its extension work."[19] The Office of Motion Pictures, however, was not established until July 1, 1922.

In the first decade of the century, the Department of War became the third largest producer of films in the government, ranking behind the Departments of Agriculture and Interior. The Signal Corps filmed most of these productions.[20] Until World War I, many of the early efforts of the War Department were simple recruitment films in the form of travelogues or short commercials that resembled posters in motion.

The advent of World War I added two additional objectives for Army film-making activities: training films, and a motion picture record of combat. In 1917, the Bray Company, a private producer of motion pictures, urged the War Department to attend a screening of sample offerings of animated teaching films they had made.[21] After the screening, the department ordered sixty-two training films, which remained in circulation until 1928.

A large collection of combat footage was accumulated by Signal Corps photographers. The Creel Committee released some of the footage to the public, and other footage was released for newsreels or was utilized in Army training films. This combat footage returned to the screen in 1924 in *Flashes of Action*, a four-reeler for soldiers described by Hartley as being "episodic, with

[18] Thomas M. Pryor, "Uncle Sam: Film Producer," *New York Times*, July 12, 1936.

[19] MacCann, *op. cit.*, 153, quoting Raymond Evans, "USDA Motion Picture Service, 1908–1943," *Business Screen*, Vol. V, No. 1 (1943).

[20] This department's interest dates back to 1908, when the Agriculture photographers filmed a Wright brothers flight by request.

[21] MacCann, *op. cit.*, 142.

little continuity."[22] Some of this Signal Corps footage was borrowed from newsreel companies by Lorentz for use in his film *The Plow That Broke the Plains*.

Following World War I, motion picture activity in the government increased. The Department of Agriculture established the Office of Motion Pictures as a separate unit on July 1, 1922; it had been placed under the Extension Service in 1918, with Clyde Warburton as director.[23]

The primary purpose of the Department of Agriculture provided the motivation for the program. John Gaus and Leon Walcott have described this purpose and its importance: "In fact, the Department might be thought of quite properly as having been established as an agricultural information center for the nation as a whole and for farmers in particular. Consequently, the program of information was one of the most important aspects of its work."[24]

Here we have a governmental department intended to provide information to the public, a fact overlooked by those who criticize information activities by the government as having no legal precedent.

During this period, the Department of Interior continued to expand its program so that by the 1930's it was producing about twenty-five reels a year.[25] Also, the Bureau of Mines in the Department of the Interior became an active film producer during this period, and various other government agencies had training films made for their employees.

Still, this production activity was sporadic. Little of it was done with a continued program in mind, and none of it seems to have been intended for general commercial distribution. The Women's Bureau of the Department of Labor, for example, produced three silent films during a ten-year period: *The Story of the*

[22] William Hartley, *Selected Films for American History and Problems* (New York, Columbia University Press, 1940), 172.

[23] Pryor, "Uncle Sam: Film Producer," *New York Times*, July 12, 1936.

[24] John Gaus and Leon Walcott, *Public Administration and the Department of Agriculture*, 361.

[25] Fanning Hearon, "Interior's Division of Motion Pictures," *School Life*, September, 1937, 6.

Women's Bureau (1927), *Within the Gates* (1930), and *Behind the Scenes in the Machine Age* (1936).[26]

Government motion picture activity accelerated considerably in the 1930's. In addition to the films mentioned above, the Signal Corps turned out an average of six films a year between 1930 and 1937. After 1933, the productions were all released with sound tracks, many on 16-mm. stock.[27]

By the time *The Plow That Broke the Plains* (1936) was produced, two additional departments had turned out single films: the Post Office Department made the single-reeler *Following a Postage Stamp* (1935); the Justice Department, a one-reel answer to Hollywood's prison films, *Protecting the Public* (1936), which concerned the Board of Prisons and such institutions as Alcatraz, Leavenworth, and Atlanta.[28]

The Department of Commerce produced films about its branches, such as the Bureau of Air Commerce and the Bureau of Fisheries, and even attempted a film on foreign trade, *Commerce around the Coffee Cup* (1936). After 1936, the Department of Commerce attempted no further films.[29]

In 1937, Fanning Hearon, then director of the Interior's Division of Motion Pictures, reported that the division had been producing about twenty-five reels per year during the 1930's.[30] Some of these films showed New Deal activities, such as the Civilian Conservation Corps, large-scale farming practices, as well as the progress of the work of the Bureau of Reclamation on Boulder and Grand Coulee dams. According to Hearon, these films were written, photographed, edited, and processed by the Division of Motion Pictures.[31]

Hearon summarized the philosophy behind the department's motion picture program in 1937: "Activities of the Division of Motion Pictures are based upon two beliefs: 1. It is the privilege

[26] MacCann, *op. cit.*, 146.
[27] John Devine, *Films as an Aid in Training Public Employees*, 5.
[28] MacCann, *op. cit.*, 49.
[29] *Ibid.*
[30] Hearon, "Interior's Division of Motion Pictures," *School Life*, September, 1937, 6.
[31] *Ibid.*

10

of the people to be thoroughly and impartially informed of the Government's business and [it is] the responsibility of Government to provide the information; 2. Pictures are made to be seen."[32]

In spite of Hearon's statement that the productions of the division should be seen by the public, no attempt was made to seek commercial distribution for these short films.

Before Lorentz's activities began in 1935, the only government agency outside the Department of the Interior to show an interest in producing motion pictures designed to have an effect on public opinion was the Works Progress Administration (WPA). The WPA, like the Resettlement Administration, Lorentz's first sponsor, was a new agency that was given the task of launching an unpopular and much criticized program. Harry Hopkins, WPA administrator, said at an appropriations hearing, "We felt that the people were not getting any adequate or proper information as to the way our funds were being expended."[33] Those in charge of the program felt that films would be an answer. One of the congressmen present at the hearing, Representative John Taber, charged the WPA with distributing propaganda; Hopkins countered that the propaganda material was simply "published reports of our work to show what we were doing."[34]

The most remarkable WPA production was a very short (one-half reel) film called *Hands* (1934). This film, released by Pathé, was a skillfully and artistically photographed and edited series of short scenes of hands, idle, at work, and finally receiving checks from the government and putting the money back into circulation. The WPA obtained commercial screenings for this film and some of its other shorts by having its state directors solicit screenings in the commercial theaters of their states.[35]

The WPA became affiliated with Pathé in another, less successful, venture. Plans were made to produce a series of six-

[32] *Ibid.*, 7.

[33] U.S. House of Representatives, *First Deficiency Appropriations Bill for 1937*, 75 Cong., 2 sess., 114–15.

[34] This same congressman would later harass the Film Service on similar grounds.

[35] James McCamy, *Government Publicity*, 124.

11

minute films to explain the work of various relief agencies such as the WPA.[36]

Before any of these films were completed, the WPA negotiated a contract with Pathé News for the production of a series of newsreels intended to accomplish the same purpose. Hopkins invited bids from forty-one motion picture producers for thirty newsreels. Only five companies responded to the invitation, and Pathé won with a bid of $4,280 per reel. An attractive feature of the contract was that Pathé agreed to distribute, without charge, one such WPA newsreel a month as a part of its own release.[37]

Pathé experienced considerable difficulty in meeting its commitments. Few of the films were delivered on schedule. The charge of "propaganda" was made by Republican and conservative opponents.[38] For example, Republican House Leader Bertrand Snell objected to having "propaganda . . . paid for out of relief funds."[39]

By 1935, increased demands for motion pictures within the Department of Agriculture resulted in the building of a sound stage in the department in Washington. This represented a substantial growth from the beginnings of production in 1908 in an eight-foot by twelve-foot attic room with one Jenkins camera and two or three pin racks for tray development.[40]

The government's basic lack of interest in producing films for theatrical distribution continued, however, until the time of the release of *The Plow That Broke the Plains* (1936) by the Resettlement Administration. The official department policy of the time was set forth by Raymond Evans, director of the Office of Motion Pictures of the Department of Agriculture:

> Though an occasional motion picture because of its scenic value has found a place on the programs of metropolitan houses, the greater part of our theatre circulation is in small rural towns where the

[36] *New York Times*, April 13, 1936.

[37] Raymond L. Fielding, "A History of the American Motion Picture Newsreel" (unpublished Ph.D. dissertation, University of Southern California, 1961), 325.

[38] *New York Times*, August 7, 1936.

[39] "WPA: Pathé Wins Film Contract as 'New Deal Goes Hollywood,'" *Newsweek*, August 15, 1936, 18.

[40] MacCann, *op. cit.*, 154.

patrons of the theatre have a constructive interest in the subject matter presented. It is contrary to our policy to produce propaganda films of the *ex parte* type and no effort is made to compete in the motion picture field.[41]

Apparently Evans was unaware of the motion picture revolution about to occur within an agency of his department.

The record of film production before Lorentz's arrival in Washington in 1935 contains no film that can be called a documentary according to the definition presented at the beginning of this chapter. Only *Hands*, the WPA's half-reeler, comes close. The Department of Agriculture, which had produced the largest number of films until that time, emphasized information rather than promotion and avoided documentary films as a matter of policy. Few government films were intended for general distribution. Only the wartime reports produced by the Creel Committee and certain of the WPA films were so intended, and distribution of most of the latter was not through regular commercial channels.

Yet the number of government productions is impressive. By 1935, twenty-two federal agencies had produced more than four hundred films. Three departments—Agriculture, Interior, and War—had set up their own production and processing units.[42] Qualitatively, the record is weak—there were no films of lasting merit. There was no co-ordination between any of the agencies producing films, no concentrated effort to secure distribution, and no central agency to assure such co-ordination and distribution. The possibilities of documentary had not been explored. No attempt had been made to explain to the public the workings of the government, the problems faced, or the solutions being attempted.

In summary, before 1935, the government was producing films in three categories: those that taught specific processes; those that gave a more or less technical description of an industry; those that described government facilities.[43] These films were being produced by the government by two basic methods: through its

---

[41] Pryor, "Uncle Sam: Film Producer," *New York Times*, July 12, 1936.

[42] Howe, "U.S. Film Service Presents," *U.S. Camera*, June–July, 1940.

[43] *Ibid*. The categories are Lorentz's, reported by Howe.

own laboratories, with technical and production staffs maintained in one of the departments (the Department of Agriculture, Department of the Interior, and War Department films were made in this way); through inviting bids from contracting film producers, a method described as "by contract" (the Social Security Board, FHA, and many of the WPA films were made in this way).[44]

Paul Rotha contends that the production of successful documentary films differs from the production of narrative films in that the production of the former is "wholly a matter of the capabilities of the individual producer."[45] Pare Lorentz, the producer of the first and most significant documentary films for the federal government, was, at first glance, strikingly unqualified to be such a producer—he had not produced, directed, written, or worked on a film in any way.

Pare Lorentz was born in Clarksburg, West Virginia, on December 11, 1905, to Pare Hanson and Alma Ruttencutter Lorentz. His father was a printer and publisher of high school and college yearbooks. His mother was a professional singer; performers at college affairs were frequent guests at the Lorentz home, as were members of the music faculty at West Virginia Wesleyan. His ancestors were among a group of Palatinates and Pietists who came to the William Penn colony between 1723 and 1776 to avoid religious persecution.

Pare's great-grandfather, Jacob Lorentz, came to western Virginia from Lancaster County, Pennsylvania, in 1800, and was among the first settlers in what became Upshur and Lewis counties; the town of Lorentz in Upshur County is named for him. He and his ten sons owned the first store in the area and had the first painted house, a sign of considerable wealth in those days.

Jacob Lorentz was given the grant of land by Governor John Tyler. These were wilderness lands owned by Lord Fairfax and surveyed by George Washington. Pare still has the original land

[44] U.S. National Emergency Council, U.S. Film Service, *Study Guide: The Plow That Broke the Plains*, 4.

[45] *Op. cit.*, 61.

14

grant; his own grandfather was a Confederate and lost the lands when the new state of West Virginia was formed in 1863.

Following his graduation from Buckhannon High School in 1921, Pare Lorentz attended West Virginia Wesleyan in Buckhannon for a year and then transferred to the University of West Virginia. He edited *Moonshine*, the university's humor magazine, and became a member of Sphinx, an honorary journalistic fraternity. He was elected president of the Southern Association of College Editors in his junior year.

After leaving the university before graduation, Lorentz went to New York and became editor of the *Edison Mazda Lamp Sales Builder*, his first job as a commercial writer. What he had learned about typesetting from his father helped him get the job.[46]

Because he needed money to continue his education, Lorentz had actually come to New York with several ideas in mind, one of which was to become a music critic. There was always music in the home, and he had studied music for ten years, although he was not a professional musician. When he first came to New York, he attended hundreds of concerts, particularly at the Damrosch School, and developed friendships with many members of the faculty there. Discussions of the role of music in motion pictures were to appear many times in his journalistic writings. For example, he often wrote about the lack of music counterpoint in background scores. At that time he felt that only René Clair and a few others used music in such a manner in their productions. Music, he thought, was being used much as sound effects were— to augment what was already on the film.[47]

In 1927, he left the *Edison Mazda Lamp Sales Builder* to become motion picture reviewer for *Judge*. At that time, he was one of the youngest American columnists with a by-line. He was never satisfied with holding one job at a time, and he was soon writing film criticism for other publications. From 1930 to 1932, he was film critic for the *New York Evening Journal* and, in 1933, for *Vanity Fair* as well. Lorentz felt honored to be on the staff of

[46] Interview with Pare Lorentz, April 25, 1961.
[47] Interview with Pare Lorentz, July 28, 1961.

15

Vanity Fair, an exciting magazine that presented some of the best photography, writing, and illustrating of the time. Its staff included George Jean Nathan and Paul Gallico as columnists on drama and sports respectively, Covarrubias as caricaturist, and Edward J. Steichen as photographer.[48]

From 1934 to 1936, Lorentz wrote a film column for King Features and also covered movies for *Town and Country.* Mc-Call's became the first woman's magazine to run serious motion picture criticism when he was added to their staff in 1935. Lorentz acquired a national reputation as a serious student and critic of films, and has been referred to as a "director's critic."[49] Many other magazines—including *Fortune, Harper's, Scribner's, Forum,* and *Story*—carried articles by Lorentz during this period. A college textbook reprinted one of his articles, "A Young Man Goes to Work," from *Scribner's.*

The first book Lorentz wrote may have been partly responsible for some of the difficulty he was to experience when he attempted to deal with Hollywood for stock footage and to secure distribution rights. This book, *Censored: The Private Life of the Movies,* written in collaboration with Morris Ernst in 1929 and published in 1930,[50] has been described as a plea for a "more adult and intelligent acceptance of realism on the screen."[51] In the late 1920's, Lorentz had written an article in *Plain Talk,* "The Coming of Super Utilities," in which he foresaw the coming of giant utilities to small towns and the consequent impact. Morris Ernst, a lawyer and spokesman for freedom of artistic expression, was also interested in this matter. The two discussed the subject and discovered a common interest in the issue of motion picture censorship. The result was *Censored.*

At the time, Lorentz was twenty-five and had been a critic and student of film for only two years; yet he clearly revealed a

---

[48] Lorentz recalls that George Jean Nathan was drama critic for *Judge* at the time.

[49] *Current Biography: 1940* (New York, H. W. Wilson Co., 1940), 519.

[50] The book was published by Jonathan Cape and Harrison Smith.

[51] *Current Biography: 1940,* 519. Actually, it was much more than that: it was a strong attack on Will Hays.

16

powerful insight into the potential of motion pictures, a potential he was among the first to fulfill in this country. In *Censored*, Lorentz and Ernst wrote: "The movie was created, tried, and developed in America. Supported by the dumb and the quick, rich and poor, it is the most powerful medium for news, opinion, and art in the world."[52] By no means were they the first to say this, but they built a powerful indictment of certain interests that they felt were responsible for the failure of movies to fulfill this potential:

> Despite its childish extravaganza the movie of today is capable of producing adult entertainment. There are too many cheap novels, true story magazines, and tabloid newspapers in existence for the movie to bear the blame of mass expression. At its worst, it is illiterate and childish. At its best, it is America's greatest contribution to art. Yet, at its best, it is unable to escape the unlearned and stupid hecklings of the censor. At its logical development, it could dwarf the stage, the press and literature with its power.[53]

Lorentz and Ernst substantiated their statements with a description of various cuts made in a long list of outstanding films, some of which had been produced abroad and others that were adaptations of famous novels or plays. The authors were also careful to point out cases in which the various state censorship boards differed in their treatment of a film, being unable to decide unanimously what was censorable and what was not. The authors also provided biographical sketches of the heads of the state boards. Then they began their attack on Will Hays, for which Lorentz accepts most of the responsibility. The complaint and lament were that the motion picture, a medium potentially more powerful and influential than the novel, had been turned over to the control of one man.[54]

Lorentz expanded the charges he leveled against Will Hays to include the motion picture producers themselves: "A fearsome lot, they have banded together and given a politician almost arbitrary power, and with no feeling for real courage, taste or dig-

[52] P. 2.
[53] P. 13.
[54] *Ibid.*

nity, he has allocated censorship power to the ladies."[55] In his opinion, the producers were offering protection money to the Board of Review when they paid to have their films pre-examined and licensed. He attacked them for not fighting against censorship as the press and publishers had.[56]

At the end of the book, Lorentz and Ernst described what they saw as the dangers of the increasing spread of censorship in American society.[57] They viewed the unification of the control of film production and distribution in the United States as an indication of the spread of censorship, and described two serious and possible consequences of the control of motion pictures and other media by large corporations: "1. the return of pre-censorship for the stage; 2. the death of political opinion and the right of free speech."[58] They noted that sound pictures made from stage plays were being censored, although the plays had not been censored when performed on the stage. Every play made into a movie was being altered in advance by the Hays Office or censored by a state board after release.

Giant utility corporations, the mutual interest that had brought Ernst and Lorentz together in the first place, elicited further dire predictions. In their opinion, the utility corporations and affiliated groups were gaining control of the movies and other media. Be-

---

[55] P. 124. Lorentz traced Hays's interest in motion pictures back to 1919. A few years before that date, Woodrow Wilson's campaign for re-election was aided by a film—*Civilization*—about peace. Hays, as manager of the Republican campaign in 1919, decided to get the support of the film industry for his party. He held meetings with Zukor, Fox, and other powerful motion picture men, and as a consequence Harding appeared in the newsreels with some frequency. In Lorentz's opinion, this was a factor in Harding's being elected. Hays was rewarded by being appointed postmaster general. His experience during the campaign provided Hays with friends who were later to place the motion picture industry under his control. He was hired in 1922 for an annual salary of $100,000 as head of the Motion Picture Producers and Distributors of America.

Lorentz contended that Hays did his job by becoming a press agent and pointing out how pure the movies were. Lorentz noted that Hays rarely censored movies himself or enforced the code, but turned these tasks over to an office force. Lorentz extended the press-agent charge when he argued that, because of the financial importance of movies, Hays functioned like a press agent or publicity department for a large corporation. Like other press agents and censors, he gave motion pictures a benign and sanctified purpose.

[56] P. 113.   [57] P. 117.   [58] P. 175.

cause of the holdings of these corporations and groups in other media, it would be possible for this one great force to control news and opinion about politics and current events before it reached the public.[59]

Ernst and Lorentz did not paint a bright picture in 1930. It was not a picture calculated to gain support from either Hollywood or Wall Street. Lorentz himself, was to be harassed by censorship through efforts to hamper the production of his films and to keep them off the motion picture screens of the nation. It cannot be said with absolute certainty that the remarks in *Censored* were responsible for Lorentz's troubles, but they certainly did not ease them.

In 1934, Pare Lorentz started writing a nationally syndicated political column, "Washington Sideshow," for the Hearst King Features, in which he commented on persons and events in national affairs. The job was extremely short-lived—in an early column he praised Secretary of Agriculture Henry A. Wallace and the New Deal's farm program, and was promptly fired by wire from Hearst's home at San Simeon, California.

Lorentz had been hired for the Hearst column by Joseph V. Connally on the basis of his second book, *The Roosevelt Year: 1933*.[60] This book actually started out to be what would have been Lorentz's first film if he could have raised financial support. He thought that the spirit of the New Deal could be captured on film and dramatized to give Americans a fresh look at their own country and the way it really was. He outlined this film with a provision for incorporating considerable newsreel footage of the significant events of the year. Then he started calling on various prospective backers. Because few persons in the United States at that time had any knowledge of, or appreciation for, the documentary, and because the film seemed to be completely without commercial possibilities (it was not entertainment and therefore

[59] P. 187. The closing paragraphs were a description of a broadcast of a declaration of war by the United States, complete with sponsors. They are a striking forecast of a column written by Art Buchwald in 1966. See Art Buchwald, "Capitol Punishment," *Washington Post*, October 6, 1966.

[60] William L. White, "Pare Lorentz," *Scribner's*, January, 1939, 7.

19

would not make any money), he was unable to find backers and so abandoned the project.[61]

Lorentz did not, however, give up the fundamental idea—a picturization of the significant events of the first year of Franklin D. Roosevelt as President. He decided to convert his idea into a book. He collected news photographs, wrote captions and a continuity, and approached publishers. The book, published in 1934 by Funk and Wagnalls, contained pictures of farm riots, bread lines, strikes, the bank holiday, and other events, with captions by Lorentz, recording "the drama of personalities, places or events, of problems to be solved, of jobs to be done."[62]

The Roosevelt Year: 1933 not only secured Lorentz a position as a political columnist, as brief as it was, but also led to his becoming a producer of documentary films for the government.

Pare Lorentz, the man who was to produce the first major documentary films for the federal government of the United States, had never produced, directed, written, or worked on any motion picture before his first production *The Plow That Broke the Plains*. He had, however, been a professional writer for more than ten years and a motion picture critic for eight. He had an avid interest in music, and was known in artistic and musical circles in New York. He had strong feelings about the potential for motion pictures to serve purposes other than entertainment, and equally strong feelings about the failure of motion pictures to approach this potential. He was interested in President Roosevelt and his ideas. He had a concern for the conservation of natural resources. He had tremendous energy, revealed, for example, by his ability to hold down more than one writing job at a time. He had determination, imagination, and charm.

In spite of these characteristics, no one could have foretold in 1935 that five short years later Lorentz would be described by Bosley Crowther, motion picture critic for the *New York Times*, as "an experimenter, an explorer in the art of the cinema."[63]

[61] Charles Rockwell, narrator, NET series "Lorentz on Film," Program I.
[62] *Ibid.*
[63] "Lorentz Experiments," *New York Times*, March 10, 1940.

20

II

The Plow That Broke the Plains

IN THE 1930's, the New Deal set out to alert the public to certain frightening conditions in the United States, the land of plenty. Almost without notice, large areas of cities had degenerated into overcrowded, unhealthy, filthy slums; farmers were being driven off their land; drought, winds, and floods were ravishing the soil; crops were failing; the land and forests were wasting away through misuse. "To all this the federal government brought a new approach and a new concern, and above all, a new confidence that these problems could be tackled."[1]

The Resettlement Administration (RA), established by executive order on April 30, 1935, represented a dramatic approach to a serious farm problem and was administered from its inception by Rexford Guy Tugwell. A year and eight months later, the RA was transferred to the Department of Agriculture and its title was changed to the Farm Security Administration (FSA).[2] Tugwell, who had been constantly under fire, resigned as administrator.

The program of the RA and the source of its funds were set forth in the First Deficiency Appropriation Bill for 1937:

Allocations of $334,000,000 have been made to the Resettlement Administration, $227,000,000 from funds made available by the Emergency Relief Appropriation Act of 1935, and $107,000,000 from the Emergency Relief Appropriation Act of 1936 funds. A major part of this total has been used to assist destitute farm families in need of assistance, but in cases of emergency straight grants have been made. In addition, the Resettlement Administration is using a portion of its funds to carry forward a program of subsistence homestead develop-

[1] Rockwell, narrator, "Lorentz on Film," Program I.
[2] This transfer was made under the direction of Executive Order 7530, December 31, 1936, and became effective January 1, 1937.

ment in rural areas and low-cost housing in suburban areas. The remaining funds of the Administration are being used to purchase and develop several millions of acres of submarginal farmlands.[3]

The program was new, experimental, and controversial. In 1962, the Department of Agriculture could assess the program by saying: "Perhaps the most significant part of them [the several rural relief programs, including the RA] was that someone was willing to try them out at a time when the Nation was going through a soul-searching experience. The accepted ways had failed."[4]

The RA was primarily a relief agency combining the emergency functions of such other programs as rural rehabilitation (FERA) and subsistence homestead developments (Department of the Interior). It, like other new agricultural programs, was based on long-range thinking. The plans of Tugwell and his advisers represented a concerted attack on the problems of the small farmer. The proposals were radical, to say the least. Tugwell's ideas were attacked as socialistic because they involved long-range planning for people, advising them where to live, how to live, when to move, where to move, and how much it would cost them.[5]

A important branch of the RA was its information staff, one of the most comprehensive in Washington until that time. In charge of the staff was John Franklin Carter, a novelist and contributor to *Vanity Fair* as well as the Washington representative for *Liberty Magazine*. Carter had persuaded Tugwell to write articles for *Liberty* in the earliest days of the New Deal. He had once told Tugwell he would like to help him some day, if the right opportunity came along.[6] In 1935, Carter's assistant was Arch Mercey.

The purpose of the information staff was to explain the action program of the RA to those whose lives it would be affecting and to those who were participating in the program by paying the taxes

[3] U.S. House of Representatives, *First Deficiency Appropriations Bill for 1937*, 75 Cong., 2 sess., 1936.
[4] Philip S. Brown, "Experiments in Survival," in Stefferud (ed.), *op. cit.*, 525.
[5] MacCann, *op. cit.*, 138.
[6] *Ibid.*, quoting an interview with John Carter, December 13, 1949, 172.

that supported it. The information staff approached its assignment by describing to the public the problems that the RA faced and the reasons for its establishment. This information program was carried out by the usual press releases as well as by more modern methods: exhibits for public display, recordings and scripts for radio stations, a large photographic service, and eventually films.[7]

For seven years, photographers of the RA and its successor, the FSA, toured the nation. Their work was to acquaint the population with the appearance of depressed areas and depressed persons. As Roy Stryker, chief of the photographic staff described it: "Our basic concern was with agriculture—with dust, migrants, sharecroppers. Our job was to educate the city dweller to the needs of the rural population."[8] Among others working for Stryker were Walker Evans, Dorothea Lange, Russell Lee, Carl Mydans, Arthur Rothstein, Ben Shahn, and John Vachon. Their pictures have been reprinted in many books, magazines, newspapers, and exhibits. A particularly brilliant collection by Walker Evans appeared in *Let Us Now Praise Famous Men*.[9]

In spite of statements made in Congress to the contrary, the Dust Bowl existed and was forcing farmers by the thousands off the land. The Dust Bowl was the result of several factors: overgrazing, overplowing, planting of marginal lands, and—most of all—the drought that began in 1932. By 1934, the Dust Bowl extended from Texas to North Dakota. On one day—May 11, 1934—an estimated 300,000,000 tons of fertile soil were swept off the Great Plains.[10] Following a nationwide survey in 1934, the

---

[7] *Ibid.*

[8] Alfred Stefferud, "Lean Years," in Stefferud (ed.), *op. cit.*, 513.

[9] James Agee and Walker Evans, *Let Us Now Praise Famous Men*.

[10] U.S. Department of Agriculture, *Little Waters*, 2. It has been estimated that more than 400,000,000 tons of topsoil a year were washed into the Gulf of Mexico by the Mississippi River. In May, 1934, dust from the plains reached the east coast. On February 24, 1935, brown snow fell through New England, caused by powdery topsoil from the Southwest. (*Ibid.*) Dalhart, in the Texas Panhandle, reported sixty-one dust storms in 1935, forty-five in 1936. (U.S. Department of Agriculture, *Farmer's Bulletin 1825*, 1.) Kansas reported an estimated three million acres subject to blowing in 1934, and 8,871,227 acres in 1935. (Kansas State Board of Agriculture, *Soil Erosion by Wind*, 9.)

Soil Erosion Service, forerunner of the Soil Conservation Service, reported that 14 per cent of the land—some 180,000,000 acres— had been ruined for further cultivation and that an additional 775,000,000 acres were in the process of being destroyed by erosion.[11] Much of the land affected was in the Great Plains.

The work of the photographic section in documenting the Dust Bowl and explaining the need for the RA program was effective, but still photographs could not reveal the violence of a dust storm in action. Motion pictures could, and in the spring of 1935 Tugwell and Carter decided to make films.[12]

Once this decision had been made, it was necessary to obtain professional advice on how to launch the project. A variety of factors brought Pare Lorentz to the attention of Tugwell and Carter. First of all, Lorentz was available; he had been unable to find financial support for his film on Roosevelt, and he had recently been fired from his job as a political columnist. Further, he had been trying to get a film produced about the Dust Bowl.[13]

Another factor that may have helped Lorentz secure the position as motion picture consultant to the RA was the lengthy piece he had written on the Dust Bowl while working for *Newsweek*. In addition, he was acquainted with John Franklin Carter, and it is likely that Tugwell was familiar with Lorentz's book *The Roosevelt Year: 1933*.[14]

The men responsible for bringing Lorentz to Washington in June, 1935, were James D. LeCron and Henry Wallace. LeCron knew of Lorentz's interest in producing a film on the Dust Bowl and of Tugwell's interest in such films. LeCron was impressed by *The Roosevelt Year: 1933*. He invited Lorentz to come to Wash-

[11] H. H. Bennett, *Soils and Security*, 6–7.

[12] Letter from Arch Mercey, March 22, 1962; also letter from James D. LeCron, October 24, 1960.

[13] For more than a year he had been trying to interest various people in such a film and had made a trip through the Great Plains in 1931. At that time he discussed the idea with James D. LeCron in Des Moines. (J. P. McEvoy, "Young Man with a Camera," *Reader's Digest*, August, 1940, 74.) LeCron was an assistant to Wallace. Lorentz's wife's sister was married to a Cowles brother, and LeCron was married to a Cowles sister.

[14] Rockwell, narrator, "Lorentz on Film," Program I.

24

ington to meet Secretary Wallace and to talk about producing films on the agricultural situation.[15] The secretary, in turn, told Lorentz about the RA. He outlined the advantages of producing films for the program: it was new, and its purpose was to provide new methods to solve awkward agricultural problems. Wallace recommended that Lorentz meet Tugwell.[16]

After talks with Tugwell and Carter, Lorentz agreed to become a consultant on motion pictures for the information staff of the RA. His recommendations for production were to be made to them. First, he examined several government films, studied distribution and production practices, and then made his recommendations.

Although Tugwell had originally suggested a series of eighteen films, Lorentz recommended that the RA concentrate on making one film that would be good enough to be shown on commercial screens. This recommendation was accepted.[17]

As Lorentz conceived it, a film of merit was to be one produced by the federal government that could stand on its own merits and share billing with commercial Hollywood productions. He developed the concept while studying government motion pictures and production and distribution methods.[18] Although he did not refer to it by name, Lorentz later explained his idea to Senator Kenneth McKellar in the Senate hearing on the budget for the United States Film Service in April, 1940.[19]

About the time Lorentz left his position as director of the Film Service, he discussed his approach to film making for the government in an article that appeared in *U.S. Camera*. There he was quoted as saying that government films should be good enough technically to bear comparison with commercial films and be entertaining enough to draw an audience.[20]

[15] Letter from James D. LeCron, October 24, 1960.

[16] Interview with Pare Lorentz, July 27, 1961.

[17] Interview with Pare Lorentz, April 25, 1961.

[18] *Ibid.*

[19] U.S. Senate Appropriations Committee, *Hearings on Department of Labor–Federal Security Agency Appropriations Bill, 1941*, 76 Cong., 3 sess., 248.

[20] Howe, "U.S. Film Service Presents," *U.S. Camera*, June–July, 1940. From the personal files of Pare Lorentz.

25

After Tugwell and Carter accepted Lorentz's recommendation to make only one film, certain important decisions were made. If the first film was to be shown on commercial screens, Lorentz decided that it could not be a dry, informative film similar to the hundreds the Department of Agriculture had already turned out. The film had to be able to hold an audience by dramatic means and, at the same time, had to make clear the causes of the national problem it treated and why the government had established the RA program.

Lorentz was aware that the film would have to merit the commercial distribution and exhibition he desired.[21] The film could not be forced on commercial theater owners by the government. The problem was how to produce on a budget of six thousand dollars a film that would earn a place on commercial screens.

The limited budget led to certain decisions. Lorentz decided there would be no professional actors, because they would be too expensive. Instead, he decided to use persons who were actually living on the Great Plains. Because the budget did not permit studio filming, he decided to shoot all footage, except visuals, on location. Too, the visuals and animated sequences were to be kept simple. He believed it would be too expensive to record sound on location, and he decided to use a narrator and background music instead.[22]

Although he made many decisions that cut the cost of his first film, Lorentz decided to hire the best men available for the various technical positions on the crew. Because he could not offer salaries competitive with those of Hollywood, he hoped that the enthusiasm many talented persons had for the New Deal would lead them to accept his offer to work on the film.[23]

When Lorentz failed to interest anyone in producing and directing the kind of film he had in mind, he decided to perform those tasks himself. He was eager to get the program under way, and he

[21] Interview with Pare Lorentz, April 25, 1961.
[22] Interview with Pare Lorentz, July 24, 1961.
[23] Interview with Pare Lorentz, July 26, 1961.

welcomed the opportunity of making a motion picture. As producer, Lorentz faced two immediate problems: how to finance the film, and how to improve salaries for technical personnel. These problems caused some delay in shooting the film.[24]

The solution to the first problem was to secure approval from the comptroller general to spend funds to make a film. Securing this approval was the task of Arch Mercey, who was assigned to work with Lorentz, and saw himself as functioning mainly by "interpreting Lorentz to the bureaucrats and the bureaucrats to Lorentz."[25] Mercey had had previous experience with the workings of bureaucracy in Washington, and had been on the information staff of the RA almost since its beginning. Mercey had V. A. Kleinfeld, an attorney for the RA, draft a letter for Tugwell to send the comptroller general.[26] This letter, submitted August 12, 1935, requested permission to spend six thousand dollars to make a sound motion picture whose subject was to be: "the extent and richness of the western plain lands before their abuse, the settlements thereon, the beginning of misuse, such as overgrazing, overproduction, mechanized farming by absentee owners, etc., and the results thereof, such as wind and soil erosion, drought, dust storms, floods, worn lands and poverty."[27]

The letter contained also the stated purpose of the film: to educate the employees of the RA and of the co-operating agencies to the problems facing them in the work of the newly formed agency. The economic aspects of the use of such a film were stressed. There was no mention of releasing the film to the general public through commercial distributors, although this was Lorentz's recommendation and Tugwell's hope.

The comptroller general replied on August 19, 1935, that his

[24] Lorentz made his recommendations to Tugwell and Carter in June. Shooting did not begin until September.

[25] Letter from Arch Mercey, March 22, 1962.

[26] The letter is to be found in Appendix A. Kleinfeld was to be legal adviser to the RA as long as it carried on film activities.

[27] Letter from Rexford G. Tugwell to Comptroller General McCarl, August 12, 1935. The letter is to be found in Appendix A. This statement accurately anticipates the actual content of the film.

27

office would not object to the RA's making the film with funds appropriated for administrative expenses.

By September, the problem of satisfactory salaries for cameramen was solved by having a new job description approved.[28] Mercey's responsibility was to work with the Civil Service Commission on the new description which was "Technical Consultant" and which called for a salary of twenty-five dollars per day plus travel expenses and the regular per diem.[29] The cameramen, the composer, and the narrator were all classified under this description.[30]

In addition to initiating these requests for job reclassification and production approval, Lorentz did research for his script of the film. While working on the script, Lorentz decided that shooting on location would present certain problems. Although the decision to shoot on location was, in part, financial, shooting on location could still be costly, especially when the three-man camera crew had to cover the thousands of square miles in the Great Plains looking for appropriate locations.

To reduce the time it would take to scout locations, Lorentz decided to take advantage of the many RA still photographs of the conditions in agricultural America. He studied these photographs and then had RA's still cameramen take pictures in various sections of the Dust Bowl. In this way he was able to preselect many of the shooting locations before leaving Washington.[31]

While doing research and developing an outline of the script, Lorentz kept in mind two principal objectives: to show audiences a specific and exciting section of the country, and "to portray the

[28] The government pay scale for cameramen at this time was very low. Civil Service cameramen were receiving about ten dollars a day. (Letter from Arch Mercey, March 22, 1962.) Lorentz reports that the average annual salary for Civil Service cameramen was about $2,600, whereas the minimum union scale in Hollywood for a "B" cameraman was three or four times as much. (Letter from Pare Lorentz, April 19, 1963.)

[29] Letter from Pare Lorentz, April 19, 1963.

[30] Approval to begin production came from the comptroller general on August 19, 1935. Civil Service approval of the new job description did not come until later, so that cameramen were not hired until September 2, 1935.

[31] Interview with Pare Lorentz, July 25, 1961.

events which led up to one of the major catastrophes in American history—to show in other words, the Great Drought which is now going into its sixth year."[32]

From reading a lecture by Nathaniel Southgate Shaler of Harvard, Lorentz learned that the United States was not a natural country, with regular cycles of rainfall, in the sense that France and England were. Moreover, one part of the United States might have an annual rainfall of a hundred inches, another only fourteen inches. Shaler warned that if the American people did not use the country properly they would turn a great part of it into a desert.[33] These ideas were incorporated into Lorentz's script. Lorentz's own earlier trip through the Great Plains and the research he did for the article in *Newsweek* helped him on the project.

When Lorentz left Washington to begin shooting, all he had was an outline of the script, which Tugwell and Carter had approved. He intended to film some dust storms building up (one was filmed near Dalhart, Texas, in the Panhandle), but the rest of the footage was not carefully planned.

The camera crew Lorentz hired was Ralph Steiner, Paul Strand, and Leo Hurwitz.[34] Each had produced documentary films of his own. Steiner had made several shorts, including *H_2O* (1929) and *Surf and Sea Weed* (1931). Strand, a protégé of Alfred Stieglitz, had recently returned from Mexico, where he had produced *The Wave* (1934) for the Mexican government. Hurwitz had produced two films, one on the WPA, and the other on the Scottsboro case. All three men were reported strongly influenced by Soviet documentary film makers.[35]

Lorentz and his crew started shooting in Montana in September,

[32] "The Plow That Broke the Plains," *McCall's*, July, 1936, 21.

[33] Pare Lorentz, "Lorentz on Film," Program I. The lectures were given early in the twentieth century.

[34] A. William Bluem, *Documentary in American Television*, 51, has written that Floyd Crosby was a member of the camera crew. Crosby did not work for Lorentz until *The River*.

[35] *Time*, May 25, 1936, 47.

worked their way into Wyoming "on the wings of a blizzard," and continued on to Colorado, western Kansas, and the Texas Panhandle. In Texas, they faced high winds and choking dust.[36]

The wandering film makers found the people in the Dust Bowl friendly and courageous. On the NET series *"Lorentz on Film,"* Lorentz recalled a few of his impressions formed on the trek. "One chap was living in a dugout underground with a quonset hut full of equipment. I went to talk to him and he warned me about a rattlesnake, a sort of family rattlesnake."[37]

The unforgettable Bam White, a seventy-two-year-old Texan from the Panhandle, gave an exceptional performance in the film. Lorentz asked a local WPA official to find him a man who had a team of horses and a sod plow. White was one of the few in the area who still owned a team. As they had talked with many others on the parched plains, they talked with White, finding him a wiry, blunt-speaking plainsman whose life and prophecies curiously matched the tone of the film.[38]

The crew found that the plains people were not self-conscious about acting before the cameras. These people did not think that it was strange that a film should be made of their plight and that they, the real victims, should portray their own tragedy. Lorentz was quoted as saying: "They still have an enormous pride. We stopped some and filmed them as they went by. When we talked to them we learned much of the cruel force that has blighted them."[39]

Although the people were co-operative, the situation within the crew became unpleasant. In fact, *Variety* announced that the photographers were "on strike" in Texas.[40] The conflict arose from several sources. For one thing, Steiner, Strand, and Hurwitz were professional film makers, and Lorentz was not. The cameramen did not understand his sketchy script. Lorentz maintained that professionals like King Vidor did understand it. He knew

---

[36] "Dust Storm Film," *Literary Digest*, May 16, 1936, 22.
[37] Program I.
[38] "Dust Storm Film," *Literary Digest*, May 16, 1936, 22.
[39] *Ibid.*
[40] *Variety*, May 12, 1936. From the personal files of Pare Lorentz.

what he wanted to accomplish in the film but was unable to express it in the jargon of the cutting room.[41] The conflict was also due to the different political views of the personalities involved. Strand and Hurwitz were already identified with leftist interests through their previous productions. Lorentz, on the other hand, was an enthusiastic New Deal Democrat.[42]

An internal conflict also developed among the cameramen. Roy Stryker told Richard D. MacCann that Strand and Steiner were regularly at odds. "One week you could mention Steiner to Strand and the next week you couldn't."[43] The basis of the conflict was political. Because of Strand's political attitude, Steiner later refused to join Strand and others in forming Frontier Films, a documentary film production group.[44]

The conflict came to a head in the "strike" reported by *Variety*.[45] Strand and Hurwitz disapproved of what they understood to be Lorentz's point of view on the subject being filmed. They prepared their own shooting script, submitted it to Lorentz, and refused to continue work until he accepted it. Lorentz rejected it because "they wanted it to be all about human greed and how lousy our social system was. And I couldn't see what this had to do with dust storms."[46] The two cameramen defended their script during a heated argument, but Lorentz refused to yield. Finally Strand and Hurwitz acquiesced grudgingly, disclaiming any future responsibility for the film.

After the dust storm sequences were completed, Lorentz fired the crew and went on to Hollywood, where he hoped to obtain stock shots to fill the gaps in the historical outline of the film; he also needed more shots of combining on the Great Plains. Ordinarily, stock footage is available at a reasonable price to anyone who wants to buy it. According to William L. White, the com-

[41] White, "Pare Lorentz," *Scribner's*, January, 1939, 8.
[42] *Ibid.*
[43] MacCann, *op. cit.*, 178, quoting interview with Roy Stryker.
[44] Lorentz retained considerable respect for Steiner because he recommended Steiner's production group, American Documentary Films, Inc., to the Carnegie Foundation to produce *The City* (1939), based on Lorentz's scenario.
[45] See p. 30.
[46] White, "Pare Lorentz," *Scribner's*, January, 1939, p. 8.

mercial film producers and stockholders and their spokesman Will Hays decided they did not want the government making motion pictures at that time, particularly if Roosevelt was involved in any way.[47] White suggests that, because this was the year before an election, the doors of every major studio were locked to Lorentz and that Hays notified all film libraries not to sell footage to him.

King Vidor, in whose home Lorentz stayed while he was in Hollywood, and others helped Lorentz get the footage he needed. Vidor does not recall exactly what he did—perhaps it was merely to suggest places where the footage could be found. He wrote, "Pare was unhappy with some of the reception he received and I do remember that he thought the government effort should give him some further entry than he apparently was receiving."[48] With the help of Vidor and other sympathetic directors, Lorentz gained admission to projection rooms so that he might screen footage they brought to him and choose what he needed. Vidor and others had prints made for him.[49]

Before Lorentz left for New York, he decided to photograph migrants arriving in California. Dorothea Lange, a still photographer for the RA, and others had been shooting near Camp Shafter, a migrant camp. Lorentz had enough money left for one day's shooting, so with the help of Paul Ivano he filmed the migrants for one day. Dorothea Lange helped by lining up the families on U.S. Highway 99.[50]

When Lorentz arrived in New York, the six thousand dollars budgeted for the project was almost gone. He had no contract for a film editor and none for a music score—and music was an integral part of his plan. After some delay in getting authorization

[47] *Ibid.*, 10.

[48] Letter from King Vidor, March 22, 1962.

[49] Interviews with Pare Lorentz, April 25, 1961, and July 25, 1961. See also MacCann, *op. cit.*, 182–83. The importance of Vidor's help is indicated by a letter to Vidor in which Lorentz writes: "Great parts of the credit for *The Plow That Broke the Plains* should be yours. We all appreciate your sympathy and interest." (MacCann, *op. cit.*, 183.)

[50] Lorentz, "Lorentz on Film," Program I.

to rent space, he moved to the Deluxe Laboratories for cutting purposes and he hired a girl to teach him to edit and wind film.

According to the scenario he had in mind, he needed some footage of World War I, which he obtained from newsreel companies in New York and from Signal Corps files.[51]

While he was assembling the rough cut of the film, Lorentz began looking for a composer for the musical score. Twelve composers were interviewed. The first eleven were excited about the project and wanted to write a symphony at his expense, not a motion picture score. They showed little interest in sitting down and working closely with the producer. The twelfth composer interviewed was Virgil Thomson.[52] Lorentz was familiar with Thomson's music and was particularly impressed with his opera *Four Saints in Three Acts.*

In Lorentz's estimation, Thomson was an expert craftsman, a fine composer,[53] and was knowledgeable in all aspects of American music. Lorentz liked him at first sight. After Lorentz explained what he wanted, Thomson's first question was, "How much money do you have?" Lorentz told him he had very little left but would pay him all that remained in the budget.[54] Thomson agreed to work with Lorentz.

Kathleen Hoover has suggested that Thomson possessed particular qualifications for this score, even though he was unfamiliar with the requirements of film music. She emphasizes his middle western background as a preparation for this particular assignment. He had grown up near the prairie, and it was natural for him to provide the accompaniment for the wheat field and grassland sequences. In the sequences of people, he quoted the settlers' songs he had known from his childhood. He also remembered something of the horrors of dust storms from the days of his military training in Texas in World War I.[55]

[51] See p. 8 for a previous reference.

[52] Lorentz, "Lorentz on Film," Program I.

[53] Thomson also had the advantage of being from the Middle West, having been born and raised in Kansas City, Missouri.

[54] Lorentz, "Lorentz on Film," Program I.

[55] Kathleen Hoover, and John Cage, *Virgil Thomson: His Life and Music,* 84–85.

Lorentz continued to work, assisted by Leo Zochling, on cutting the film at the Deluxe Laboratories, which developed and printed the final rushes. He assembled the film in rough form and made obvious cuts. He worked closely with Thomson on the composition of the score and by himself on the narration. The visual, musical, and narrative aspects had to be closely co-ordinated.

Lorentz and Thomson worked together on the film and the score in an unusual manner. Thomson credits Lorentz with "an extreme sensitivity to the expressive powers and dramatic uses of music."[56] The two men held lengthy and frequent discussions about what melodic material they both thought would be appropriate for the film. Lorentz illustrated his points by strumming at a guitar once or twice. Thomson found all the cowboy and western settler music available in books. After developing his themes, he played each one for Lorentz on the piano for his approval.

In addition to his use of old plains tunes, such as cattle- and dirt-farmer songs, Thomson used a brief passage of authentic—as opposed to Tin Pan Alley—war themes in the score. The dust storm had a hymn thematic background.[57]

After Lorentz had rough-cut the film, Thomson composed his musical selections according to time requirements of the episodes. As a double check, he played these selections on a piano for Lorentz while the film was being projected. Following Lorentz's approval of the piano selections, Thomson orchestrated the score. Then the sound track was recorded at General Service Sound Studio in Astoria, Long Island.[58]

Thomson made another contribution to the film almost as important as his original score. He persuaded Alexander Smallens to conduct the score with an orchestra of about twenty of the first-chair performers of the New York Philharmonic, whom Smallens had assisted in recruiting.

Thomas Chalmers, a close friend of Lorentz and a fellow member of the Players club, was selected to do the narration. Chalmers

[56] Letter from Virgil Thomson, December 14, 1961.

[57] *Literary Digest,* May 16, 1936, 22.

[58] Letter from Virgil Thomson, December 14, 1961.

had been a leading member of the Metropolitan Opera Company in the days of Enrico Caruso and Geraldine Farrar until an operation had damaged his singing voice. He then became an actor and appeared in several Broadway productions. From 1931 he served as film editor of *Pathé Topics*, but had done no motion picture narration until he worked on *The Plow That Broke the Plains*.[59] Chalmers recorded over the finished recording of the score, fitting his words to the music. In this way Lorentz controlled the relationship between music and words.

Thomson has a strong impression of how Lorentz produced the final cutting after the score was recorded. According to Thomson, Lorentz differed from other directors in that he preferred to cut his film to a pre-existing musical background, at least for the production of his first two films. Thomson explained that the point toward which Lorentz had been waiting and working was a completed score to which he could cut and fit his pictorial sequences. Further, Thomson recalls:

> Since a background [score] can't be composed, orchestrated and recorded (that is, a background specifically designed for a given film) until the film has been cut and the lengths of the shots and sequences fixed, Pare has to go through a cutting for visual narration; but his heart is not in it. When he gets the final recorded music track, then he goes back to the cutting room, finds inspiration for expressive visual narration through the musical detail, and wholly recuts his film. At least that's what he did on *The Plow* and *The River*.[60]

This approach to editing would account for the expressive power and unity that are held responsible for much of the artistic success of Lorentz's films.

The musical score gave Lorentz a form. He could tighten the visual sequences to match the emotional content of Thomson's score, letting the latter serve as counterpoint at times, a technique Lorentz had learned from René Clair. Karel Reisz describes an example of this contrapuntal use of music and sound:

59 U.S. Farm Security Administration press release, n.d. From the personal files of Pare Lorentz.

60 *Ibid.*

35

Another instance of a similar use of commentative sound occurs in Pare Lorentz's *The Plow That Broke the Plains*. A sequence examining the state of American agriculture during the 1914–1918 war shows a series of shots of the countryside with farmers working on the land. Behind this we hear a military march, the steps of marching soldiers, gunfire, and a commentary spoken as if on a parade ground. Partly, of course, this implies that the steady, regular routine of the farmers' year goes on while soldiers are fighting at the front. But there is an additional overtone of meaning: the continuity suggests that wartime farming had assumed something of the urgency and controlled discipline of an army. These sentiments are not directly expressed in the commentary: the comment provided by the contrast in the rhythm and comment of the sound and images in itself conveys the desired result.[61]

It was possible for Lorentz to achieve an expressive power and unity *after* the score was composed. We cannot know whether the same power and unity would have resulted if the film had been edited in its final form before the score was composed. We do know that Lorentz preferred to work this way.[62]

The outline of the finished film was rather simple. It was summed up tersely by a reviewer in *Time* following its public release in New York. "*The Plow* begins with lush, billowy grass, ends with the bulk of a dead tree surrounded by sun-baked desert."[63] Lorentz demonstrated what happened between by showing the arrival of cattle on the four-hundred-million–acre pasture of the plains and the inrush of speculators in the wake of the railroads. A homesteader's plow is seen biting into soil held together by the deep roots of the prairie while Chalmers' voice warns, "Settler, plow at your peril." A grizzled farmer watches the first sign of drought without comprehending. Next is seen the wartime sequence. This is followed by the economic boom, during which higher and higher prices are followed quickly by more and more wheat planting as part of the war effort ("Wheat Will Win the War!"), until the grass that once held the plains together has

61 *The Technique of Film Editing*, 164.

62 It should be remembered that Lorentz had a background in music and had considered the possibility of being a music critic when he came to New York.

63 May 25, 1936, 47.

36

given way to endless open fields under a scorching sun. The result of man's abuse follows. To the accompaniment of Thomson's dirgelike music, Lorentz disclosed the ravages of the drifting dust that followed when drought, heat, and winds struck the acres that should never have been plowed. Thirty thousand refugees roll out of the Dust Bowl heading west in a tired procession. The epilogue of the film shows how the RA was relocating 4,500 stranded families in new houses on small farms in ten states.[64]

Among the unforgettable sequences of the film is the dust storm. In an impressive combination of picture and music, Lorentz brought the horror of the black blizzard to life to millions who had only read about what was happening far away on the Great Plains.

Lorentz reviewed his own film in *McCall's*:

> Thus, with some outstanding photography and music, *The Plow That Broke the Plains* is an unusual motion picture which might have been a really great one had the story and construction been up to the rest of the workmanship. As it is, it tells the story of the Plains and it tells it with some emotional value—an emotion that springs out of the soil itself. Our heroine is the grass, our villain the sun and the wind, our players the actual farmers living in the Plains country. It is a melodrama of nature, the tragedy of turning grass into dust, a melodrama that only Carl Sandburg or Willa Cather perhaps could tell as it should be told.[65]

Lorentz remained objective in reviewing his first film, and could see its shortcomings. The film was rarely criticized for its pictorial beauty or Thomson's score, but critics did find fault with its construction and story.

It was not possible to complete the film for the six thousand dollars originally allotted for its production. Its final cost was $19,260.[66] When he returned to Washington early in 1936, Lorentz was anticipating some difficulties with the Treasury Department. Richard D. MacCann says: "He had only the slightest acquaintance with budget justifications, Civil Service require-

[64] This epilogue was eventually cut from the film.
[65] July, 1936.
[66] William Pinkerton, Associated Press news release, October 13, 1938. From the personal files of Pare Lorentz.

ments, travel vouchers, and disbursing agents. It seemed that the bundle of receipts he brought back from his midwestern expedition—some of them were scratched on wrapping paper—were not instantly exchangeable for cash."[67]

For example, Lorentz had hired farmers to drive their horses and tractors for the film and paid them in much-needed cash. Costs for recording the music had to be added. He had obtained authorization to rent editing facilities in New York, but he had not taken time to get approval for many of the expenses incurred on location. He had paid for these himself in order to save production time.

It was difficult for his aides to get approval of vouchers based on receipts written on envelopes and other scraps of paper. At a meeting with the chief disbursing officer of the Treasury Department, Lorentz was able to convince the government official that Lorentz himself should be disbursing agent. Nevertheless, Lorentz lost a great deal of his own money on his first film for the United States government.

With the film completed, Lorentz's goal was only half-reached. He believed he had produced a film of merit, one good enough to be seen on commercial screens. Now the problem was how to get it on commercial screens. Because of his earlier experience in having stock footage denied him in Hollywood, Lorentz reasoned that the major producers, through the large booking concerns, would be opposed to distributing and exhibiting his film. But the commercial industry was not completely opposed to government films. Just a week before the New York premiere of *The Plow*, the Capitol Theatre, a key house in the Loew-MGM chain, had shown *Around the World in a Coffee Cup*, a Department of Commerce production. Further, the motion picture industry had been producing and distributing gratis what could be called New Deal propaganda in the form of NRA shorts.[68] Still, Lorentz was worried about distributing *The Plow*.

Lorentz believed that if he could show the film to President Roosevelt and get his approval of it, he would be more likely to

[67] *Op. cit.,* 181.
[68] Peter Ellis, "The Plow That Broke the Plains," *New Theatre*, July, 1936, 18.

get wide distribution. Consequently, the world premiere of *The Plow That Broke the Plains* was on a Sunday evening on the second floor of the White House in early March, 1936. The President invited senators and representatives of the Dust Bowl states, Rexford Tugwell, John Carter, Pare Lorentz, and a few other guests. Following dinner the film was screened. When it was finished, President Roosevelt was brimming over with enthusiasm, and had a long talk with Lorentz, praising him for his work.[69]

Lorentz told the President that he wanted to show the film to professional Hollywood people because he feared that the dislike of Roosevelt, his ideas, and the New Deal among the motion picture and newspaper industries might destroy any chances the film had for wide spread distribution.[70] He believed that he had to get professional comments for the film based on merit, not on politics, or he would be unable to get distribution.

Soon after the White House screening, he flew to Hollywood with the film. King Vidor arranged to have several top directors, including Rouben Mamoulian and Lewis Milestone, attend a showing of *The Plow*. Later, they laughed at Lorentz's concern and told him he had a good film. Given this assurance, Lorentz returned to New York anxious to find an appropriate way to present his film to the public.

Several private screenings of the film followed in New York in March. Lorentz held a private showing in New York for fifteen friends representing a variety of professions.[71] Virgil Thomson sent out invitations on March 5, 1936, announcing two performances of the film on the following day at 4:30 P.M. and 5:15 P.M. in the Little Theatre in the Chanin Building. The invitation specified that these were unofficial showings and that the press was not to be informed.

Two months later *The Plow* received a full-dress Washington

[69] *Time*, May 25, 1936, 47. This was Lorentz's first personal meeting with the President.

[70] Interview with Pare Lorentz, July 27, 1961.

[71] Letter from Pare Lorentz, May 29, 1964. Because this screening was acclaimed by his friends and because he was superstitious, Lorentz gave the screenings for fifteen friends of *The River* and *The Fight for Life*.

premiere at the Mayflower Hotel on May 10, 1936. The evening's program was sponsored by the Museum of Modern Art and included documentaries from Europe. In attendance were members of the White House staff, the diplomatic corps, and the Supreme Court. The Museum of Modern Art provided a master of ceremonies to introduce the films. He announced that five European films would be shown to illustrate what was being done in the field of documentaries. The other films were *The Face of Britain* (1934), produced by Gaumont-Instructional, a private firm, and directed by Paul Rotha; *Color Box* (1935), an experimental short film by Len Lye, produced by the British General Post Office Film Unit; *Harvest Festival* (1935), by Ukrainfilm of Kiru, U.S.S.R.; *Midi* (1935), by the French State Railways; and an excerpt from *The Triumph of the Will* (1935), directed and produced by Leni Riefenstahl for the German Nazi government. *The Plow* was the last film on the program.

Both the Russian film and Lorentz's were concerned with agriculture. Their approach was entirely different, as can be gathered from the reaction of one reviewer, Edward T. Folliard, who headlined his piece in the *Washington Post* "Tugwell's Farmer's Lot Is Sad Compared to Russian Film Idyll."[72] Folliard wrote that the Russian film was the best one shown that evening. He complimented Lorentz and his crew for doing a "splendid job technically," but he thought their film was "sad from a emotional standpoint."[73] In his opinion, the Russian film was "more than a movie, it was an idyll."

The Plow received excellent press coverage as a result of this second Washington screening. Fred Othman, of the United Press, wrote a full-column rave review that appeared on the front page of twenty-one newspapers, thrilling the RA information staff.[74]

[72] May 11, 1936. Folliard later told Lorentz that he had to leave before *The Plow* was shown in order to meet his deadline and was instructed by his publisher to pan the Tugwell film because of the paper's editorial policy toward Tugwell. (Letter from Pare Lorentz, April 19, 1963.)

[73] Folliard, "Tugwell's Farmer's Lot Is Sad Compared to Russian Film Idyll," *Washington Post*, May 11, 1936.

[74] White, "Pare Lorentz," *Scribner's*, January, 1939, 10.

Film reviews did not make the front page then any more often than they do now.

Representative Maury Maverick, who had attended the showing, placed Othman's review in the *Congressional Record* of May 7, 1936.[75] In his own remarks Maverick specifically criticized the *Washington Post* for the headline and its good words about the Russian film. Maverick continued by noting the educational value of such films as Lorentz's:

> While criticisms may be made of the Resettlement film because it shows the horrible waste of our natural resources, I think that films of that character must by all means be shown to awaken our citizens to the necessity for immediate steps in conservation. Moreover, the whole field of documentary films, which show the real problems of American life, offers a tremendous opportunity of development on the part of private companies.[76]

Continuing, Maverick criticized the commercial producers for not making films like *The Plow*. He forecast the content of Lorentz's later films when he wondered why commercial producers had made no films on unemployment, poorly planned cities, lack of sanitation, or the plight of sharecroppers and tenant farmers.[77] He also attacked the government for being the "most backward government of any civilized, first-class nation in our utilization of the motion picture," in spite of the fact that this country was the most advanced in making motion pictures. He endorsed the production and use of high-quality motion pictures by the government for educational and informational purposes, and he placed in the *Congressional Record* letters Lorentz had received from King Vidor and Lewis Milestone praising the film. Then Maverick quoted from three reviews that appeared in Washington newspapers on May 11, 1936, including Othman's, whose headline read, "The New Deal's First Major Movie Effort Packs a Terrific Punch": "Before the final fadeout it had diplomats, Congressmen and New Dealers holding to the edges of their gilt chairs. It

[75] U.S. *Congressional Record*, 74 Cong., 2 sess., 1936, LXXX, Pt. 6, 6882–83.
[76] *Ibid.*, 6883.
[77] *Ibid.*

41

may have been preaching a sermon, but it surpassed many a Hollywood epic for sheer drama and technical excellence."[78] Betty Hynes, drama critic for the *Washington Herald,* called it the most dramatic film on the program. "An amazing, stirring picture," Bob McCormick wrote in the *Washington News.* "It may have been equalled by other pictures shown in Washington but it is doubtful it has been excelled."[79]

The response to *The Plow* was greater than the staff had hoped for. Lorentz decided to use these reviews to establish the merit of his film with bookers and exhibitors. By May 15, however, newspapers were reporting opposition to plans to distribute the film commercially. The *New York Times* reported a variety of reasons why the film could not be distributed.[80] The film was said to be propaganda, although the RA preferred to call it instructional because it was designed to instruct the public about certain problems. Rumors that it was boycotted because it was New Deal propaganda were reportedly denied in informed quarters. Exhibitors were reported to have said that its length was not suitable for commercial screening and that it was too specialized in nature to be a commercial success. The *New York Times* continued by saying that spokesmen for several major companies denied blacklisting the film. Their argument was that educational films were having trouble getting bookings through regular channels. (However, as noted earlier, a large Loew-MGM theater had recently offered a Department of Commerce film on its program.) The Hays Office claimed to know nothing about the matter.[81]

The Hays Office did have an official position on propaganda at this time. In his annual report to the directors of the Motion Picture Producers and Distributors Association of America, Will Hays called for a common-sense attitude in determining the dis-

[78] *Ibid.*

[79] *Ibid.*

[80] According to Lorentz, Arthur Hays Sulzberger, publisher of the *New York Times,* was so upset by the article that he ordered the Sunday editor to devote two full pages in the rotogravure section to stills from the film. (Letter from Pare Lorentz, April 17, 1963.)

[81] "Theatre Heads Balk at Tugwell's Movie," *New York Times,* May 15, 1936.

tinction between motion pictures with a message and those dealing with self-serving propaganda.[82]

Not only was Lorentz having trouble securing commercial distribution, but his sponsor, the RA, was running into severe opposition at this time. On May 18, 1936, the United States Court of Appeals for the District of Columbia, in a divided opinion, ruled as unconstitutional the provisions of the Federal Emergency Appropriations Act of 1935 that set up the RA.[83] By May 20, sentiment was growing in administration circles not to appeal the court's decision. The administration feared that such an appeal would result in a challenge to the constitutionality of the entire work relief program. In any event, an appeal would not come before the court until fall, by which time almost all the current work relief funds, as well as most of the new appropriation, would have been spent.[84] The constitutionality issue was being raised because the Federal Emergency Appropriations Act of 1935 permitted what the Court of Appeals, in its ruling on May 18, called an unlawful delegation of powers to the President.

The court ruling possibly provided Hollywood with further justification for refusing to help distribute *The Plow*. Frank Nugent was prompted to write, "Hollywood can now plead constitutional loyalty for raising bars against a valuable documentary film,"[85] but he could find no justification for barring the film as propaganda or because the public was disinterested. Nugent wrote, "Hollywood has turned thumbs down on *The Plow*," basing his remark on an interview with Lorentz. According to Nugent, when Lorentz asked for help in distributing the film, one official told him, "I wouldn't release any government picture, not even if it were *Ben Hur*."[86] Another distributor said: "If any private company or individual made this picture, it would be a documentary film. When the government makes it, it auto-

---

[82] *New York Times*, March 31, 1936.
[83] *New York Times*, May 19, 1936.
[84] *New York Times*, May 20, 1936.
[85] "Raw Deal for the New Deal," *New York Times*, May 24, 1936.
[86] *Ibid.*

matically becomes a propaganda picture."[87] When Lorentz asked the distributor what he objected to in a film showing dust storms, drought, market collapse, the exodus of farmers, and the government's plan for resettlement and conservation, the Hollywood official replied that he objected to nothing in particular but simply to the principle involved—that is, government competition with Hollywood.

Business Week also reported that, although producers and distributors maintained publicly that *The Plow* was too long for a short feature and too short for a long feature, what they were really objecting to was the government's entrance into the competitive production of entertainment.[88] This objection seems partly justified because for the first time, in *The Plow*, the government was using highly professional talent. Even more important, Lorentz had shattered Washington film-making precedents by adding drama to a government film. He had added precisely what Hollywood had for sale.[89]

Unfortunately, the film was released in 1936, the year of a bitter presidential campaign. Thomas M. Pryor pointed to a campaign-issue ingredient in Hollywood's objections when he said: "Hollywood refused to distribute *The Plow* because it was New Deal electioneering."[90] By encouraging labor unions and collective bargaining also, the New Deal was having an effect on the labor force of the motion picture industry, which producers resented.[91] This resentment toward the New Deal is further emphasized by Lorentz's assertion that slips were placed in the pay envelopes of Hollywood employees before the election informing them that they would be fired if they voted for Roosevelt.[92] King

[87] *Ibid.*

[88] "Federal Movie Furor," *Business Week*, July 11, 1936, 14. This magazine recalled these charges a year and a half later while reviewing *The River*. It recalled that Hollywood refused to distribute *The Plow* because "they distrusted government propaganda, it was an election year, and they didn't want to encourage government competition." ("Federal Film Hit," *Business Week*, February 19, 1938, 35.)

[89] *Business Week*, February 19, 1938, 35.

[90] "Uncle Sam: Film Producer," *New York Times*, July 12, 1936.

[91] C. M. Black, "He Serves Up America," *Collier's*, August 3, 1940, 22.

[92] Letter from Pare Lorentz, April 17, 1963.

44

Vidor has also reported that the producers were extremely hostile toward the government's new film activities under Lorentz.[93]

Despite the stiff and unbending opposition, Lorentz was determined to secure commercial distribution. Part of the over-all plan had been to produce a film good enough to be distributed commercially and to secure such distribution. It is not possible to say whether Lorentz anticipated the opposition of the industry when the plan was originally conceived, but such opposition must have been clear to him when he was unable to secure the stock footage he needed through legitimate and open channels.

With eight large booking firms refusing to distribute the film, a way had to be found to deal directly with theater operators. Lorentz packed the film cans containing *The Plow* into suitcases and set out with a team of government press agents to circumvent the booking blockade. Upon arriving in a town, they would arrange a preview for the press. The national reputation Lorentz had developed as a writer and critic helped him. Managing editors and motion picture critics knew his work and were willing to help him, especially after seeing the film. Just before the screening, Lorentz would say to them, "If you like it, please say that this picture can't be shown in your town."[94] The lever of the press worked to a degree, prying open a few theaters that had been closed to him. Lorentz filled a press book with reviews that would have been the envy of any production.

Typical of the reviews supporting Lorentz's approach and demanding distribution for the film was the one that appeared in *Christian Century*:

> Nine old men keep you from seeing it. There is nothing in the Constitution which authorizes the government to make and release movies for commercial distribution. If this is so, and we have only Mr. [William L.] White's word for it—then it is one more proof that some things are basically wrong with our system. A successful working of Democracy depends on giving each voter a maximum of understanding of government policies in order that he may vote with the utmost possible intelligence. If the government is debarred from

[93] Letter from King Vidor, March 22, 1962.
[94] *Current Biography: 1940*, 519.

45

using this modern method of spreading information to the electorate as to the nature of a major national problem and its proposals for dealing with it, then there is a need for a new deal. The commercial film interests have already shown (in the defeat of Upton Sinclair for California Governor) their readiness to use this agency to serve and protect their selfish interests.[95]

As a result of this campaign, *The Plow* was booked into a few first-run houses, but in many instances these bookings were mysteriously canceled. Another problem was that government regulations did not allow the RA to charge for the film, and the theater chains would not take it as a gift.

The key to Lorentz's campaign became a booking for the film in a major theater in New York City. The imaginative and enterprising Arthur Mayer, prompted perhaps by Nugent's article, offered to book it into the Rialto Theatre on Times Square. Lorentz never forgot this favor. The film opened at the Rialto on May 28, 1936, on a bill with *Florida Special*, starring Jack Oakie and Sally Eilers.

Mayer took full advantage of the line Nugent used in the *New York Times*. In front of the theater, he placed an enormous poster of a large hand with the thumb pointing toward the sidewalk; "Hollywood Says Thumbs Down!" was emblazoned across it. His ads in the newspapers also referred to Nugent's review. "The *New York Times* said: 'It is unusual, timely, entertaining.' . . . Yet Hollywood has turned its manicured thumb down!" The ad also proclaimed, "The picture they dared us to show!"[96]

The next day the *New York Times* reported that the audience at the Rialto greeted *The Plow* with even heartier applause than it gave a companion short feature of Haile Selassie protesting against Italian imperialism.[97]

Once the booking blockade was breeched in New York, Lorentz curtailed his activities in promoting the film. He had secured a booking in Chicago with the help of Louis Rupple, who at the time was managing editor of the *Chicago Times*. Rupple ran a double-

[95] "The Movie No One Will See," *Christian Century*, June 3, 1936, 788–89.
[96] *New York Times*, May 28, 1936.
[97] "The Screen in Review," *New York Times*, May 29, 1936.

page spread of stills from the film. His method was taken over by the various RA information officers, who secured further bookings. Among these information officers were George Gercke (New York), Dean S. Jennings (Chicago), and Paul Jordan (Lincoln, Nebraska). Arch Mercey was responsible for the Southeast. California was attacked later.[98]

Following the premiere at the Rialto, *The Plow* soon had three other major eastern bookings: in Philadelphia at the Europa, in Boston at the Fine Arts, and in Washington at the Little Theatre. By July 15, 1936, the film had received wide circulation in the Middle West through a large chain of independent houses: six hundred theaters in Illinois, five hundred in Ohio, two hundred in Wisconsin, with smaller circuits in Texas, Arkansas, Tennessee, Indiana, and other states.[99] Mercey later reported that the campaign by the regional information officers resulted in more than three thousand independent theater bookings.[100]

Lorentz's campaign and the subsequent tireless efforts by members of the RA staff put to rest the lament of the critics. While the film was being circulated during Lorentz's campaign, one critic voiced the fears of many when he wrote of his concern that *The Plow* would be relegated to playing "the old federal circuit of army posts, naval vessels, CCC camps, clubs, Sunday Schools, and colleges."[101] Now it was playing from coast to coast in first-run theaters, and was also receiving indirect publicity and advertising in newspapers as the result of continued front-page stories and pictures on the drought and dust storms.

The methods of Lorentz's campaign were not new. Similar methods had been tried at least twice before to promote Hollywood productions, once by Lorentz's close friend King Vidor, and a second time by Barrett Kiestling in the spring of 1936. Vidor's

[98] MacCann, *op. cit.*, 188, note 56.

[99] RA Memorandum, July 16, 1936, from Arch Mercey to Grace E. Falke, executive assistant, Subject: "*The Plow* distribution as of July 15" (MacCann, *op. cit.*, 188).

[100] Arch Mercey, "Films by American Governments," *Films*, Summer, 1940 (MacCann, *op. cit.*, 188).

[101] "New Deal Movie Wins Critics but Theatres Bar Doors to It," *Baltimore Sun*, May 13, 1936.

all-Negro film, *Hallelujah* (1929), was having trouble getting bookings outside New York. Vidor went to Chicago with a print of the film and showed it to the critics, who wrote glowing reviews that were published even though the picture was not showing in Chicago. The interest of an independent theater owner (a spiritual brother of Arthur B. Mayer, no doubt) was aroused, and he booked it into Chicago. Vidor's film was so successful it was booked for a second run at other theaters in the Loop.[102] Barrett Kiestling used similar techniques when he showed *Romeo and Juliet* (1936) to many different civic leaders and critics. The result of his drive to organize patronage for the film made it the box-office champion for 1936 and one of the top ten films of the year 1937–38.[103]

Audience reaction to *The Plow* was varied. For example, Richard D. MacCann reports that Senator Alva Adams declared the film to be "a vivid dramatic presentation of the unplanned cooperation of land-hungry men, war, drought, and wind in the destruction of grass lands of the West. It is a remarkable presentation."[104] Later, however, the senator had a change of mind during an Appropriations Committee hearing in 1939. At that time he accused the film of "deviating from the facts."[105] Some politicians reacted violently, even considering that their states were being maligned in the film. Harlan J. Bushfield, a Republican state chairman from South Dakota, criticized the RA and said that the film would put South Dakota in the Republican column in November. The picture "in one savage blow ruthlessly destroyed all that South Dakotans have built up in a generation," he declared, "by picturing the state as a wasteland. If there was any doubt about it before, *The Plow That Broke the Plains* has made South Dakota definitely Republican."[106] Incidentally, Landon failed to carry South Dakota. A Texan reacted even more violent-

---

[102] King Vidor, *A Tree Is a Tree*, 184–85. Vidor bases the start of his friendship with Lorentz on a fine review Lorentz wrote after seeing *Hallelujah* in New York.
[103] Raymond Moley, *The Hays Office*, 151–53.
[104] *Op. cit.*, 186.
[105] *Ibid.*
[106] "Says a Film Loses a State," *New York Times*, August 4, 1936.

ly. Representative Eugene Worley threatened to punch Tugwell in the nose, and announced that he wanted the Democratic National Convention to pass a resolution requesting that Tugwell destroy the film. Worley, a delegate to the convention and a resident of the Panhandle, charged, "That picture is a libel on the greatest section of the United States. The cameraman selected isolated spots."[107] Another resident of the Panhandle reacted differently to the film. Mrs. R. L. Duke, of Dalhart, sent a personal letter to Pare Lorentz:

> I keep track of your criticisms of the movies of talkies in *McCall's* magazine. Last year on June 1 I was in Washington, D.C., and saw the picture "The Plow That Broke the Plains." I told Lady Eleanor Cole of Kenya, South Africa that it [the picture] was like our High Plains and the only criticism I could offer was that you did not have the worst things that happened out here: people dying from dust pneumonia, cows being shot and BLACK dusters.
>
> What I want to say about this picture is this; you told the truth and a lot of Chambers of Commerce flew up in the air. They did not fly long when I was around, I got the picture here in Dalhart and even if some did not want to look, they looked anyhow. I have lived in this country since 1900. I have seen my country go from the country of Parkman's *Oregon Trail* to sand dunes. I have seen this country in the happy time 1900–1914. I am afraid I will never see it again in the happy time.

Obviously, the film was able to provoke all sorts of response. Lorentz's favorite story is of two women sitting in front of him during a screening of *The Plow* at the Rialto in New York. At the end of the film one turned to the other and remarked, "They never should have plowed them plains."

---

[107] "Dust Bowl Film Brings Threat to Punch Tugwell," *New York Times*, June 10, 1936.

III

The River

BY the spring of 1936, there had been many frustrations, irritations, and disappointments in the brief motion picture career of Pare Lorentz. Film making for the government had not been what he had expected. As King Vidor remarked of Lorentz's Hollywood experience, "I do remember that he thought the government effort should give him some further entry [to motion picture studios and stock film libraries] than he apparently was receiving."[1] His Hollywood experience was, however, not the only frustration and disappointment Lorentz encountered. He had his troubles with government agencies as well.

The problem was not one of red tape and procedures alone. According to John Carter, there was opposition to Lorentz's efforts within the executive branch of the government:

> At almost every point his [Lorentz's] superiors tried to sabotage the enterprise. The Department of Agriculture film chief was allowed to make a public speech ridiculing the documentary film program, high agricultural sources privately assured Henry Wallace that Lorentz would not be allowed to make another government film, his budgets were cut down and funds already assigned him were tied up by petty bureaucratic tactics. Political dynamite was required to blast officials into a realization that these films were the sort of thing the White House wanted.[2]

Perhaps Lorentz's drive and flamboyance were too much for a conservative Department of Agriculture. There may have been concern that his films would draw attention and finances away

[1] Letter from King Vidor, March 22, 1962.
[2] Jay Franklin [John Franklin Carter], "We the People" [syndicated column], October 29, 1937. From the personal files of Pare Lorentz.

50

from problems other than the one dramatized in *The Plow That Broke the Plains* or those to be treated in future films. There may have been professional jealousy of his ability to produce a quality film for the government and get it distributed nationally on commercial screens.

Lorentz had produced *The Plow* for less than twenty thousand dollars—no mean feat—although only six thousand dollars had originally been allocated for the film. Many of these expenses had not been paid, owing in part to the lack of proper government receipts. Other financial aspects of making films for the government were irritating to Lorentz. He complained about "the necessity of counting pennies and accounting for pencils."[3] Nor had Lorentz been paid excessively for his labors and ideas. He drew $18.06 a day for his efforts, less than the cameramen and others he had classified under the new Civil Service position.

Fortunately, Lorentz had continued writing for magazines, and he paid many of the expenses for completing and promoting *The Plow* out of this income and his wife's stage earnings.[4]

Added to these irritations and frustrations was the fact that Lorentz really had no staff besides Arch Mercey. Much of the fight for distribution had to be handled by the field information officers of the RA, who had not been successful in securing bookings until Lorentz himself broke the barrier in New York. Also, they could not have been expected to give their full attention to promoting the film. There was no other distribution machinery within the government to which Lorentz could turn. His work seemed to have little permanence in the form of a staff and facilities, and lacked financial support. Consequently, Lorentz's work had no future, in the form of either more films or scheduled screenings.

In June, Lorentz walked into Tugwell's office to resign.[5] He told Tugwell that he had made a valuable film according to expert opinion and had succeeded in getting commercial distribution. The film was running in New York, and bookings were beginning

[3] White, "Pare Lorentz," *Scribner's*, January, 1939, 10.
[4] She was the actress Sally Bates.
[5] Letter from Pare Lorentz, February 21, 1967.

to materialize elsewhere. He had done what he had set out to do, and there seemed to be little future.[6]

As he turned to leave Tugwell's office, he found himself facing a profile map of the Mississippi River. "There," he said, "you people are missing the biggest story in the world—the Mississippi River."[7] Tugwell called him back, asked what he meant, and began to discuss a project for a new film.

In the course of his research for *The Plow*, Lorentz had read the *Mississippi Valley Committee Report*,[8] which had given him the basic idea for the design of the new film. "Having read the report, and knowing that 51% of the population of the country lived in the Mississippi Valley, my proposal was simple—to take an engineer's boat, put a couple of pick-up trucks on it, and start at Minneapolis and go clear to the Gulf."[9] Lorentz changed these plans considerably once production began, but he convinced Tugwell that day that this idea would make an excellent film.

Tugwell communicated with the White House in an effort to secure funds. On July 4, Lorentz received a phone call at his home in Sneeden's Landing, New York, recalling him to Washington. John Carter told him that fifty thousand dollars had been provided by the President to be used specifically for the production of the proposed film. Lorentz's salary was raised to thirty dollars a day. Both the success of *The Plow That Broke the Plains* and the need for such films had been recognized in a concrete manner.[10]

Considering the problems and disappointments that must have driven Lorentz to offer his resignation, one must come to the conclusion that he thought that the obstacles, frustrations, and irritations of the first attempt could be overcome.

---

[6] Lorentz, "Lorentz on Film," Program I.

[7] White, "Pare Lorentz," *Scribner's*, January, 1939, 10.

[8] U.S. Public Works Administration, *Mississippi Valley Committee Report*.

[9] Letter from Pare Lorentz, April 5, 1962.

[10] About his meeting with Tugwell, Lorentz has been quoted at times as saying that Tugwell had never heard of the Mississippi. What Lorentz meant was that Tugwell had not thought of the river in terms other than land and commodities. After studying the map and discussing the project with Lorentz, Tugwell began to grasp

Pare Lorentz, 1963

Pare Lorentz, 1937

A cattle herd in eastern Colorado. "It was a cattleman's paradise."
From *The Plow That Broke the Plains*.

Bam White looks for rain. "Settler, plow at your peril!" From *The Plow That Broke the Plains.*

Baby playing in a dust-choked field in the Texas Panhandle. "Many were disappointed, but the great day was coming . . . the day of new causes—new profits—new hopes." From *The Plow That Broke the Plains*.

U.S. RESETTLEMENT ADMINISTRATION
PHOTOGRAPH BY ROTHSTEIN

Dust storm on the Great Plains. "This time no grass held moisture
against the wind and sun. . . . This time millions of acres of plowed
land lay open to the sun." From *The Plow That Broke the Plains.*

House buried in dust. "Baked out—blown out—and broke! Year in, year out, uncomplaining they fought the worst drought in history." From *The Plow That Broke the Plains*.

U.S. RESETTLEMENT ADMINISTRATION
PHOTOGRAPH BY DOROTHEA LANGE

Migrant farm workers at Camp Shafter, California. "No place to go . . . and no place to stop. Nothing to eat . . . nothing to do . . . and homes on four wheels . . . their work a desperate gamble for a day's labor in the fields along the highways." From *The Plow That Broke the Plains.*

U.S. RESETTLEMENT ADMINISTRATION
PHOTOGRAPH BY WALKER EVANS

Rialto Theatre, New York, 1936.

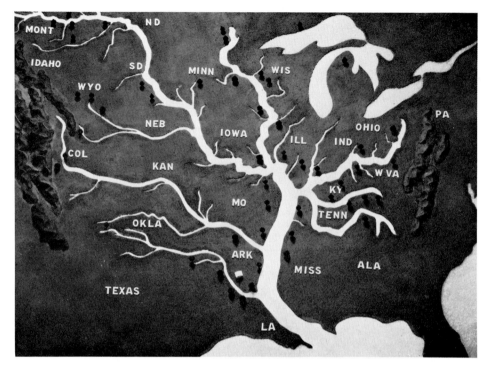

U.S. DEPARTMENT OF AGRICULTURE,
FARM SECURITY ADMINISTRATION

Map used in *The River*. "There is no such thing as an ideal river in nature, but the Mississippi River is out of joint."

Mississippi River levee, north of New Orleans. "We built a dike a thousand miles long. Man and mules; mules and mud." From *The River*.

Cotton loading, south of New Orleans. "And we made cotton king—we rolled a million bales down the river for Liverpool and Leeds." From *The River*.

Watershed destruction. "Black spruce and Norway pine; Douglas fir and red cedar; scarlet oak and shagbark hickory; we built a hundred cities and a thousand towns, but at what a cost." From *The River*.

U.S. DEPARTMENT OF AGRICULTURE,
FARM SECURITY ADMINISTRATION

The flood, 1937, Cairo, Illinois. "Food and water and clothing needed for 750,000 flood victims . . . the Mississippi claimed her valley." From *The River*.

Flood refugees, Arkansas. "But spring and fall the water comes down—" From *The River*.

U.S. DEPARTMENT OF AGRICULTURE,
FARM SECURITY ADMINISTRATION

Nature avenges herself. "And 400 million tons of topsoil—400 million tons of our valuable natural resources—have been washed into the Gulf of Mexico every year." From *The River*.

In spite of his eagerness to produce the Mississippi film, Lorentz could not afford another personal financial fiasco like *The Plow*. John Bridgeman, a Treasury clerk, was assigned to Lorentz to accompany him as agent cashier. Lorentz and Bridgeman got along well, making the financial situation much more congenial.[11]

Lorentz knew the Mississippi River Valley from personal experience. He had spent some time on the river as a youth before he enrolled at West Virginia University in 1923. He has written that he remembered the feeling of the big river.[12]

During the early summer of 1936, Lorentz was busy on two fronts: doing research for the new film, and trying to get the first one distributed nationally. In this period of research he was especially drawn to the *Mississippi Valley Committee Report*, Mark Twain's *Life on the Mississippi*, Lyle Saxon's *Father Mississippi*, and blueprints of the river made by Army engineers.[13]

Lorentz included Virgil Thomson in the plans for the music for the second film. Both men were familiar with the folk music and literature of the river and hill country. Lorentz had been impressed by Honegger's *King David*, and was particularly interested in the possibility of building up a score for the film in the form of work songs with a boss singer and a workers' chorus engaging in calls and responses, somewhat similar to the form of Honegger's oratorio.[14]

Lorentz prepared a script in outline form based on his research and headed for the Mississippi Valley in the summer of 1936 to check the script and his original idea of floating down the Mississippi from its source to its mouth at the Gulf of Mexico. He quickly saw the impracticality of his plan.

From Cairo, Illinois, south, the big river is rather dull from a photographic point of view. "You can't take a thousand feet of

the concept of the entity of the river basin. (Letter from Pare Lorentz, January 21, 1962.)

11 MacCann, *op. cit.*, 191.
12 Letter from Pare Lorentz, April 5, 1962.
13 Interview with Pare Lorentz, July 24, 1961.
14 Lorentz, "Lorentz on Film," Program I.

nothing," he said.[15] Such a presentation would not hold an audience.

At Vicksburg, Mississippi, he visited the massive hydraulics laboratory maintained by the Corps of Engineers and learned that the key to controlling floods in the lower valley was controlling the smaller streams and tributaries of the river.

Consequently, he decided to tell his story by working down from small mountain streams and rivers—especially the Tennessee—along the tributaries, and finally to the big river itself. As a matter of fact, there are few shots of the Mississippi River in the film.[16]

He returned east, revised his script, and set about hiring a camera crew, which was eventually composed of Stacy and Horace Woodard, Floyd Crosby, and Willard Van Dyke.

Stacy and Horace were the cameramen, in the firm of Woodard Brothers, who had been producing a series of nature films called "The Struggle to Live." They had won two Motion Picture Academy awards for their work: a second prize for short pictures in 1933 for *The Sea*, and first prize in 1934 for *City of Wax*. Floyd Crosby had worked as a cameraman on two outstanding exterior films, *Matto Grosso* and *Tabu* (1931), the latter produced and directed by F. W. Murnau. He won an Academy Award for his work on *Tabu*. He had had experience in a variety of foreign locations with scientific expeditions. Willard Van Dyke had studied photography with Edward Weston and had made a picture for the WPA in California.[17]

First public notice that a second film was under way appeared in the press on October 6, 1936. The *New York Times* commented on the report two days later on its editorial page and quoted Lorentz: "We are not going to argue that only man is vile. There never was such a thing as an ideal river. . . . But we do want to

[15] Pare Lorentz, in a public lecture at Wisconsin State University, Oshkosh, Wisconsin, May 5, 1966.

[16] Lorentz, "Lorentz on Film," Program I.

[17] U.S. Farm Security Administration press release, n.d. From the personal files of Pare Lorentz. King Vidor was partly responsible for Lorentz's new crew. He recommended Crosby to Lorentz. He also recommended Lloyd Nosler, who had worked with him in Hollywood and who was to be Lorentz's editorial assistant on the next two films.

show that if man will only adopt practices slowing down the flow of the river he will get the full benefit of it in fields free from erosion, in power, in clean water."[18] According to Lorentz the worst flood in the Mississippi Valley had been in De Soto's time.

Although Lorentz was hired in July to produce the new film, various problems kept the project ensnarled until October. This was a longer delay than Lorentz had experienced on the first film, and it was to affect the film through changes in the shooting schedule.

Original plans were to start shooting at Lake Itasca, Minnesota, near the source of the Mississippi. Lorentz hired a camera crew from the University of Minnesota under the direction of Robert Kissack to film footage. Because of bad weather and a peat-bog fire, the footage was not shot until spring.

Lorentz's own cameramen were divided into two crews. The Woodards accompanied Lorentz to West Virginia, where the first footage was shot overlooking what had been his grandfather's land at Tygart's Valley.[19] Horace Woodard left the crew after a short stay and returned home.[20]

In Alabama, Tennessee, and Mississippi the two crews filmed footage of erosion, the barren hillsides, the poverty of the share-croppers, reclamation in the TVA area, and, of course, dams, both completed and under construction. As shooting continued into December, the crews were plagued by rains. Stacy Woodard left near the end of December. King Vidor had recommended Floyd Crosby. Lorentz wired Crosby to join the crew in New Orleans.[21]

As producer-director, Lorentz developed considerable new skill during the production of *The River*. Two anecdotes illustrate this growth. In the sequence of the Negro roustabouts unloading

---

[18] *New York Times*, October 8, 1936. The report originally appeared in the *New York Herald Tribune*, October 6, 1936.

[19] Letter from Pare Lorentz, April 5, 1962. MacCann's interview with Van Dyke corroborates the trip to West Virginia to shoot the first footage. (MacCann, *op. cit.*, 194.)

[20] MacCann, *op. cit.*, 194, quoting an interview with Willard Van Dyke, April 9, 1949. Lorentz gave Van Dyke an assistant to hold the slate and act as financial agent to pay the bills.

[21] Letter from Floyd Crosby, December 10, 1961.

bales of cotton from a Mississippi River steamboat, the workers could not accept the fact that they were to do real work. There was to be a series of shots of bales tumbling down the gangplank toward the camera, with the heads of two Negro roustabouts looming above each bale as it neared the lens. The Negroes thought it was playacting and began mugging ferociously as they neared the camera. At other times they moved listlessly, without the characteristic rhythm of such work. Lorentz had to order retakes time and time again. Everyone was getting tired, stiff, and sore. Finally, Lorentz had the mate on the steamboat shout orders to the men. They put their backs into the work, forgot the camera, and Lorentz had his footage.[22] Crosby was the cameraman.

A further proof of Lorentz's growth is the fact that he no longer left matters to chance. He did not photograph what he happened to find along the way, as he had done much of the time in producing *The Plow*. Now he made plans in advance for necessary footage. For example, through William Alexander, the Farm Security administrator, he obtained information about the time of cotton loadings in New Orleans and in the valley in order to get the needed footage.[23]

The last shots for the script were made on January 16, 1937, near New Orleans. Shortly after the crew broke up, it became apparent that the flood coming down the Ohio and some of the other tributaries was going to be a serious one. Lorentz recalled Van Dyke and Crosby to Memphis on January 21 and told them to start filming, but, as Van Dyke has told Richard MacCann, there were a thousand miles of disaster to cover and they did not know where to start.[24] Lorentz flew to Memphis, prepared a script for the flood scenes, and supervised the shooting. Since the shooting budget was almost expended, he wired Henry Wallace for more money; the secretary granted permission to film the flood.

The unexpected flood disaster provided the crew with some of the most thrilling unstaged photography ever included in a motion

[22] Howe, "U.S. Film Service Presents," *U.S. Camera*, June–July, 1940. From the personal files of Pare Lorentz.

[23] MacCann, *op. cit.*, 194, note 66.

[24] *Ibid.*, 195.

picture. This was truly an unexpected stroke of luck for Lorentz and the film. Lorentz had planned to include a flood in the film, but he anticipated that it would have to be done through stock footage. Not only did Lorentz now have exciting flood footage of his own, but the disaster itself served to focus attention on the film when it was released, just as the dust storms of 1936 had aided the promotion of *The Plow*. Whole communities were evacuated, and tent cities were built to house the refugees. Distribution centers for food, fuel, water, and medical supplies were set up. An extensive first-aid program was put into action. When the floodwaters receded, the WPA went to work removing silt and repairing the damage.[25]

Lorentz and his crew worked their way back up the river, filming the rising, rushing, rampaging waters and the human suffering. They went up from Memphis along the Mississippi River levees to Illinois, often working as long as thirty-eight hours at a stretch.

When they arrived at Cairo, they ran into opposition from relief directors. They were told they could go no further. Only one boat was to be allowed on the river, and that was a government boat. Because Lorentz was working for the government, he assumed that he and the crew could go on the boat. They were told they could not, although press and newsreel photographers were on the boat with government permission. Lorentz asked whose permission he needed in order to go along. He was told by a relief official that the man from Paramount was in charge. Lorentz is then reported to have said:

> Let me see if I've got this straight. This is a government boat and I'm making pictures for the government—the one that owns this boat and that you're working for and I'm working for. The same government that has to have thousands of feet of motion pictures of this flood for the Army Engineering Corps and the Department of Agriculture. If they don't get these pictures from me, they're going to have to buy them from commercial newsreel men, and meanwhile I

25 U.S. National Emergency Council, U.S. Film Service, *Study Guide: The River*, 15–17.

am being paid to take them and I can't get on a government boat to
do it without permission from Paramount.[26]

The official agreed with Lorentz's interpretation of the situation.
Lorentz went over the heads of the officials to the Corps of
Engineers, who were supervising matters along the river, and
soon had his crew on the boat.

After the episode at Cairo, the crew continued up the receding
Ohio River, shooting pictures of the ruined cities, until they
reached Ironton, Ohio, not far downstream from West Virginia,
the starting place of the film. They finished their work on March
1, 1937.[27]

Lorentz returned to New York and began his assembly of the
film. He started screening what he had photographed, began his
editing plan for the film, and called in Virgil Thomson to work
on the score.

Lloyd Nosler joined Lorentz as editor on *The River* at the
recommendation of King Vidor. He remained with Lorentz as
chief of the technical department and worked on Lorentz's later
films for the government. He did not edit any of the films alone, in
the sense that Lorentz gave him raw footage and told him to put it
together. The two men assembled the scenes together, working
closely and amicably for long hours. Nosler enjoyed the opportunity to experiment, and much of the pictorial continuity of the
film is the result of his talent.

Lorentz, inspired by the *Mississippi Valley Committee Report*,[28] had decided that the opening of the film should stress the
problem of runoff in the highlands and along the tributaries. Too,
the initial section of the film should show the Mississippi growing
from a drop of water to the wide expanse of its mouth. Lorentz
planned much of the editing as moving from left to right and top
to bottom.[29]

The other theme in the film—the close relationship between

[26] McEvoy, "Young Man with a Camera," *Reader's Digest*, August, 1940, 74.
[27] U.S. Farm Security Administration press release, n.d. From the personal files
of Pare Lorentz.
[28] P. 62.
[29] Lorentz, "Lorentz on Film," Program I.

land, water, and people—is also to be found in the *Mississippi Valley Report*. Consider this quotation from the sound track of the film:

> But you can't plan for water unless you plan for land. . . .
> But you cannot plan for water and land unless you plan for people.[30]

The foreword (page ii) to the report begins: "We cannot plan for water unless we also consider the relevant problems of the land. We cannot plan for water and land unless we plan for the whole people."[31]

The rough cutting took several months, with Lorentz and Nosler working as much as eighteen hours a day in the cutting room. Some of the assembling was determined by Lorentz's own reactions to the river: "The bigger the scene, or rather the landscape, the faster you should cut. A big panorama of a river might be impressive to the movie maker, but it gets real dull to an audience and very quickly."[32]

While the film was being assembled, there were two problems of content to be faced. The flood presented one problem: "If you build it to a climax, what else can you say about the other problems? The problem was solved by music in part."[33] The other problem was how to include Civil War material to add historical flavor. This had to be done in such a way as not to offend either the South or the North. It was decided merely to show the letter General Robert E. Lee wrote to his troops on the day before the surrender at Appomattox.

Lorentz originally wanted Thomson to experiment with the form of the musical score, but, because of lack of time and money, this experimentation was out of the question. Thomson set to work on a score similar in form to the one for *The Plow That Broke the Plains*. As in his preparation for *The Plow*, Thomson did considerable musicological research, systematically studying

[30] Sound track from *The River*.

[31] U.S. Public Works Administration, *Mississippi Valley Committee Report*, ii.

[32] Letter from Pare Lorentz, April 5, 1962.

[33] Lorentz, "Lorentz on Film," Program I. The solution will be discussed in detail later.

folklore and old hymns. He corresponded with George Pullen Jackson, a specialist in these fields and a faculty member at Vanderbilt University. Jackson provided Thomson with a large number of white spirituals.[34]

In the third program of the NET series "Lorentz on Film," Lorentz explained how he and Thomson worked together on *The River*:

> Virgil made piano sketches of each section of the movie, each large sequence, and then the crew and I tried to edit it down to a pre-conceived time, at which point Virgil would get some ideas, genius ideas, and we would work back and forth so that you didn't have a completed score put on top of a completed movie or vice versa. The words were then written to the music and to a concept of music.[35]

The fact that the score was composed and the film assembled simultaneously seems to have helped maintain a close relationship between the two, resulting in an integrated film and score, as in *The Plow*, not "a completed score put on top of a completed movie or vice versa." The pictorial and musical unity of *The River* drew praise from many reviewers.[36]

Because of the nature of the pictorial content of *The River*, it was necessary for film and music to play roles of varying dominance throughout the assembled motion picture. For example, in order to keep the flood scenes, with their tremendous dramatic punch, from overshadowing the more important but less exciting parts of the film that follow, the flood music was made loud and dramatic but rather obvious and shallow. The score for the later scenes relied on folk music, and was "full of the emotional content inherent in anything essentially human."[37] Kathleen Hoover also comments on the technique of fitting music to specific pictorial content: "For the human episodes he [Thomson] drew on folk tunes, but his idiom was modern and individual. For the

[34] Hoover and Cage, *op. cit.*, 86.

[35] Lorentz, "Lorentz on Film," Program III. This process is almost identical to the way Thomson described the method the two followed. See pp. 34–35.

[36] See Chapter VIII for critical comments on *The River*.

[37] Howe, "U.S. Film Service Presents," *U.S. Camera*, June–July, 1940. From the personal files of Pare Lorentz.

landscape sequences he invented material that captures the Mississippi's changing moods with electric immediacy."[38]

The narration was not written until the score had been composed and the film edited in its final form. The text was published later as a book with stills from the film.[39] In the preface, Lorentz wrote, "It was intended as a functional text to accompany Mr. Virgil Thomson's score, and fit the tempo of the sequences in the picture."

The narration for *The River* developed into its particular form rather unexpectedly. A poetic form had not been planned. Otis L. Wiese, editor of *McCall's*, asked Lorentz to write a report on the flood for his magazine. Lorentz, the movie critic for *McCall's* at the time, agreed because he felt that the report might provide a basis for the narration for the movie. He wrote a five-thousand-word narrative report, which he later decided would be unsatisfactory for the readers of *McCall's* because it was "too specific, too statistical, and too long." He reviewed all the material he had collected, including Forest Service reports and news accounts of the flood, and began work on a lyrical report, written in one weekend in a nonstop effort. He submitted both versions to Wiese, who published the lyrical version.[40] After 150,000 requests for copies had been received from readers of *McCall's*, Lorentz was convinced that this poetic approach would be suitable for the film.[41] With only a few changes, it became the narration for the film.

Chalmers recorded the narration, and then it was put together with Virgil Thomson's score and Lorentz's edited film. The story line and construction—weak points in *The Plow*—were strong in *The River*. Added to the previous combination—excellent photography—music by Thomson, and narration by Lorentz, spoken by Thomas Chalmers—is the imaginative use of sound: "Effective use is made of natural sounds merely by repetition. For example,

[38] Hoover and Cage, *op. cit.*, 86.

[39] Pare Lorentz, *The River*.

[40] Pare Lorentz, "The River," *McCall's* (May, 1937). From the personal files of Pare Lorentz.

[41] Lorentz, "Lorentz on Film," Program III; interview with Pare Lorentz, July 27, 1961.

the sounds of the steel mill early in the film are imitated in the frantic whistle of a coast-guard boat later."[42]

The completed sequences of *The River* are arranged chronologically. The initial sequence shows the growth of the Mississippi River from its many tributaries, the waters flowing calmly and naturally between their banks. This was the state of the basin before the coming of the white man with agriculture and industry. The following sequences show cotton farming, the impoverishment of the South by the Civil War, and the growth of lumber and steel industries. The results of the exploitation of the valley are chronicled in the next sequences: floods, naked and eroding hillsides, displaced and impoverished people, the relationship between poor land and poor people. The epilogue depicts the Tennessee Valley Authority at work putting the valley together again.

Lorentz spent nearly six months completing *The River* after the dispersal of the crew in March. The film cost approximately fifty thousand dollars, in comparison with about twenty thousand dollars for *The Plow*. The difference in cost is accounted for in part by the increased number of personnel, the greater distance traveled on location—fourteen states for the second, five for the first—and the cost of shooting the unexpected flood.

Word of the cost of *The River* must have leaked out early. Several months before the film was released, the *New York Times* reported that the Senate Special Committee on Government Reorganization was going to investigate motion picture production in the RA. The committee, with Senator Harry Byrd as chairman, was concerned with the cost of the two films. The RA officials were reported as welcoming such an inquiry since "they regard the films as one of their most successful and least expensive experiments."[43] Apparently, the investigation was dropped.

The second film of merit was now complete. Because of the confidence Lorentz had gained from the success of the first film and the encouragement he had received from his sponsors, in-

[42] A. R. Fulton, *Motion Pictures: The Development of an Art from Silent Films to the Age of Television*, 197–98.

[43] "RA Film Inquiry to Begin," *New York Times*, June 6, 1937.

cluding President Roosevelt, he was able to proceed in a different manner in securing the release of this film. It was not necessary to take it around to friends in the profession to seek their approval. Lorentz knew he had a good film, and he began to make plans to get it distributed.[44]

Secretary of Agriculture Henry Wallace was the first ranking official to see the film. Arrangements were made for him to see it at 10:00 A.M. in a caucus room. Lorentz objected: "No one looks at films at 10:00 A.M." But Wallace did look at it at 10:00 A.M. When it was over, he rose, walked to the door, turned, and said, "There's no corn in it."[45] The secretary's Iowa heritage was showing. Actually, it had been too late to get good footage of a corn harvest.

After this experience Lorentz was eager to get the President's reaction. He did not know how to get an invitation or arrange an appropriate screening. George Gercke, who had been Albany correspondent for the *New York World* when Roosevelt was governor of New York and was familiar with the President's habits, likes, and dislikes, found the answer. He decided that the President might not mind a postscript to his evening's film program at Hyde Park, and arranged an invitation for Lorentz and himself.

Lorentz, Gercke, and *The River* arrived at Hyde Park on a rainy night in September just after dinner, about 9:00 P.M. By coincidence, the President had been asking at dinner what had happened to the new Lorentz film. It was a typical, quiet evening at Hyde Park. As Lorentz recalls, "I think the Japs had bombed Shanghai, the stock market had crashed, and there had been an intercollegiate regatta on the Hudson."[46]

The President looked at several newsreels and then a feature film, Sonja Henie in *Thin Ice*. About 12:30 A.M. *The River* was shown. When the lights came on at the end, Roosevelt turned to

[44] Tugwell's approval was no longer needed for the film. He resigned before the election in 1936, about the time Lorentz began work on location. The motion picture unit, along with most of the other activities of the RA, was transferred to the new Farm Security Administration while the crews were out on location.

[45] Lorentz, "Lorentz on Film," Program I.

[46] *Ibid.*

Lorentz and said: "That's a grand movie. What can I do to help?"[47] According to Lorentz, the President wanted to show the film to a joint session of Congress, but Lorentz demurred.

Did Lorentz anticipate the President's question or not? It is likely that, as they made the trip up the Hudson by train, he and Gercke had discussed what the President's various reactions might be. Lorentz was ready with an answer. He was facing two problems: the problem of distribution and his own future, and the role of movies in the government. He posed both problems to the President.

Thomas Corcoran, a presidential adviser and coauthor with Ben Cohen of several New Deal measures, was visiting Hyde Park that weekend. He was called from upstairs and joined the discussion. The result, according to Richard D. MacCann,[48] was that Corcoran began immediately to work on plans for the United States Film Service.

The next step Lorentz had in mind for distributing the film was motivated by its content and his experience while filming it. He decided to give the people most concerned—the residents of the Mississippi Valley—the opportunity to see the film first. He did not want Southerners to be offended by the film, and was worried that they might be if they learned of it first through a review. If he could win them over first, he felt that there would be much less misunderstanding later.[49]

The world premiere of *The River* took place in New Orleans on October 29, 1937. If Lorentz had been worried about southern reaction before the New Orleans premiere, he had no need to worry when the screening was over. The audience stood up and cheered when General Lee's name appeared on the screen. The manager of the Strand Theatre, where the premiere was held, sent the following telegram to Lorentz:

[47] *Ibid.*

[48] *Op. cit.,* 196.

[49] Lorentz, "Lorentz on Film," Program I. Lorentz held another semiprivate screening in New York for fifteen friends, as he had done for *The Plow.* He also took *The River* to Hollywood and screened it for Charlie Chaplin, King Vidor, and others. (Letter from Pare Lorentz, May 29, 1964.)

Held world premiere of River October 29th three hundred and fifty leading people at New Orleans. Reaction was wonderful. I personally contacted several hundred of those people after premiere. They congratulated me for being able to bring film of that nature to my screen. Nineteen schools of the city had a representative from their history class to see River. Also showed Rivers [sic] to some 20,000 patrons. Audience reaction great. The public needs more history shorts like The River. Hoping Minneapolis enjoys it as New Orleans did.[50]

The film was next shown in Memphis on November 1 and in St. Louis on November 10. Other cities on the schedule were Des Moines and St. Paul.

The success of the river-city openings is revealed in excerpts from a brochure distributed by the Farm Security Administration:

New Orleans State: This is a cinema which will live in your memory. It should make America sit up and take notice.

New Orleans Times-Picayune: It is a story which concerns America and Mr. Lorentz has told it in a manner which will make America listen.

New Orleans Item: The River is an extraordinarily well-done documentary film and is a worthy successor to *The Plow That Broke the Plains*.

Memphis Commercial Appeal: . . . should thrill audiences everywhere, not merely because of the importance of its content, but also by virtue of the masterful manner in which its makers have dramatized the subject.

Memphis Press-Scimitar: The River is more compelling and exciting drama than its predecessor, *The Plow That Broke the Plains*.

St. Louis Post-Dispatch: An accomplishment exceeding that of the previous picture, and a work of exceptional pictorial quality.

St. Louis Globe-Democrat: It is a film for the nation to see and ponder over and never forget.

Des Moines Register: It is a splendid job. We recommend that people see it.

St. Paul Dispatch: It is an extraordinary piece of work.[51]

50 From the personal files of Pare Lorentz.

51 U.S. Farm Security Administration, *"The River"* [brochure], n.d. From the personal files of Pare Lorentz.

The reviewer for the *St. Louis Post-Dispatch* rated *The River* better than *The Plow*. He also foresaw that opponents of the New Deal would see it as New Deal propaganda, but pointed out that the picture had very little argument for any specific project.[52] Almost twenty-five minutes of the total twenty-nine in the film were devoted to photography of the Mississippi and its tributaries, industrial development, the flood, and erosion.

The River was inextricably tied up with politics from the time of its release. Two days before the Washington premiere, the political significance of the film was pointed out in the *Washington Star*:

> Just as *The Plow* appeared at a time when the Government was emphasizing the need of widespread soil conservation and relief for sharecroppers, so *The River* is released at a time when the Government is on a new quest. Pending before Congress is the Norris Bill proposing to create seven national authorities to build dams, abate floods, recreate farming, improve navigation—and generate power. The President advocated enactment of the legislation.[53]

The Washington premiere was held at the Rialto Theatre on December 7, 1937. Invitations were sent out by the secretary of agriculture. Lorentz attended, and must have been thrilled by the spontaneous and sustained round of applause that burst forth from the audience at the conclusion of the film. The next day the Washington papers were full of praise:

> *Washington Post*, Nelson B. Bell: In *The River* Pare Lorentz has produced a brilliantly illuminating screen treatise upon the irresistible power for both good and evil of the Mississippi, father of waters.
> *Washington Herald*, Mabelle Jennings: *The River* proves momentous film in Rialto preview.
> *Washington Star*, Jay Carmody: If you do not believe there is drama and poetry and excitement in the documentary motion picture, it can only be because you have not seen *The River*.

The *Washington Daily News* praised the film but was concerned about the propaganda for the TVA at the end. In the edition of

[52] November 11, 1937. From the personal files of Pare Lorentz.
[53] December 5, 1937. From the personal files of Pare Lorentz.

December 10, this paper reprinted Nelson B. Bell's review from the *Post*.

A reviewer from the *Christian Science Monitor* also attended the Washington premiere:

> Official Washington had a thrill last night when it saw Pare Lorentz's second documentary film with music, *The River*, prepared for the Farm Security Administration.
>
> In effect, the senses of the audience were assailed on three sides simultaneously as they looked at the picture.
>
> Some of the sequences are masterpieces of oblique suggestion, and all drive home the central philosophy or "propaganda," that it is man's denudation of the forests that has wrought the erosion and floods, and that what man has wrecked man can put together again . . . by TVA dams, let us say.[54]

The first major city to book *The River* for an extended run was Chicago. Oliver Griswold, who had arranged the screenings at St. Louis and Memphis, worked out a special rotogravure Sunday section with Louis Rupple, managing editor of the *Chicago Times*. The material in this section was based on news coverage of the flood and the river-city premieres. Griswold arranged a conference with executives of Balaban and Katz Theatres, showed the film, and told them of the publicity material prepared with Rupple. The officials agreed to book the film into the Apollo Theatre. As Griswold wrote, "The film sold itself. My job was just to get it before the right people."[55]

Following the run at the Apollo, Joe Strut, of the Balaban and Katz Corporation, wrote to Griswold on December 15, 1937, quoting a memo from the Apollo Theatre:

> We are very pleased with the comments we are receiving on the government short, *The River*. Our audiences applaud it after every showing.
>
> During the last day or two we have received numerous calls on the telephone inquiring how long we are going to run it. Many of the inquiries are on the nature of people asking if we intend to show it in our outlying houses.

[54] December 9, 1937. From the personal files of Pare Lorentz.

[55] Letter from Oliver Griswold, December 10, 1963.

In short, it is our belief that this subject has received more favorable comments than any short of this nature we have ever shown.[56]

During December, *The River* had a run at the Little Theatre in Washington, where applause was noted at every showing. An increase in business, instead of the usual slump during the Christmas shopping season, was noticed by the management.

Before the film was released generally, many critics firmly endorsed *The River* and urged their readers to see the film. Gilbert Seldes wrote, "Nothing more useful to the entire industry can be accomplished than to force distributors to go outside their commercial contracts to show this picture."[57] After attending a preview of the film in New York, William Boehnel recommended that his readers see the film.[58]

The government had made the film available without charge to any theater owner who wanted to show it, but the film was still not enjoying wide distribution. The river-city campaign, the Washington premiere, and the Chicago run were beginning to arouse interest, but a national distribution contract was needed. Many exhibitors were still wary of showing a government film.[59]

The River was spared the fate of being a film of merit that would rarely be seen. Paramount Pictures agreed to distribute it. Lorentz completed negotiations with Paramount Pictures and signed the contracts himself. *Business Week* reported that the film was available without charge, except for transportation charges from the Paramount distribution centers in thirty-eight cities throughout the country.[60] Barney Balaban, chairman of the board of Paramount Pictures, must have been impressed with the film's run in his chain in Chicago. The three-week run in Chicago, as well as bookings elsewhere, had proved that the film could draw cus-

56 Letter from Joe Strut, Balaban and Katz Corporation, to Oliver Griswold, Farm Security Administration, Documentary Film Section, December 15, 1937. From the personal files of Pare Lorentz.

57 "The River," *Scribner's*, January, 1938, 42.

58 "New Film Tells Story of Floods," *New York World-Telegram*, January 29, 1938. From the personal files of Pare Lorentz.

59 "Movies: The Mississippi's Power for Good and Evil," *Literary Digest*, November 20, 1937, 34.

60 "Federal Film Hit," *Business Week*, February 19, 1938, 36.

tomers, the only measure of merit that concerned exhibitors and distributors.

The first public showing of *The River* in New York was at Loew's Criterion on February 4, 1938. The companion on the bill, *Scandal Street*, lasted about a week, but *The River* was held over.[61] It ran five weeks in Boston at a first-run theater in February and March.

Lorentz had won a major distribution battle on the merits of his second film, but Hollywood was going to withhold the well-deserved glory of an Academy Award. When the list of nominees for the 1938 awards was released, *The River* was conspicuous by its absence from the short-subject categories. The explanation was that documentary films such as *The River* did not fit any of the existing categories, including cartoons, black-and-white shorts up to a thousand feet, black-and-white shorts up to three thousand feet, and color films of three thousand feet. The committee did recommend that a new category for documentary and educational pictures be established.[62]

Lorentz received support from the Screen Directors Guild, the only professional film organization he ever joined. The FSA announced a protest by the guild to the Academy of Motion Picture Arts and Science over the exclusion of *The River* from consideration for an award.[63] As Lorentz recalls, no one member was responsible, but several of his friends, including Milestone and King Vidor, joined the protest.

Dean Jennings, a newspaperman who was working for the FSA and had officially submitted the film, told Lorentz that all the producers of shorts, including Lorentz's friend Walt Disney, objected to its inclusion on the grounds that the government was competing with private industry. For this reason they did not allow the film even to be screened in competition.[64]

Although *The River* was denied an Oscar, awards did come.

61 Frank Nugent, "One Down, Two Doubled," *New York Times*, February 13, 1938.
62 " 'River' Omitted from Oscar Nominations," *New York Times*, February 7, 1938.
63 "Protest Ban on Film," *New York Times*, March 10, 1938.
64 Letter from Pare Lorentz, April 5, 1962.

The first major award that the film received was the J. Emanuel Plaque for 1938. This award was presented annually to the best three-reel dramatic film, and was based on a vote of 4,200 motion picture exhibitors.[65] This award led to Lorentz's being called to Washington to receive the congratulations of the President. On this date—June 19, 1938—public notice was made for the first time that the President was considering a permanent bureau or agency to produce motion pictures, with Lorentz as its head.

Praise for the film kept coming in from many quarters. From the South, Oscar Johnson, president of the Delta and Pine Land Company of Mississippi, wrote Lorentz to say that *The River* was "excellently done and provides an object lesson which should be beneficial in the effort being made by the Federal and State governments to promote soil conservation and the prevention of erosion."[66] The chief of the Motion Picture Section of the Pan American Union wrote that he thought *The River* was excellent and offered to discuss with Lorentz the possibility of having the film dubbed in Spanish for official South American release.[67]

While on his way to England to direct a film based on A. J. Cronin's *The Citadel*, King Vidor stopped off in New York to see Lorentz. Vidor had a script which had been prepared at the MGM studio but with which he was not completely satisfied. He invited Lorentz to go to England with him to discuss the objectives of the book and some of the ideas that could be worked into the script. He hoped it might be possible to get Lorentz on the crew in England as a writer or assistant, but this plan did not materialize. Vidor found that the employment quotas were so strict in England that it would have been impossible to have Lorentz as a writer along with the other Americans working on the film.[68] Lorentz felt a need to get away for a while and rest. He accepted the offer to go along but did not intend to stay. In twenty-four hours, with the

[65] "Roosevelt Studies a New Movie Bureau," *New York Times*, June 19, 1938.

[66] Letter to Pare Lorentz from Oscar Johnson, November 9, 1937. Most of the scenes of sharecroppers were filmed on this man's plantation, and Lorentz thought it only proper that he be invited to see the finished film. (Letter from Pare Lorentz, May 29, 1964.)

[67] Letter to Pare Lorentz from William B. Larson, February 8, 1938.

[68] Letter from King Vidor, March 22, 1962.

70

help of his crew and clearance from the White House, he was ready to go. He took along only a small suitcase, a typewriter, and a guitar, and sailed with Vidor on the *Manhattan* on April 20, 1938.

By what Lorentz calls "an extraordinary circumstance," there was a print of *The River* on board. Captain Randall of the *Manhattan* had sailed as skipper of Roosevelt's sailboat, the *Malabar X*, and was an ardent admirer of the President. He liked *The River* so much he had the film screened twice daily during the crossing.[69]

While on board ship, Lorentz received word from Iris Barry, curator of the Film Library of the Museum of Modern Art, informing him that she had cabled John Grierson and Robert Flaherty in London that Lorentz was coming. When Lorentz arrived at the Savoy Hotel, Flaherty and Grierson were waiting for him, along with Charles Laughton and Elsa Lanchester, whom Lorentz had met in New York. When they heard that Lorentz had a print of *The River* with him, they made arrangements to have it shown the next night at the annual showing of the work of various members of the General Post Office Film Unit, which Grierson headed.

The River was a big success at the showing. Later, Laughton invited Flaherty, Lorentz, and several others to his apartment for a party. During the weekend that followed, Flaherty introduced Lorentz to several friends. Lorentz was flattered by Flaherty's courtesy and interest. Before Lorentz left England, Flaherty said to him, "I left America because of Herbert Hoover, but now I'm tired of the understatement of the British Empire and would like to work for the U.S. Government, if they're allowing people to do such things as *The River*."[70] Lorentz told Flaherty that he would hire him to direct a film for the government if an opportunity arose.[71]

The River was shown in theaters throughout the United King-

[69] Letter from Pare Lorentz, April 5, 1962.

[70] *Ibid.*

[71] Although Mrs. Flaherty does not remember any of the details of her husband's meeting with Lorentz in London, she does recall that *The River* made a deep impression on those who saw it, including her and her husband. (Letter from Frances Flaherty, December 29, 1961.)

dom. Lorentz remembers a white-tie opening night at the smart West End Carlton Theatre in London, attended by Ambassador Joseph P. Kennedy and some of his family. The opening was arranged by Elsie Cohen of the Henry Bernstein Theatres.

Before Lorentz left England, arrangements were made to show *The River* to the British public on television. The week following the telecast a British critic wrote: "There was history made in the cinema on Monday evening last week, when one of the noblest films that America has ever produced, *The River*, was shown to the English public for the first time—on television."[72] Another critic reported to the *New York Times*: "It came through clear as a diamond with just the homely sense that fits it, of a good story told quietly by one man to another over his smoke and highball."[73]

According to Lorentz, the various screenings of *The River* in Great Britain had a rather amusing consequence. The telecast of the film resulted in some revenue for the United States government. The BBC is reported to have paid a hundred dollars to televise the film.[74] As a representative of the government, Lorentz signed a contract with Henry Bernstein, who owned a chain of theaters in the United Kingdom. The contract provided that half the proceeds were to go to the American government. Bernstein sent the money to the Guaranty Trust Bank in New York. The arrival of the money upset officials in the FSA because they did not know where to have the money sent. As Lorentz recalls, the money finally ended up in general receipts in the Treasury.[75]

On the voyage back to the United States aboard the *Queen Mary*, Lorentz wrote a script outline for what he hoped would be his next film. He and his staff had already begun the research. The film was to be called *Ecce Homo!* and was to be a study of unemployment. He later based a radio script on this outline and he submitted it to the Columbia Broadcasting System.[76] The radio

[72] C. A. LeJeune, "Films of the Week," *London Observer*, June 5, 1938. From the personal files of Pare Lorentz.

[73] C. A. Jenkins, "Progress on the Thames," *New York Times*, June 19, 1938.

[74] Pinkerton, Associated Press news release, October 13, 1938. From the personal files of Pare Lorentz.

[75] Letter from Pare Lorentz, May 29, 1964.

[76] The story of the broadcast and the uncompleted film will be told in Chapter V.

script was in a sense an audition because it gave Lorentz the opportunity to experiment with a new medium. He returned to New York with a new script, refreshed and eager to begin production again.[77]

The next international activity involving *The River* was at the Venice International Film Festival of 1938.[78] In June of that year, Lorentz was concerned with the possibility of new projects and the growing possibility of a permanent office, and he was not at first interested in devoting any of his time to the festival. It should also be remembered he had only recently been denied one prize that would have given him and those connected with the film immense personal satisfaction—an Academy Award.

When George Gercke and Arch Mercey insisted on submitting the film to Venice, Lorentz consented. The confident anticipations of Lorentz's staff were shaken rudely when it was discovered that someone in the State Department had learned of the entry and blocked it. No explanation was given for the action.

Lorentz's superiors at the FSA arranged an interview for him with Sumner Welles, then undersecretary of state. Lorentz explained why the film had been submitted and was told by Welles that the office of the secretary had been misinformed. They had

[77] Lorentz's activities on behalf of *The River* did not keep him from helping Vidor with *The Citadel*. They discussed the film for some time on the way over. Vidor considers these talks to have been of great value. (Letter from King Vidor, March 22, 1962.)

[78] It seems that *The Plow That Broke the Plains* prepared the way for *The River* at Venice. *The Plow* had been submitted to the festival of 1937. Lorentz was not aware that *The Plow* had been entered in the previous festival until he received a letter from the chief archivist of the festival stating that someone had dropped a film can at his office at festival headquarters on the evening of the last day of the competition. The film can was not accompanied by any information about title, source, or explanation of the entry, nor was it accompanied by foreign-language translations, as required by the rules of the festival. The chief archivist reported, however, that *The Plow* was screened when the festival was over and that the members of the committee felt it would have been competitive if it had been submitted properly—that is, in time and with the necessary translations. (Interview with Pare Lorentz.)

Mercey has written that he, Guy Bolte, and Philip Martin were in New York in the summer of 1937 when they heard of the festival. They decided to send *The Plow* over on the *Bremen*. Mercey even considered accompanying the film but decided against it after talking with Tugwell on the phone. The film was shipped over on the *Bremen*, but they did not know that specific material should have accompanied the film. (Letter from Arch Mercey, February 4, 1964.)

been told that Lorentz was selling the film in Europe, and felt that, because of the rise of the Fascists, neutrality sentiment in the United States, American prestige abroad, and the conditions revealed in the film, it would not be wise to sell this particular film abroad. Welles agreed with Lorentz that a film festival was another matter entirely and offered to do everything possible to ensure the success of *The River* in Venice.

Welles personally ordered the film sent to Venice as quickly as possible and translated into three languages. He also cabled Ambassador William Bullitt, requesting that he personally go to Venice to attend the festival as the official representative of the United States government. This request was made, at the suggestion of Lorentz, to counteract the lack of recognition of the arts by the government. Lorentz pointed out to Welles that Virgil Thomson had once been invited to Buckingham Palace with six other foreign artists and composers and that not one official of the State Department had attended the affair. Lorentz emphasized to the undersecretary that the attitude of the United States toward artists and art festivals was well known and was damaging American prestige abroad as well as the prestige of individual artists.[79]

The River was first shown at the Venice Festival on the evening of August 9 in two simultaneous screenings that were well attended and received. Italian Minister of Propaganda Dino Alfieri, who was among the spectators, personally congratulated the American representatives present.[80] A few days later it was announced that *The River* had received first prize as best documentary at the festival, winning over Leni Riefenstahl's film about the Berlin Olympics, *Olympiad*. It was the first time an American film had been honored in this category.

The importance of the award at Venice cannot be overlooked. Lorentz and his productions for the government, especially *The River*, were now internationally known. Lorentz had established the merit of his productions.

[79] Interview with Pare Lorentz, July 24, 1961.
[80] "Venice Sees 'The River,'" *New York Times*, August 10, 1938.

Some discussion of the use of the first two films of merit seems in order. Both were used politically in a way that Tugwell, the sponsor, and Lorentz, the producer, had not foreseen. Tugwell's letter requesting approval for funds for the production of *The Plow* had stated that the film was to be used to educate the staff of the RA and those of associated agencies. Lorentz, however, intended that it should be shown to the general public to inform them about a particular problem, what the causes of the problem were, and what the government was doing about the problem.

Because of its availability and the fact that many Democratic politicians were proud of the film, *The Plow* was used in the 1936 political campaign. Richard D. MacCann[81] reports two specific instances of congressmen using *The Plow* in their campaigns: Maury Maverick in Texas, and Fred H. Hildebrandt in South Dakota.

The comments of Fred Hildebrandt are especially interesting, particularly in view of the fact that another South Dakota politician, a Republican, had an entirely opposite reaction to the film.[82] Hildebrandt wrote in a newsletter to his district:

> It was vivid from a dramatic standpoint, but what is more important, it was true to facts in every detail. No more accurate and graphic portrayal of the exhaustion of the soil in the Great Plains extending from the Texas Panhandle up through the Dakotas and intermediate states to the Dominion of Canada, of dust storms and their fearful damage ... and of the transformation now being effected by the RA could have been provided than is found in this exceptionally interesting and instructive film.[83]

The film was available to all who wanted to use it. There is no record of Republican congressmen using it as an aid in their campaign in 1936. The film was produced by an agency that was highly unpopular with opponents of the New Deal. If anything, the Republicans attacked the film, as did the South Dakota Republican state chairman.

[81] *Op. cit.*, 202–203.
[82] See p. 48.
[83] MacCann, *op. cit.*, 208, note 86.

Neither were Democrats unanimous in their praise. Criticism came from Texans who wanted *The Plow* censured at the 1936 Democratic National Convention. Staff members of the regional RA office in Dallas wrote a letter to Tugwell expressing their dissatisfaction with the film, calling it inaccurate. Maverick, on the other hand, thought enough of the film to want to show it to his constituents and to read its reviews into the *Congressional Record*.

The Plow was linked inextricably with politics because it was intended to be an action-inducing film. Tugwell and Carter hoped that by presenting a problem, it causes, and a solution, the film would win support for the RA.

The first film of merit, *The Plow That Broke the Plains*, was eventually withdrawn from circulation. Addison Foster, the executive officer of the Office of Government Reports, informed the House Appropriations Subcommittee that the film had been withdrawn on April 18, 1939, and had not been reissued. He reported that the United States Film Service had plans to revise the film in light of improved agricultural conditions but that it had been unable to do so because of a lack of funds.

However, through the efforts of Secretary of Agriculture Orville Freeman, it is now available for educational distribution; it was seen on educational television stations throughout the country in 1961 and 1962 as part of the NET series "Lorentz on Film."[84]

The River was used for political purposes during the election campaign in 1938. For example, Thomas Amlie, Democratic congressman from Wisconsin, wrote the FSA from Elkhorn, Wisconsin, on July 27 requesting both films for use during the next two months or more of the primary campaign.[85] But 1938 was not a major election year, and the use of the film seems not to have caused much comment.

There are other reasons why the political uses of *The River* did not receive as much criticism as the uses of *The Plow* did. There was not so much to get angry about or criticize. In the first place,

[84] Prints may be ordered from the National Archives and Records Service after obtaining clearance from the Department of Agriculture. (Letter from May Fawcett, National Archives and Records Service, March 12, 1965.)

[85] MacCann, *op. cit.*, 208.

the overt political message for the TVA at the end of *The River* was only about half as long as the message about Tugwell's Beltville community at the end of *The Plow*. Second, the sympathy of the country had already been aroused by the devastation and suffering caused by the great flood of 1937 before Lorentz's film was released, whereas part of the purpose of *The Plow* had been to awaken sympathy for the devastation in the Dust Bowl. Third, there tended to be less controversy about the causes of the floods in the Mississippi Valley than there was about the causes of the Dust Bowl. Fourth, there was less controversy about the extent of the former tragedy than there was about the latter. For some reason, many people living in or near the Dust Bowl did not wish to acknowledge its existence. There is one final possible factor: when Lorentz was ready to release *The River*, he took it first directly to the people most involved—the residents of the valley—for their approval.[86]

The two films assumed greater importance through their effect on individual congressmen when budgets for further film activities were considered. Republicans and Democrats alike could find factors in the use of government motion pictures which would lead them to vote against the continuance of the production of similar films.

The success of *The River* was not alone responsible for the sudden interest in documentary films in the United States in 1938, although it was certainly a major factor. Paul Rotha[87] has mentioned several other factors that resulted in increased production of documentaries: the quality of the "March of Time" series, the lectures on documentary films at the New School of Social Research, and the Museum of Modern Art series of British documentary films. The General Education Board of the Rockefeller Foundation was also showing interest in documentaries by supporting research, experimentation, and distribution of films. A

[86] Although the TVA is depicted at the end of *The River*, no money from the TVA was used in the production of the film, nor is there any evidence from the period that the TVA endorsed the film.

[87] "The Outlook for American Documentary Films," *New York Times*, May 1, 1938.

group of expert film technicians had recently formed American Documentary Films, Inc., to produce films. The future of documentary production in the United States seemed brighter, and *The River* had played an important part.

Both *The Plow* and *The River* were parts of a particular mood or attitude typical of the sponsoring agency as well of the public at that time. It was an attitude of concern, widespread in the administration, Congress, and the general public, about preventing as much as possible the recurrence of such events as the stock market crash of 1929, the dust storms of 1933 to 1936, and the great flood of 1937.

The various action programs of the New Deal and the production of these two films illustrate a law of society described by Gilbert Seldes: "When individuals do not do the necessary work, the government will step in and do it."[88] Hollywood had little concern for social issues other than sensational exposés and gangster films. As Seldes said at the time: "In this case the federal government has not only done something worth doing, but—on past performances—has done it better than private enterprise, so lamentably unenterprising, could possibly have done it."[89]

The Plow and *The River* were truly meritorious. They were films of high technical quality, and they focused attention on two vital problems in the United States. People wanted to see the films. Lacking the support of the motion picture industry, the government had no choice but to continue to produce films.

[88] "The River," *Scribner's*, January, 1938, 67.
[89] *Ibid.*

IV

THE FORMATION AND FINANCING OF THE UNITED STATES FILM SERVICE

DURING 1938, the year *The River* began its run in New York and the United States Film Service was formed, a major development in commercial motion picture content was under way, a development of interest to the federal government.

Although America was avowedly neutralist at this time, Hollywood began a long series of films in 1937 glamorizing the armed forces. Among these films were *Dawn Patrol, Riding the Waves, Navy Blues, The Singing Marine,* and *Men with Wings.* The last mentioned is of interest because the War Department intervened in its production and had the film's original pacifist ending changed to one stressing air preparedness and the building of bombers.[1]

In a sense, Hollywood began co-operating with the government in the production of a number of films. These films did not, however, underline the government's concern with social and economic reforms. Instead, they reflected the Administration's growing interest in military strength and preparedness.

There was another somewhat surprising example of co-operation between the government and Hollywood. In 1938, when Walt Disney released *Snow White and the Seven Dwarfs,* his first full-length animated cartoon, he encouraged exhibitors to run *The River* on the same bill.

American attitudes toward documentary films were beginning to crystallize by the time *The River* had won its awards. Hollywood seemed to be suspicious of documentary films. For example, Douglas Churchill wrote, "Hollywood has long viewed this phase of entertainment with distrust, for the commercial screen has an

[1] Jacobs, *op. cit.,* 529.

abhorrence of becoming involved in thoughtful discussions which might lead to charges of bias."[2] On the other hand, a writer for the *Christian Science Monitor* held the view that motion pictures, especially documentaries, offered a possible solution to the problem of educating the general public, whose lack of knowledge about public affairs limited the benefits of democracy.[3]

In 1938, the American public seemed to be showing an interest in films designed to provoke thought, as indicated by its acceptance of *Blockade, The Plow, The River*, and the "March of Time."[4] At this time the government was making increasing use of documentary films. Reed N. Haythorne described the growing use of documentary films by the government: "It can be readily understood that motion pictures are fast becoming popular with the government and that our government is certainly doing its part in visual education, documentary film work and research, through the use of good motion picture production."[5] He cited the use of documentaries as elements of research programs, as feature films for the public, and as educational materials for farmers, CCC boys, and men in service. He also noted that "these films serve as constructive propaganda for the entire country."

Three years after Lorentz came to Washington in June, 1935, as a motion picture consultant, he had produced two outstanding films and had written, produced, and directed a radio program on unemployment. This program was entitled *Ecce Homo!* and had developed out of research and the detailed script outline for what Lorentz hoped would be his third government-sponsored film.[6]

If he was to continue producing films for the government, he needed recognition for his work in the form of funds and a more permanent base of operations. His first sponsor had been eliminated from the government, and his second sponsor, the Farm

[2] "Caught on the Wing in Hollywood," *New York Times*, April 24, 1938.

[3] "Gap in Our Armor," *Christian Science Monitor*, February 24, 1937.

[4] The "March of Time" series was begun early in 1935, created by Louis de Rochemont, and sponsored by *Time*. (Jacobs, *op. cit.*, 537.)

[5] "Uncle Sam Busy Lenser," *American Cinematographer*, September, 1937, 398.

[6] The story of the broadcast of *Ecce Homo!* and the uncompleted film is presented in Chapter V.

Security Administration, was about to drop him and his unit from their future plans.

The opportunity for Lorentz to make a plea for a consistent film production policy arose when he was called to Washington in June, 1938, to receive the J. Emanuel Plaque for *The River*. The opportunity was coming none too soon, because Lorentz's staff was due to break up on June 30.[7] The fate of the existing film unit had been sealed as far as the Department of Agriculture was concerned. On June 13, just before Lorentz met with the President, Henry Wallace wrote to Sumner Welles:

> I regret that it is impossible for the Department of Agriculture through the Farm Security Administration to continue to produce pictures of the type similar to *The River* and *The Plow That Broke the Plains* but it appears that there is no legal basis for this agency to continue this activity. The General Accounting Office has recently taken exception to the use of funds appropriated for relief purposes in the distribution of films of this character.[8]

In an attempt to obtain further funds and to produce a film on unemployment problems, Lorentz had been calling on various relief agencies with a transcription of the broadcast of *Ecce Homo!* and his script outline. He had not been able to find sponsors.

The meeting with Roosevelt to receive the J. Emanuel Plaque took place some time in the week ending June 19. When asked about this meeting, Lorentz provided the following background. He had already presented a three-page outline of *Ecce Homo!* to Tom Corcoran. Corcoran and Steve Early arranged for the meeting with Roosevelt at the time because Lorentz, in his own words, "was getting restless. Nothing was happening."[9]

Following the formal presentation the President made some jokes about the plaque, which seemed to be adorned by a man in his underwear—that is, it was a short award for shorts. Roosevelt

---

[7] "Roosevelt Studies a New Movie Bureau," *New York Times*, June 19, 1938.

[8] Letter from Henry Wallace to Sumner Welles, June 13, 1938, MacCann, *op. cit.*, 222.

[9] Interview with Pare Lorentz, July 28, 1961. Corcoran had been at Hyde Park when Lorentz screened *The River* for Roosevelt and, according to MacCann, had been directed by the President to work on plans for a permanent film bureau. See p. 64.

told Lorentz he had a lot of work for him to do—about thirty movies, three to five minutes long, on public works programs.

Lorentz objected, pointing out that they had just won an award for thirty minutes of screen time. On a four-hour, double-feature bill, three minutes would be like film titles—it would be impossible to make an impression on an audience. He told the President that he wanted to make a feature-length motion picture that would present the basic problems of public works in one large, powerful message.

Roosevelt asked him what the theme of the picture would be. When Lorentz answered, "Unemployment!" the President "went cold" according to Lorentz.[10] They discussed the project for a time, and then the President told him to go ahead on the project and prepare an outline for him to look at.

Lorentz also pointed out to the President that he would soon be without a crew and was already out of funds. He was about to leave the Department of Agriculture, as Wallace's letter of June 13 made clear. This gave Lorentz and Corcoran the opportunity to present preliminary recommendations for establishing a permanent film bureau.

A news story of June 19 reported the President's interest in establishing a permanent film agency for the production and distribution of documentary films. The story reported that this would be a small agency, under the jurisdiction of the National Emergency Council (NEC), and that its purpose would be to coordinate the efforts of various departments that were producing films.[11]

Lorentz buried himself in a room at the Carlton Hotel and went to work on the script in earnest, developing the half-hour radio play into a two-hour feature film. A few weeks later he asked Corcoran to arrange an interview with the President so that he could show him the script. The interview was arranged for July 13.

When Lorentz and Corcoran entered, Roosevelt greeted Lorentz with the remark that he noticed Lewis Gannett had nominated

[10] Interview with Pare Lorentz, July 28, 1961.

[11] *New York Times*, June 19, 1938.

Lorentz for the Pulitzer Prize in poetry on the basis of the narration for *The River*.[12] Lorentz handed the President his script, keeping the last page in his pocket. The President read the script carefully and asked Lorentz, "How are you going to end it?"

Lorentz replied, "Sir, how are you going to end it?" He handed the President the last page of the script, which was based on the regional development program the President was preparing for Congress. This program called for the area development of resources patterned on the TVA. Lorentz reports that the President was pleased and told him to proceed with all possible speed.[13]

The United States Film Service was established under the NEC by a series of letters, all dated August 13, 1938, from President Roosevelt to the various parties concerned. Pare Lorentz was named director; Arch Mercey, assistant director; and Floyd Crosby, director of photography. George Gercke and John Bridgeman from the old crew, were also on the new staff.

The first letter was sent by the President to Lowell Mellett, director of the National Emergency Council.[14] In this letter, a few days after *The River* had won the award at the Venice Film Festival, the President mentioned two purposes of the films to be produced by the Film Service: educating government employees, and informing the public about present-day problems.[15] The President gave to the new service control over the distribution and exhibition of films produced by other departments and agencies, and gave Lorentz the authority to proceed with the production of *Ecce Homo!* and provided funds for that purpose. The funds for the new film were to come from the budgets of the WPA and PWA as provided for in the Emergency Relief Appropriations Act of 1938. The closing paragraph of the President's letter stated, "This project shall be subject to all the restrictions and limitations of said act."

12 Letter from Pare Lorentz, February 1, 1967. For Gannett's nomination, see Lewis Gannett, "Of Books and Things," *New York Herald Tribune*, July 13, 1938.

13 Letter from Pare Lorentz, February 1, 1967.

14 The complete text of the letter is to be found in Appendix B.

15 The purposes include both of those for *The Plow*. The first purpose is the official one of *The Plow*. (See Appendix A.) The second was Lorentz's recommendation to Tugwell in 1935.

President Roosevelt also sent a letter to Henry Wallace requesting funds for the Film Service from the Department of Agriculture.[16] The letter outlined the purpose of the new agency and specifically stated that the President intended the NEC to produce and distribute a motion picture on unemployment. Agriculture funds intended for relief were not to be involved in Film Service projects; the President asked that the money come from funds allocated for administration. Now Lorentz had three sponsors for his film: the Farm Security Administration, the Works Progress Administration, and the Public Works Administration.

A third letter pertaining to the establishment of the Film Service was sent by Mellett to Lorentz. The letter, the first to refer to the United States Film Service by name, described the authority by which the service was established and outlined rules and regulations for its operation, fixing the official birth date of the service as August 13, 1938. The major purpose and duties of the new organization were outlined in the first paragraph of the letter:

> 1. The functions and duties of the United States Film Service shall be to coordinate the activities of the several departments and agencies which relate to the production or distribution of motion picture films; to maintain a film library of governmental and other film subjects of interest and educational value to educational and institutional organizations and groups; to distribute and exhibit such motion picture films; to act as consultants to governmental, education, and foundation organizations on motion pictures; and to produce motion pictures in conjunction with other federal agencies at the direction and with the approval of the Executive Director.[17]

This was Lorentz's official directive from the President to get production under way on *Ecce Homo!*

From the administrative point of view, there was a great deal of work necessary to get the Film Service started. Arch Mercey, who had much of the responsibility along with John Bridgeman, described the work as "another laborious job of developing a plan of work, organization chart, preparation of job descriptions,

---

[16] The complete text of the letter is to be found in Appendix C.

[17] Letter and enclosure from Lowell Mellett to Pare Lorentz, August 13, 1938. The complete text is to be found in Appendix D.

etc."[18] Bridgeman, who had served as Lorentz's financial clerk during the production of *The River*, was an expert on governmental procedures and a big help to Mercey.

After Mellett reported that the Film Service had been established, Roosevelt wrote him again, this time on September 20, 1938.[19] In the letter the President set forth other responsibilities of the Film Service: to establish a system of minimum standards of technical quality; to examine all production and processing contracts; to examine scripts for all other agencies; and to approve the use of government personnel and property in commercial productions.[20]

According to Lorentz, the final paragraph was added to the original draft of the letter in pencil by the President himself.[21] The purpose of this paragraph was to indicate what Roosevelt and Lorentz saw as the justification for the production of motion pictures by the government. It also set forth what they saw as the relationship between Hollywood films and government productions. In their minds, the production of films was a natural and legal function of the federal government.

The base for Lorentz's work—the NEC—was far from permanent. It had been established by executive order in 1933, then almost abolished eight months before the Film Service was assigned to it, but extended by another Executive Order until June 30, 1938, when it was again extended by another executive order for one more year.[22]

Not only was the NEC far from being a solid base for opera-

---

18 Letter from Arch Mercey, March 22, 1962.

19 The complete text of the letter is to be found in Appendix E.

20 Lorentz sought the first two responsibilities because he was dissatisfied with much of the technical work done for the government and had discussed this matter with the President. He thought that a film of merit required the highest possible standards in the quality of raw film and processing. (Interview with Pare Lorentz, July 20, 1961.)

21 I have seen the original letter in the files of Pare Lorentz. The letter is typed on blank stationery. The last two paragraphs are added in pencil in a handwriting quite unlike Lorentz's and similar to the President's—although I do not profess to be a handwriting specialist.

22 The original order was 6433 A, November 17, 1933. The order continuing the NEC was 7906, June 6, 1938.

tions, but also it was unpopular with Congress. Some congressmen viewed it as an imposition on state legislatures because one of its responsibilities was to act as a liaison between federal agencies and state administrations.[23]

In spite of this shortcoming, an important step had been taken by the government. For the first time it looked as if government documentary films would have a chance for real sponsorship. Although the Film Service did not have a production budget of its own, it did have the authority to initiate films and encourage various agencies and departments to sponsor them.

In certain quarters the establishment of the Film Service was looked upon as a significant event. Paul Rotha hailed the move on the part of the government.[24] Philip Sterling wrote in the *New York Times* of the importance of the event a year after its occurrence.[25] T. R. Adams emphasized the impact on adult education:

> The most helpful development in the educational use of films of Government origin lies in the recent operation of the United States Film Service. . . . Educational and cultural groups throughout the country are now able to obtain information concerning the availability of Government films directly from this single body. As this obviates inquiries to perhaps twenty-six different Government departments and sub-departments it should facilitate a wider use of Government films by adult educational groups. . . . On the other production side, it is to be hoped that departments seeking to make films for general educational purposes will use the advisory service of the agency under the direction of Pare Lorentz.[26]

Having a base did not, of course, remove all the problems. A full month passed after the Film Service was authorized under the NEC before it received funds for operations, and four months elapsed before it had enough money to set up an administrative office and start making films.[27]

In 1939, the United States Film Service received the first se-

[23] MacCann, *op. cit.*, 228–29.
[24] Rotha, *Documentary Film*, 308.
[25] "Following 'The River,'" *New York Times*, October 15, 1939.
[26] *Motion Pictures in Adult Education*, 49.
[27] William O. Player, Jr., "Cut," *New York Post*, May 28, 1940. From the personal files of Pare Lorentz.

rious challenge to its existence when its budget was presented to Congress for approval. While Lorentz was on location filming *The Fight for Life*, Arch Mercey kept him informed of the situation in Washington. By spring it was apparent that the future of the Film Service was uncertain. What made the situation more critical was that it was difficult for Mercey and Lorentz to give their attention to both film projects in progress as well as to the hearings before Congress.

On May 15, 1939, Mercey wrote to Lorentz about the effect that a proposed reorganization plan would have on the Film Service. Under this plan the NEC was to be abolished on June 30, 1939, and its various functions and offices were to be placed with other agencies.[28] The main problem was, however, to get a good presentation before Congress on the proposed budget. Mercey indicated in the letter that he would be working on clarifying the relationships and operation of the Film Service under the reorganization plan.

Shortly after Mercey wrote to Lorentz about the effect of the reorganization plan on the Film Service, Mercey and Mellett made a rather significant decision. On May 19, 1939, Mercey wrote to Lorentz, "We are asking for our budget just as if reorganization matters had not come up at all."[29] The wisdom of this decision can be questioned. It put Mellett in the strange position of asking for funds for an agency that was about to be eliminated, and his argument for the service was weakened. On May 9, the day they received Reorganization Plan II, Congress knew that the NEC was to be abolished and the Film Service sent elsewhere. Why argue as if this were not taking place?

To make matters worse, the Budget Bureau had accidentally left the Film Service out of the budget. Mercey wrote Lorentz that Isadore Lubin had told him that a grave error had been made by the Budget Bureau in leaving out a proposed budget for the Film Service.[30] Lubin told Mercey that everything possible would be

[28] Letter from Arch Mercey to Pare Lorentz, May 15, 1939.

[29] Letter from Arch Mercey to Pare Lorentz, May 19, 1939.

[30] Lubin was a high-ranking adviser on wages and prices and a member of the Temporary National Economic Committee at the time.

done to correct this. From Mercey's letter to Lorentz on May 19, it seems that Lubin is the man who suggested that they proceed with their request as if nothing were to change.

Mercey's letter of May 19 also indicates the direction in which the Film Service was headed in the plans for reorganization. Mercey wrote Lorentz that Lubin was in agreement that if they transferred to the Federal Security Agency as part of the Office of Education, they should get a letter from the "top man" (Roosevelt?) to the administrator to the effect that the Film Service was to proceed without restrictions. This would permit Lorentz to continue with the various projects under way.

Mellett and Mercey went before the House Appropriations Subcommittee on May 25, 1939—not a pleasant experience. For example, while discussing films, Mellett and Representative John Taber contradicted each other three times in rapid succession. Democratic members of the subcommittee inquired about the present and proposed future salaries of the staff of the Film Service. After answering their questions, Mellett tried to make the point that the Film Service would have an economizing effect by cutting down on the number of films produced by other agencies, but other testimony indicated that one of the main objectives of the Film Service was to increase production.

When Democratic members of the subcommittee asked Mellett about future film projects, he mentioned: "A full-length feature on American maritime history for the U.S. Maritime Commission, a series on public agencies and their health programs, a training film for census takers, another fire prevention movie for the Forest Service."[31] Other projects were also suggested, such as a plan to send American films to Latin American countries and import films from those countries for distribution in the United States. Mellett reported that this plan had the backing of Secretary of State Cordell Hull. To anyone who had doubts about the necessity of the Film Service, these plans for the future could not have sounded much like economizing.

[31] U.S. House of Representatives, Appropriations Subcommittee, *Hearings on Work Relief and Relief Appropriations Act, 1939*, 76 Cong., 1 sess., 327.

The overriding concern of the subcommittee was what the cost would be and where money for the Film Service had come from previously. In fact, some Republican members of the committee wanted assurance that the Film Service would produce all films for all departments and agencies. Mellett maintained that the Film Service did not have the authority to produce all government films. It is doubtful that the Departments of Agriculture, War, and the Interior would have easily given up their production units or would have been willing to submit them to Lorentz's supervision. The subcommittee dropped the matter because the budgets for the other agencies involved had already been approved, and there was no way to direct their funds to the Film Service.[32]

After the hearings, the subcommittee made two recommendations about the Film Service. First, "No provision is made for the United States Film Service, which has been set up during the current year from funds appropriated to other agencies and allocated to the National Emergency Council."[33] Second, the subcommittee wrote a provision into the Emergency Relief Appropriations Act, which was approved by the House at large, that made it difficult for the Film Service to continue producing films with funds from relief agencies. It read, "Except as authorized in this joint resolution, no allocation of funds should be made to any other Federal agency from the appropriations in this joint resolution for any Federal agency."[34]

Before the hearings, there was evidence in the House that certain of its members were prejudiced against the Film Service. On February 16, 1939, Karl Mundt lashed out at *The Plow* for maligning South Dakota. In his opinion, the film showed that "seeing is deceiving."[35] He maintained that conditions were not as shown in his home state or elsewhere—which is likely since by that time the drought had ended. He attacked the film as propa-

[32] *Ibid.,* 324–25.

[33] U.S. House of Representatives Appropriations Subcommittee, *Work Relief and Relief Appropriations Act, 1939,* 76 Cong., 1 sess., 1939, *House Report 833,* 18. The Radio Service received $20,000, although its value had been questioned also.

[34] U.S. Congress, *Emergency Relief Appropriations Act, 1939,* 76 Cong., 1 sess., 1939, *Public Resolution 24.*

[35] U.S. *Congressional Record,* 76 Cong., 1 sess., 1939 LXXXIV, Pt. 7, 7340.

ganda, objected to having the taxpayers' money spent to spread a falsehood, and indicated that he had written to Lowell Mellett the day before to have circulation of the film stopped. Representative Herman Eberharter defended the film in the brief discussion that followed, but several other congressmen supported halting circulation of the film.[36]

A further indication of congressional attitudes toward the Film Service and the NEC can be determined from debates on the approval of the Work Relief and Public Works Appropriation Bill of 1939. Following the reading of Section 8, which provided an appropriation for transferring the activities of the NEC to the Executive Office of the President and transferring the Radio Service to the Office of Education, Representative Everett Dirksen offered an amendment to strike out Section 8 entirely. He attacked the propaganda activities of the NEC through the Radio Service, Film Service, and Information Service, and stated that the item had no business in a relief bill.[37] Representative Clifton Woodrum replied by praising *The River*, and stated that he hoped the Film Service would continue producing films even though its budget had been cut out.[38] Dirksen's amendment lost.

Later in the same debate, Representative J. William Ditter lashed out at the Film Service. In his opinion, information activities in radio and film were probably legitimate but should be financed by regular funds and not by relief funds as proposed in the measure being discussed.[39] He thought that the Film Service and Radio Service should have been financed through the Budget Bureau. As far as he was concerned, the future of the Film Service

[36] *Ibid.*, 1522–24.
[37] *Ibid.*, 7340.
[38] *Ibid.*, 7341.
[39] *Ibid.*, 7349. Ditter's statement is very ironic. The Film Service and the Radio Service were the only NEC activities *not* placed in the Executive Office of the President. The defeat of the Reorganization Act of 1938, which would have given the President broad powers to reorganize the executive branch of the government, would have made it possible to set up the Film Service as an autonomous agency. Late in 1938 there was talk of reviving the old Reorganization Bill, but the one that cleared both houses in 1938 was different from the original bill. It is not known why the Film Service was not placed in the Executive Office in Reorganization Plan II. This omission was a great disappointment to Lorentz. (Letter from Pare Lorentz, May 29, 1964.)

and the Radio Service in the Office of Education was not good. He added, "The Office of Education is primarily a promotional agency; its chief job is to lobby for more funds for education."[40] He correctly summarized the activities of the Film Service, including production, and went on to report that the centralization of all film activities had not taken place and that the transfer to the Office of Education would neither eliminate duplication nor bring about centralization. He reviewed the financial structure of the Film Service for the current year and its proposed budget for 1940.[41] In addition to the funds it received from various agencies, Representative Ditter noted, the President had proposed giving the Film Service $176,500 for the Latin American motion picture program.[42] Ditter called salaries proposed for Film Service personnel "very high"—they averaged $2,745 a person per year.[43] He also itemized the films the service was working on and enumerated the money involved in each production.[44] "All told over a million dollars is proposed for this Film Service for 1940."[45] Apparently the congressman's major objection to the films was what he assumed to be their propaganda character:

> The most vicious thing about the program is the character of the documentary films. Most of them have been very definitely of a propaganda nature. *The Plow That Broke the Plains* was obviously designed to promote the soil conservation program of the AAA. And it is easy enough to surmise that the film that is soon to be made for the AAA will point out the glories of the Wallace farm program. Motion pictures may have a limited place in the work of the Federal

40 U.S. *Congressional Record*, 76 Cong., 1 sess., 1939, LXXXIV, Pt. 7, 7349.

41 *Ibid*. Funds transferred to the Film Service in fiscal 1939 totaled $265,000, of which $35,000 came from the Department of Agriculture, $120,000 from WPA, and $110,000 from PWA. It can be seen that most of the money came from relief funds. For 1940 the Film Service requested $335,840, including $211,140 for personal services and $124,700 for other obligations. Ditter's attention had been drawn particularly to an item of $40,600 for travel.

42 *Ibid*. See pp. 234–38 for a discussion of this program.

43 *Ibid*. The top ones included: "Film Service Director—$10,000; Chief of Production—$9,000; Motion Picture Director—$9,000; Director of Photography—$9,000; Assistant Director—$7,500; General Counsel—$6,500; Business Manager—$5,600; Chief of Distribution—$5,600."

44 *Ibid*. "*Ecce Homo!*—$165,000; *The Fight for Life*—$50,000–$75,000; *Power and the Land*—$20,000; *The Land*—$40,000."

45 *Ibid*. His arithmetic was faulty. The total was approximately $813,000.

Government, but it seems certain that they have expanded beyond reasonable limits. Before any additional funds are appropriated for such work a thorough survey of the present use of motion pictures by the government should be made and a definite policy decided upon.[46]

No one answered Ditter's remarks, no one proposed a survey of the use of motion pictures by the government, and no one decided upon a definite policy. At least no one in Congress promoted any of these projects or provided the money for them.

The Film Service was not dead, in spite of the fact that the House refused to give it an appropriation. The salaries of the supervisory personnel could be covered within the administrative budget of the Office of Education, and money could still be found for production. The information budgets of several agencies had already been approved and could have been used to provide funds. Hearings by the Senate Appropriations Committee pointed out the feasibility of this method. Questions by Senator James F. Byrnes particularly made this clear. He wanted the economy promised by the Film Service to be effected as soon as possible. Because information budgets of other agencies had already been approved, an appropriation to the Film Service might not mean any savings. These agencies could still transfer funds to the Film Service for production. For these reasons, Byrnes suggested that the Film Service continue as it had been doing.[47]

During June, 1939, the Film Service ran out of funds and was unable to pay even its office girls. Lorentz talked to such friends as John Steinbeck and Dr. Paul de Kruif, who urged the President to give his attention to the situation. The President directed Treasury Secretary Morgenthau to provide money from bureaus with funds available for information to keep the Film Service alive until its transfer to the Office of Education.

The search for funds continued. Arch Mercey noted that additional funds would be needed to finish *The Fight for Life.* With the help of Lowell Mellett, who became director of the Office of

[46] *Ibid.*

[47] U.S. Senate, Appropriations Committee, *Hearings on Work Relief and Public Works Appropriations Act, 1940,* 76 Cong., 1 sess., 1939, 253.

Government Reports after the NEC was dispersed, funds were found. Two steps were then initiated to make certain that the transfer of funds to the Film Service was legal. A detailed memorandum concerning "the law, the use of funds, the picture, etc." was prepared with the help of the Treasury Department and submitted to the comptroller general. Following a lengthy conference with his legal counsel, the comptroller general decided that use of the funds in accordance with the memorandum would be legal. The money was soon transferred to the Film Service.[48]

The Film Service and the Radio Service were transferred to the Federal Security Agency as parts of the Office of Education. The move was effective July 1, 1939, when Reorganization Plan II went into effect.

On the same day, the President wrote the commissioner of education outlining the responsibilities of the Film Service as they had been originally described to the executive director of the NEC:

(In order that all proposed pictures to be produced by departments or establishments of the government might be improved, wastage prevented, and real economies in production effected), to develop a system of minimum standards of quality in motion pictures produced, exhibited and distributed by the federal government; to see to it that these requirements were included in all motion picture contracts into which establishments of the government might desire to enter; to examine all such contracts prior to their execution, and to provide the contracting representatives of the government with a clearing approval of the many technical points involved; and to examine all scripts (which should be cleared through it) for such proposed motion pictures and provide the several establishments with the benefit of constructive technical and professional criticism. It is my further desire, as indicated in my letter of September 20, 1938, that the Film Service examine in advance of production, scripts or portions which may be used by private commercial producers who in connection with such scripts are utilizing federal property or the services of federal personnel.[49]

[48] Letter from Arch Mercey, May 18, 1964.

[49] Letter from President Franklin D. Roosevelt to the commissioner of education, July 1, 1939. The complete text is to be found in Appendix F.

The President also made reference to the clearance and distribution functions of the service, its current consultant activities, and the four films under way. He explained that the transfer to the Office of Education was being made "in view of the fact that the functions of the Film Service appeared clearly to be a part of the educational activities being carried on in the Office of Education."[50] He directed the commissioner to make certain that the functions of the Film Service were carried out. The President emphasized the importance of completing the two films on relief, and mentioned that the administrator of the FWA and the secretary of agriculture had approved the projects. He directed the transfer of funds to the Film Service for this work as follows: from the FWA, $168,500; from the WPA, $91,800; from the Public Works Administration, $60,000; and from the Farm Security Administration, $16,700.[51]

The transfer of the Film Service to the Federal Security Agency and the Office of Education was unsatisfactory to Lorentz. In 1940, he described his objections to William O. Player, Jr.:

> The Office of Education not only hadn't produced a single picture or put up one penny toward producing one, but it had for years had many pleasant connections with the Will Hays Office in Hollywood and with Hollywood Corporations. And the Hays offices [sic] from the beginning had been opposed to my making pictures—particularly pictures that were good enough to get on commercial screens.[52]

That trouble existed between Lorentz and the Office of Education and the Federal Security Agency is implied by a letter that Roosevelt wrote to Paul McNutt, administrator of the Federal Security Agency:

> I have been informed that there exists a need for clarification of a portion of my letter which reads ". . . administered in the Office of Education under the direction and supervision of the Administrator of the Federal Security Administration." I feel that the unique needs of a Federal film service . . . require that both authority and responsi-

[50] *Ibid.*

[51] *Ibid.*

[52] "Cut," *New York Post*, May 23, 1940. From the personal files of Pare Lorentz.

bility for the prosecution of this program be centralized as much as possible.

I direct, therefore, that the Director of the Film Service assume complete executive and administrative responsibility, under your direction and supervision, for the successful carrying out of the entire program of the United States Film Service.[53]

The President reiterated his desire that all films under way be completed, and said that they were not to be construed as being in competition with the commercial product but bore the same relation to Hollywood films as government-printed pamphlets and reports did to commercial books and magazines.

The future did not look bright. Lorentz did not give up hope but proceeded in the way he felt was best, the way he knew best—producing films of merit. On November 25, 1939, the date of the letter from Roosevelt to McNutt, Lorentz had four films in production.

[53] Letter from President Franklin D. Roosevelt to Paul V. McNutt, administrator, FSA, November 25, 1939.

V

Ecce Homo! and *The Fight for Life*

AN exploratory script for *Ecce Homo!* was written aboard the *Queen Mary* during Lorentz's return from England in 1938.[1] After the success of *The River* and before he left for England, Lorentz had received an offer from CBS to do a radio show called "Sunday Magazine," on which he would present word and sound pictures of the United States.

While discussing the show at CBS, Lorentz asked William Lewis, vice-president in charge of programing, about the restrictions to be imposed upon him, and suggested that the first show be devoted to the TVA. Lewis replied that there would never be a show about TVA on CBS. According to Lorentz, "That was the end of a very amiable interview."[2] The interview did not really end there, although Lorentz was no longer interested in the "Sunday Magazine." Lewis then offered Lorentz the opportunity to use the "CBS Workshop" to try out some of his ideas, and Lorentz decided to try the script for *Ecce Homo!* on this program.[3]

The idea for *Ecce Homo!* developed out of the first piece of serious writing Lorentz had attempted, an unpublished novel based on the life of a North Carolinian he had met years earlier. This man, an officer in the United States Marine Corps in World War I, became #7790, the central character in the script. Lorentz wrote about what he considered a major problem of industrial society—men displaced by machines.[4] Lorentz's experiences in movie making, as well as his desire to experiment with sound and a lyrical style of narration, seem to have influenced the form of

[1] For details of this trip, see pp. 70–73.
[2] Letter from Pare Lorentz, May 29, 1964.
[3] *Ibid.* He had tested the lyrical narration for *The River* in the article in *McCall's.*
[4] Interview with Pare Lorentz, July 28, 1961.

the script. In fact, the program sounded a great deal like the sound tracks of his first two films.[5] CBS had no objection to such experimentation; in fact, experimentation was one of the purposes of the program. The broadcast was scheduled for May 21, 1938.

In his preparations, Lorentz enjoyed the full co-operation of William Robson, producer of the "Workshop," and worked closely with Bernard Hermann, a staff conductor and composer. To Lorentz, radio drama required too much time for scene setting. For example, he thought that in the broadcast the scene of the men gathering under the tree could have been done more rapidly on film. Lorentz discussed the problem with Hermann. By the time of the broadcast, these sequences moved to Lorentz's satisfaction, and he credits Hermann's music for the improvement.

There were four long narrations supported by background music. For example, the hymn *There Is a Fountain Filled with Blood* was used behind the narration by the New Englander; a chain-gang song was used behind the southerner; Lorentz had Virgil Thomson's permission to use some of the score from *The Plow* as background music for the westerner.[6] Hermann composed the rest of the music including the industrial theme music at the opening and closing of the program.

Lorentz devised many of the sound effects to create a realistic or documentary effect. He used hammers and other tools to re-create factory noises, achieving an assembly-line sound, for example, by using a barber's massage device. Because of the complexity of the sound patterns, Lorentz, the cast, and crew, with Robson's encouragement, spent considerable time rehearsing and recording the sound effects. The two principal members of the cast were Van Heflin, who played the character #7790; and Thomas Chalmers, who did most of the narration.

None of the officials at CBS saw the script until the morning of the day of the broadcast. After hearing a rehearsal that day, William Lewis wanted to cancel the program because of its controversial nature, but Lorentz convinced him to let it go on.

---

5 I have heard Mr. Lorentz's personal air check of the original broadcast.

6 Interview with Pare Lorentz, July 28, 1961.

Ben Gross reviewed the broadcast the next day in the *New York Daily News,* calling it an "especially interesting experiment."[7] He was impressed with the symphonic combination of words, vocal and instrumental music, and sound effects. In his opinion, the program was like a "dramatic musical movie of panoramic proportions, projected through the medium of sound alone." This comment is interesting because there are many similarities between the broadcast of *Ecce Homo!* and the sound tracks of *The Plow* and *The River* in the lyrical quality of the narration, the realistic sound effects, and the use of music as counterpoint to the narration. The broadcast was conceived, like the films, in the form of successive, short sequences. But a new element had been added —the element of people, of human interest—through dialogue. In the program, four men meet under a tree at a filling station on the Kansas prairie. They tell stories of being displaced by machines and speak of hopes and plans for finding work elsewhere. Lorentz based this material on interviews with applicants for relief.

The script was broadcast on at least three more occasions— twice by the BBC and once by the CBC. Lorentz heard the Canadian broadcast while on location at Grand Coulee Dam shooting film footage for *Ecce Homo!*

The British made some changes in the script. First, they changed its name to *Job to Be Done.* Second, they objected to the way Lorentz used the character Mama at the filling station. She never spoke and was constantly being sent on errands by her husband, who ran the filling station. At the BBC, lines were added for her.

Lawrence Gilliam of the BBC, who produced the broadcast, forwarded to Lorentz everything he could find in the press about the broadcast. He wrote that the script had been well received, making "a deep impression on both the radio and film specialists, and in a section of the press, as well as with listeners generally."[8] He had played a transcription of the broadcast for King Vidor

---

[7] "Listening In," *New York Daily News*, May 22, 1938. From the personal files of Pare Lorentz.

[8] Letter from Lawrence Gilliam to Pare Lorentz, August 22, 1938.

and Robert Flaherty, and they were both impressed by it. Response had been so favorable that he wanted to do another Lorentz script.

The clippings Gilliam forwarded to Lorentz show how well the broadcast was received.[9] The reviewer for *World Film News* noted the change in Lorentz's writing technique from *The River* to *Job to Be Done*:

> It was said of *The River* that it humanized nothing. *Job To Be Done* humanizes a lot. The industrial stuff of the opening can be forgotten. . . . But the personal stories of the four men fetched up from four parts of the country is new. It shows us Lorentz as a writer of dialogue. [And that dialogue is] the personal, intimate stories that make this one of the best bits of radio of the summer.[10]

Following the broadcast on CBS, Lorentz used recordings of the program to try to raise money for the film. During the rest of May and early June, the recordings were played at a number of government agencies.[11] However, no funds were available for production until after the establishment of the United States Film Service in August, 1938.

When Lorentz began planning the film *Ecce Homo!* he intended to follow the radio script but to expand it into a two-hour production. He compressed the experiences of the four men into the story of #7790, to cut the cost of dialogue recording. Music was to play a major part: he wanted to use a chorus, as he had on the broadcast and as he had wanted to in *The River*.

Lorentz described his plan for the script:

> So as he worked his way west my unemployed man was not going to be in montages, but he was going to be a man competent to repair tractors, to run "cats," to get a job wherever anybody could get a job, but ending up at the gigantic construction project, Grand Coulee. That was the promise for the migrants arriving in the Northwest. We had footage of them coming up following a rumor that there

[9] See the following reviews: Joyce Grenfell, "Broadcasting," *London Sunday Observer*, August 21, 1938; Spike Hughes, "There's Another Job to Be Done," *London Daily Herald*, August 17, 1938.

[10] "Job to Be Done," *World Film News*, September, 1938, 219.

[11] Interview with Pare Lorentz, July 28, 1961.

would be irrigated land, and they worked their way picking apples until the jalopies fell apart. Mostly unskilled workers.[12]

The film was to follow the pattern of many of the sequences in the broadcast; specific places and persons would not be identified until the final sequence.[13]

The staff of the Film Service set to work. Some collected material on the industries and places where unemployment was heaviest. For the opening sequence, one member went to the Ford River Rouge plant to record a guide's description of an assembly line. Others collected case histories of unemployed persons. Three still crews had gone out in the spring to find industrial and general travel locations, while Lorentz and Crosby headed for the Northwest.

Once funds were assigned to the Film Service, Crosby and Lorentz went to Cleveland to start filming. Floyd Crosby, director of photography for the Film Service, recalls the filming:

> The original story called for the picture to start in the Midwest in the manufacturing area and then for the leading character to go to the West Coast to California and then work his way up the coast to work on Grand Coulee Dam. I shot all the way up to Grand Coulee and back again and got some beautiful footage of the dam and the scenery on the way.[14]

Lorentz and Crosby ran into considerable opposition from the automobile manufacturers while shooting the film; some plants flatly refused to admit them. After they had gained admittance to White Motors in Cleveland, they proved that they could shoot film for several days without interrupting the work of the plant.[15] This helped them gain admittance to other plants.

Crosby also shot sequences at the Plymouth plant, the Eaton Axle Works, Dodge Forge and Foundry, U.S. Rubber, and other plants. No cast was involved, nor was any sound recorded.[16]

[12] *Ibid.*

[13] *Ibid.*

[14] While shooting near Grand Coulee, Crosby was thrown out of a junk yard by the owner, who was a rabid Republican. (Interview on tape with Floyd Crosby, March, 1962.)

[15] Interview with Pare Lorentz, July 28, 1961.

[16] Letter from Floyd Crosby, September 6, 1962.

Erosion, Mississippi Delta. Location photograph for *The River*.

U.S. DEPARTMENT OF AGRICULTURE,
FARM SECURITY ADMINISTRATION

Workers picking cotton. "And poor land makes poor people—
poor people make poor land." From *The River*.

Site of Hiwassee Dam, North Carolina. Location photograph for
The River.

Pare Lorentz (left) and assistant, on location, Norris Dam, Tennessee. *The River.*

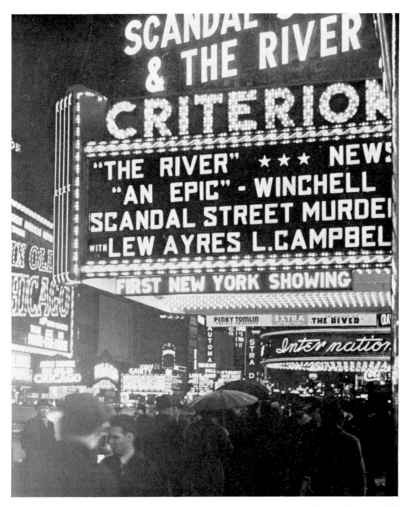

Loew's Criterion Theatre, New York, February, 1938.

Jackhammer crew, Grand Coulee Dam, Washington. From *Ecce Homo!*

Pare Lorentz and Floyd Crosby (at end of scaffold) checking
shot for *Ecce Homo!*

Pare Lorentz and crew at Fontana Dam, North Carolina, shooting footage for *Ecce Homo!*

Pare Lorentz and crew on location, engine-block room, Detroit, shooting footage for *Ecce Homo!*

PHOTOGRAPH BY EDWIN LOCKE FOR
U.S. FILM SERVICE

Automobile door welding. From *Ecce Homo!*

Automobile body welding in jig. From *Ecce Homo!*

PHOTOGRAPH BY EDWIN LOCKE FOR
U.S. FILM SERVICE

Sign at used-car lot. From *Ecce Homo!*

Floyd Crosby and crew shooting footage for *The Fight for Life*.

PHOTOGRAPH BY EDWIN LOCKE FOR
U.S. FILM SERVICE

Pare Lorentz (at right) watching Floyd Crosby (at camera) and assistant shooting Chicago Maternity Center from a roof across the street. *The Fight for Life.*

PHOTOGRAPH BY EDWIN LOCKE FOR
U.S. FILM SERVICE

Interested spectators on location. *The Fight for Life.*

The three principal actors in *The Fight for Life*. Left to right: Myron McCormick, Storrs Haynes, and Will Geer.

There were many delays. In addition to those caused by industrial management, there was a long one at the very beginning caused by the failure of the NEC to provide funds. Time out from production had to be taken in May and June, 1939, for a congressional investigation of the budget request for the Film Service. The Film Service continued to have trouble securing funds for the film, which proved to be an expensive project. Filming in the Northwest was especially costly because the rainy season hampered shooting.

After the industrial sequences, Lorentz and Crosby filmed the Columbia River Valley and the high steel construction at Grand Coulee. They returned to the TVA project and filmed construction of Fort Loudon and Fontana dams.

At this time production on *Ecce Homo!* was postponed when Lorentz was recalled to Washington to help produce a film for the Public Health Service. Lorentz was anxious to complete a major work as soon as possible to prove the merit of the newly organized Film Service, and thought that such a film could be made quickly from Dr. Paul de Kruif's book *The Fight for Life.* Details of the production of this film will be presented later in this chapter.

Following the completion of *The Fight for Life*, Lorentz and the crew resumed work on *Ecce Homo!* The President told Lorentz he wanted to show congressional leaders a rough cut of the film in May when he would submit legislation for the Columbia Valley Authority.[17] The crew reviewed all the footage and found they had about two-thirds of what was necessary for the script, including the River Rouge assembly line, the Plymouth assembly line, and various types of forges, foundries, and automatic machinery. They put together several sequences. The Columbia River gorge sequence was put together to satisfy the President's request. The first reel, which Lorentz called "the industrial symphony," and the westward movement of #7790 were also assembled[18] to establish the mood of the film and show others how far the picture

---

17 Letter from Pare Lorentz, May 29, 1964.

18 "The industrial symphony" contained shots of dawn, lines of cars, traffic, parking cars, men going in to work, and then the total straight line.

had progressed. However, the President never saw the rough cut.

Lorentz showed the assembled sequences to John Carmody, for whose agency the Film Service produced *Power and the Land,* and won him over to the project.[19] Carmody tried to raise funds to finish the project but failed. Lorentz showed the assembled footage to many people, but no one was interested in investing funds in the film.[20] Hitler had surged through France, and the attention of government was turning to national defense. *Ecce Homo!* was never finished.

The extensive footage for the film did not go to waste, however. Because of its outstanding quality, much of it was used by the OWI during the war. John Carmody said that Crosby's industrial footage and the scenes from the Columbia River "looked like Rembrandt."

In the spring of 1939 a project for a new film came from a totally unexpected and exciting source. President Roosevelt recalled Lorentz from his work on *Ecce Homo!* to say that a film was needed that would help dramatize an over-all health program the President intended to propose to Congress. Surgeon General Thomas Parran, who wanted to propose an all-out attack on five diseases, directed Lorentz to Dr. de Kruif.

The two men met in New York at the home of a mutual friend, George Woods.[21] Dr. de Kruif offered Lorentz the film rights to any of his books, including the latest, *The Fight for Life.* There was no contract between author and producer, the author making only one stipulation—that Lorentz must film it. It is reported that de Kruif said: "Take the book. It's yours. Do anything you want with it. I don't want to see the picture until it's finished. We're working on the grounds that we both are trying to tell the facts, and that is all any author wants."[22] The two discussed possible sub-

[19] Carmody was very much interested in Lorentz's films. *The River* and *The Plow* were shown at the theater in the FWA exhibit at the New York World's Fair in 1940.

[20] Interview with Pare Lorentz, July 28, 1961. This lack of interest by others in what Lorentz thought was an important project was one of the factors that prompted him to resign.

[21] Letter from Pare Lorentz, February 15, 1965.

[22] "Surveying a Struggle," *New York Times,* December 17, 1939.

jects in the book. Dr. de Kruif, who shared with Dr. Parran a concern about syphilis, suggested a film on this disease. Lorentz countered with a suggestion for a film on the start of life, the first section of the book. As they continued their discussion, de Kruif told Lorentz that he and Parran were interested in producing an entire series of films on public health problems.[23]

The section of the book that Lorentz decided to film described the work of the Chicago Maternity Center. The center was the successor to the Chicago Lying-in Hospital and Dispensary, founded in 1895 in the Chicago slums by Dr. Joseph B. De Lee. Dr. De Lee was one of the first to call attention to certain dangers in childbirth and was a pioneer in the training of obstetricians. When Lorentz first met him, Dr. De Lee was professor emeritus of gynecology and obstetrics of the University of Chicago Medical School.[24] The locale of the Chicago Maternity Center made it possible to combine two subjects: the problems of childbirth, and problems of the unemployed, such as malnutrition. Relief funds were to help pay for the production.

Arch Mercey described the reason for producing the film during the hearings of the House Appropriations Subcommittee in 1940:

> It is really a picture on human erosion. Medical experts have found that as soon as a great national health problem becomes apparent to the people, various agencies interested will take some action in alleviating the problem. . . . It dramatizes the efforts which are being made in a certain area by modern science in reducing the infant and maternal mortality rate.[25]

Recently, Lorentz has explained his purpose in making *The Fight for Life*:

> At the time of the movie we had a shockingly bad record for infant and maternal mortality compared with the United Kingdom,

[23] "De Kruif Breaks Tradition," *Dayton Journal Herald*, March 8, 1940. From the personal files of Pare Lorentz.

[24] Interview with Pare Lorentz, July 28, 1961.

[25] U.S. House of Representatives, Appropriations Subcommittee, *Hearings on Department of Labor–Federal Security Agency Appropriations Bill, 1941*, 76 Cong., 3 sess., 1940, 299–300.

Scandinavia, Canada, etc. If you will look at it again, you will find all the facts and figures given in the sequence where the doctor speaks to the students. That sequence contains the major reason for the film, and those figures were exact for that year. Of course, I wanted to show the housing conditions of the industrial middle-west as a background to the medical story. In fact, I wouldn't have made the movie had I not been allowed to broaden it to give some indication of the unemployment and living conditions as prevailed then, not only in Chicago, but in all the industrial United States.[26]

Originally, it was planned that *The Fight for Life* would be only three reels long, but as work progressed Lorentz decided that it should be a feature-length film.[27]

Considerable time was spent in research and preparation for the filming. A research worker, Elizabeth Meyer,[28] was sent to live at the Chicago Maternity Center, where she compiled an encyclopedic report of details of the workings of the institution. A location scout and a still photographer mapped the area around the center and accumulated an exhaustive pictorial report of the institution, its patients, and their lives.[29] An unexpected member of this advance crew was John Steinbeck.[30] Crosby, assisted by William Clothier, began shooting exteriors of the poverty in the slums.

For the first time in a film, Lorentz worked with professional actors. Myron McCormick was Dr. O'Donnell, the central character, Storrs Haynes was Dr. Benaron; Will Geer, Dr. Tucker; Dorothy Adams, the mother who hemorrhages after childbirth; Dudley Digges, the old doctor; and Dorothy Urban, the old woman in the hemorrhage sequence. These performers worked for the same wages as Crosby and Lorentz—twenty-five dollars a day plus expenses.[31]

[26] Letter from Pare Lorentz, April 5, 1962. Similar comments were made in "Lorentz on Film," Program II.

[27] Letter from Arch Mercey, February 4, 1964.

[28] Elizabeth Meyer later married Pare Lorentz.

[29] *New York Times*, December 17, 1939.

[30] Letter from Pare Lorentz, May 29, 1964. See also Bosley Crowther, *New York Times*, April 7, 1940. Steinbeck's novel *The Grapes of Wrath* had just been published, and, according to Lorentz, he was eager to get away from literary teas. He offered to make himself useful in any way.

[31] Letter from Pare Lorentz, April 5, 1962.

Haynes, Geer, and McCormick were selected and hired before the others and sent to Chicago to study and be trained as clinicians at the center—Lorentz wanted the picture to be as accurate as possible. McCormick provided a description of the training program. He said that for six weeks they went through the daily routine of the center. They learned how to pack medical kits and to prepare tenement rooms for a delivery; how to provide the most sanitary possible conditions in inadequate situations; how to take blood pressure, body temperature, and pulse; how to wear medical gowns and masks; how to put on gloves; and how to talk to patients. At night they returned to their hotel and practiced handling instruments and other equipment. They criticized one another's technique. McCormick said:

> We lived with the internes and learned their ways and their minds until we behaved and thought as they did. Except when we were asleep or actually shooting the picture, we were doing the work of the Center.
>
> Our emotions had to be professional emotions. . . . There was no scene in which we did not have an actual doctor or student or nurse to work with.[32]

To secure accuracy in detail, the shooting of the film and the training of the actors were supervised by the real Doctors Benaron and Tucker, who were in charge of the center at the time.[33]

Lorentz and the rest of the crew arrived after the training period. Lorentz had studied the material collected on location by the advance crew, read de Kruif's book, and prepared a script before shooting began at the center. For the first time, he used a detailed script.

Except for the performers mentioned above, most of those appearing in the film were not professional actors. Lorentz had to combine performances by professionals with those by amateurs in a dramatization based on fact. As noted in the biographical sketch in *Current Biography: 1940*, "Mothers in the waiting

[32] *New York Herald Tribune*, March 17, 1940. From the personal files of Pare Lorentz.

[33] Dr. De Lee had retired because of his age.

rooms of the Maternity Center, undernourished children playing dangerously in the streets—the people of the tenements themselves, are the real actors of this film."[34]

Lorentz utilized an unusual technique in directing some of the scenes. The actors did their work in the delivery scenes to the beat of a metronome. Lorentz told Ira Woolfert, "A baby's heartbeat is 150 to the minute and a woman's 100, and that's the way the metronome worked and the actors worked because I didn't have the music written."[35]

Technical problems during shooting were considerable. Because some scenes were shot in hospital delivery rooms, every piece of equipment had to be sterilized. For the exterior scenes in the slums, Crosby, Clothier, and Nosler worked in an old station wagon. They prowled the slums filming tenements, children at play in traffic, and adults digging refuse from garbage dumps behind dilapidated buildings.[36]

Because of the nature of the locations and to keep down expenses, everything filmed in Chicago was shot silent, all dialogue being dubbed in later. In Lorentz's opinion, Crosby accomplished a "real tour de force" with his camera work on location: he overcame bad lighting, took out windows, and even had walls removed in order to shoot the required footage. Sections of the Maternity Center and a tenement flat were later re-created in Hollywood on a sound stage. In order to match location and sound-stage sets, a WPA architect in Chicago took samples of everything at the Maternity Center and the tenement flat and later accurately reproduced the wood, paint, and wallpaper in Hollywood. The crew bought secondhand furniture on the streets in Chicago and shipped it to Hollywood to furnish the flat.[37]

[34] "Pare Lorentz," 518.

[35] Ira Woolfert, "Talk of Hollywood," *Baltimore Evening Sun*, October 29, 1940. From the personal files of Pare Lorentz. The technique was not new. King Vidor had used a metronome with a bass drummer beating in time to set the tempo for the troops marching to the front in *The Big Parade* (1925). (King Vidor, *A Tree Is a Tree*, 116–17.) Vidor had used the same technique again in *Our Daily Bread* (1934). (*Ibid.*, 225.) Lorentz's use of the technique indicates that he was giving a great deal of thought to the total concept of the film, picture, music, and dialogue.

[36] "The Fight for Life," *Time*, March 25, 1940, 92.

[37] Interview with Pare Lorentz, July 28, 1961.

The process of shooting on location in Chicago presented one challenge after another:

> To the movie technicians this was genuine novelty. Working in the crowded quarters of the Center's tiny rooms photographing people who had never seen a motion picture camera before, working long hours, odd hours, always under the fluctuating dictates of reality, instead of the next shooting schedule of a fiction script, they more nearly lived the lives of doctors than a camera crew.
>
> The daily life of the patients of the Center was a challenge to the skill of the cameramen. The difference between photographing actors and recording the actual people of Chicago was immense. For hours they froze or sweltered in their cramped camera car behind a hidden camera to catch the people at work, at play and in myriad aspects of their workaday lives. They lugged the camera into tenement homes, where doctors brought the marvel of science.
>
> One day they would perspire beside the death-fighters in a slum household; the next location would be in the cool antiseptic whiteness of a fine hospital. Or the change might be from the confusion of downtown traffic to the deliberate calm of a public health laboratory.[38]

The result was described as "some of the most candid footage of human life ever caught by the camera."[39]

One of the finest sequences in *The Fight for Life* is the "Night Walk," but only a stroke of luck made it possible—luck and Crosby's talent as a cinematographer. In the sequence, McCormick leaves a hospital after the death of a mother in childbirth. He walks the darkened streets of Chicago and wonders about her death. He walks in and out of patterns of light from the illuminated store windows. Footage to precede this sequence had been shot after a rain—the reflection of the lights on the sidewalks would be very effective. The crew waited for rain to shoot the rest of the sequence, but it was summertime in Chicago, when showers can be far apart. Finally one evening Crosby arranged with the Fire Department to wet the sidewalks. Unfortunately, this attracted a crowd, and onlookers got in the way of McCormick and the crew. Crosby asked the police to clear the street, but people

[38] *New York Times*, December 17, 1939.

[39] W. E. Oliver, *Los Angeles Herald Express*, June 26, 1940. From the personal files of Pare Lorentz.

kept coming out of doorways and alleys along McCormick's path. Crosby's assistant turned to him and said, "Do you really need rain?" Crosby said, "And how!" The assistant clambered to the top of the camera car and on his knees said a prayer to a rain god. Within twenty minutes it rained, dispersing the crowd and wetting down the sidewalks. Crosby wrote, "This sounds like a fable, but it actually happened."[40] The sequence was shot on a special highly sensitized film—the fastest available. The only light used was that available from the windows and street lights. McCormick walked along the sidewalk through the various patterns of actual light while the camera car drove alongside with Crosby and camera on top.[41] The sequence was filmed in one take, and the crew left for Hollywood the next day.

The challenge of unusual conditions on location was not the only problem faced by Lorentz's crew. The lives of the crew were even threatened, arousing the interest of the Justice Department, which asked for a complete report on Lorentz's experiences in Chicago.[42] Lorentz said on the NET program: "Chicago is not depressing, it's a fight for life. We had an all-union crew, but you don't do things straight away in Chicago."[43]

All of the last sequence, in which Dorothy Adams played a mother who hemorrhages, was filmed on a sound stage at MGM, where Lorentz's crew re-created, with shocking realism, a Chicago tenement flat. Another scene Lorentz had to shoot in Hollywood was the monologue by the old doctor, who was an interpretation of Dr. De Lee. This monologue was based on a speech by de Kruif to the graduating class at the University of Chicago Medical School in 1938. Dudley Digges had agreed to play the role after seeing rushes of the incomplete film. It was a difficult scene to perform, a three-minute monologue delivered to Myron McCormick as Dr.

[40] Letter from Floyd Crosby, March 21, 1963.

[41] Lorentz noted that the same technique was used in *The Lost Weekend* (1945) and called Crosby "one of the greatest outdoor cameramen in the history of Hollywood." (Lorentz, "Lorentz on Film," Program III.)

[42] Letter from Arch Mercey to Pare Lorentz, May 10, 1939. The problem revolved around union technicians and renting some lighting equipment.

[43] Lorentz, "Lorentz on Film," Program II.

O'Donnell, who appeared in the scene but did not speak. The scene took eighteen consecutive hours on a sound stage at Goldwyn Studios.[44]

This monologue, the last footage shot for *The Fight for Life*, was filmed on September 3, 1939. While they were working, Lorentz, Digges, and the crew learned that Great Britain had declared war on Germany. In Lorentz's opinion, that event sealed the fate of the Film Service, because the attention of the President and the government would swing from domestic to international affairs.[45]

As in the earlier films, music was destined to have an important role in *The Fight for Life*. Lorentz described the unusual requirements for the score:

> Before deciding on a composer for *Fight for Life*, my assistant and I reviewed the compositions of every living American composer, young and old, knowing that it would be the longest score ever done for a nonmusical picture in the United States; and also thinking in terms of women and children, the requirements were to find a composer with the ability to command a long score, and also one who would write simple melodies, including lullabies.[46]

Composer Louis Gruenberg fit these requirements. He knew the demands of film music because he had scored many motion pictures, including *Stagecoach*. He had demonstrated his ability to handle a long score by composing the score for the opera *Emperor Jones*, based on the Eugene O'Neill play. He had written lullabies for his own newborn child. Just as important, he was living in Santa Monica. Lorentz showed the rushes to Gruenberg, who joined forces with Lorentz. They worked together for twenty-two weeks on the score.[47] Gruenberg provided much of the suspense in the picture by orchestrating the sound of the human heartbeat. Lorentz had access to recordings of a variety of heartbeats.

[44] Interview with Pare Lorentz, April 25, 1961. At the time Digges was reportedly making $2,500 a week playing in *Raffles* for Goldwyn.

[45] *Ibid.*

[46] Letter from Pare Lorentz, April 25, 1962.

[47] For some of the problems Gruenberg faced, see Appendix G for a letter Pare Lorentz wrote to him.

Lorentz played these recordings for Gruenberg, and Gruenberg devised a sound based on the F chord, achieved by simultaneously plucking a bass viol string, striking a tympani, and tapping E-flat on the piano.[48] The desired counterpoint between music and picture was not always achieved in the first music submitted. For example, after Gruenberg saw rushes of the Chicago slums, according to Lorentz, "he went home and composed a score that sounded like the 'Ride of the Valkyrie.' He was going to blow the screen down. I objected. It doesn't need trumpets. The movie stands by itself, but I want to get the sense that there are decent human beings behind some of those buildings."[49] Gruenberg then composed a new theme, "Men of the City," for fourteen strings. The completed score ran fifty-five minutes. After Gruenberg played it for Lorentz, he slammed his hands down on the keyboard and exclaimed in amazement, "I've written a symphony!" In Lorentz's opinion, Gruenberg had not realized until then the immensity of his task.[50] There are several three-minute segments of the film without dialogue or narration. In these segments, the music, used not as a background but as the predominant medium of sound to explain the action on the screen, heightened the suspense as words could not, according to one critic.[51]

Lorentz planned to begin *The Fight for Life* in an unusual way —with the death of a woman on the operating table in a hospital. Lorentz was concerned about holding the audience after such an opening. The next sequence was to be "Night Walk," and Lorentz wanted the accompanying music to sound like jazz and be full of life. Gruenberg was unable to provide the music that Lorentz wanted to solve the problem of holding the audience.[52] Gruenberg told Lorentz that if he really wanted jazz he should get jazz musicians.

When Lorentz arrived in New York with Gruenberg's score, he talked to jazz critic John Hammond, who suggested pianist Joe

[48] Lorentz, "Lorentz on Film," Program III.
[49] *Ibid.*
[50] *Ibid.*
[51] Black, "He Serves Up America," *Colliers*, August 3, 1940, 22.
[52] See Appendix G.

Sullivan and the band he was currently leading at Cafe Society Downtown in Greenwich Village. The band was made up of Edmond Hall, clarinet; Danny Polo, tenor saxophone and clarinet; Andy Anderson, trumpet; Benny Morton, trombone; and Billy Taylor, bass.[53] Lorentz met the band at the RCA Victor studios. Sullivan asked Lorentz what kind of music he wanted. Lorentz told them what he had written to Louis Gruenberg: "It's ten below zero on Clark Street and there's a pot-bellied stove and there's ten-cent gin with a piece of lemon peel in it." Sullivan thought for a minute, gave a cue to the musicians, hit descending chords on the piano, and the musicians began improvising.[54] The beat was set by Lorentz's metronome to the pace at which McCormick walked in the "Night Walk" sequence.

Sullivan described the session: "I started out and the boys followed the mood of a lone man walking past darkened and sometimes empty stores. The cameras didn't scare the boys but the intensive heat from the studio lights caused us to perspire like it was 100° in the shade. Back to C.S. [Cafe Society] and we blew our brains out."[55] Lorentz maintains that this improvised jazz is the key to the film:

> The picture opens with death. My concern was that the audience would see it and say, "That's that!" and go home. For that reason we had the Night Walk and jazz music. You have a woman die but a big, vital, roaring city with two million souls, and that background music would lift the audience's attention and they wouldn't be so distressed that they would lose interest.[56]

An orchestra of Los Angeles' finest musicians recorded Gruenberg's score at a Samuel Goldwyn sound stage. The exhausting process of cutting the film to length began once Lorentz had the

[53] Letter from Joe Sullivan, April 21, 1964. There was a drummer also, but Sullivan does not remember who he was. He does recall that it was bitterly cold when they drove from the club to the recording studio.

[54] Lorentz, "Lorentz on Film," Program III. See also *New York Times*, April 7, 1940.

[55] Letter from Joe Sullivan, April 21, 1964.

[56] Lorentz, "Lorentz on Film," Program III. See also Woolfert, "Talk of Hollywood," *Baltimore Evening Sun*, October 29, 1940.

111

full score recorded.[57] The film was planned to be one hour and ten minutes long with a score of fifty-eight minutes. The major problem Lorentz faced in the editing was that the film was found to be one hour and thirty-five minutes long. Cutters spent considerable time trying to trim the film down to the desired length, but it was still long. Lorentz and Lloyd Nosler spent a night studying the film and trying to shorten it. At dawn they decided to cut out an entire sequence, thus bringing it down to the required length.[58]

Lorentz summarized the plot of the finished film for critic Bosley Crowther:

> In the beginning, a young obstetrical interne looks at a woman and she is dead; in the end, he looks at a woman and she is alive. In between he goes through the tortures of doubts—first doubts of himself, his profession, and then doubts of the economic system. There is no pat conclusion. The young interne—and the audience—has been through an emotional experience with certain philosophic overtones. You draw your own conclusions.[59]

This time Lorentz did not take his film around to find out what others thought about it. He went straight to the President. The first showing of *The Fight for Life* was at the White House on New Year's Eve, December 31, 1939. The President, members of his family, and intimate friends attended. The film was preceded by an hour of war newsreels. After the screening Roosevelt said, "I think it will do a lot of good." He asked Lorentz about the status of *Ecce Homo!* (It was at this time that he requested a rough cut of the film to be assembled to show congressional leaders in May.[60])

Lorentz held a few private screenings of *The Fight for Life* in New York early in 1940, including one for fifteen of his friends. Following one of these showings, Arthur Mayer, the first theater

---

[57] Lorentz had waited to make the final cut on both the earlier films after he had the score recorded.

[58] Interview with Pare Lorentz, April 25, 1961. Lorentz always had a strict time limit in mind for his films and the scores and edited each film to meet the time limit.

[59] "Grim Reality Note," *New York Times*, March 10, 1940.

[60] Letter from Pare Lorentz, February 15, 1965.

112

owner to book *The Plow,* wrote to Lorentz: "Thanks for letting me see *Fight for Life* last evening. Each of your pictures seems to me to grow in power, resourcefulness, and human understanding. I envy you, admire you, and hail you. Good speed."[61]

At the preview for his fifteen friends, Lorentz was stunned when Lieutenant Colonel Higgins, the New York director of the WPA, walked out during the hemorrhage sequence in the film. Lorentz followed him to the hall, where he found Higgins walking fretfully up and down. When Lorentz began to tell him what he thought of his behavior, Higgins interrupted to explain that his own wife had died in childbirth because of poor prenatal care.[62]

The premiere was on March 6, 1940, at the Belmont Theatre in New York, a small theater seating about five hundred. Lorentz and the staff selected the guest list and assigned each reserved seat, his club, The Players, occupying the balcony. The Film Service staff was spread out in the theater to catch audience reaction. Lorentz went to the theater alone and later joined Dr. de Kruif and his wife at George Woods's apartment, where de Kruif and Lorentz had first met. While the group at Woods's apartment waited for the reviews, de Kruif kept reassuring Lorentz that any bad reviews would be due to critics' failure to understand what he was doing. Technically, de Kruif told him, Lorentz was ahead of his time. More than an hour later Arch Mercey and George Gercke burst in tossing copies of the *Times* and *Herald Tribune* around the room. The reviews were excellent. Lorentz's first feature-length film, the Film Service's major production, had won an important victory.

Howard Barnes, in the *Herald Tribune,* declared: "The result is a stirring and eloquent drama, as well as a document of profound significance.... Here is a memorable tribute to the medical profession, accented by challenging social overtones."[63] Frank Nugent, in the *Times,* wrote: "... it's as dramatic as life itself.... We wish there were some form of Pulitzer award for the kind of

61 Letter from Arthur Mayer to Pare Lorentz, February 2, 1940.

62 Letter from Pare Lorentz, February 20, 1967.

63 *New York Herald Tribune,* March 7, 1940. From the files of Pare Lorentz.

113

cinema journalism Mr. Lorentz has been doing."[64] William Boehnel, in the *World Telegram*, said, "Pare Lorentz presents a bitter indictment of slum conditions and a gripping plea for greater medical knowledge among obstetricians in *The Fight for Life*."[65] Kate Cameron, of the *New York Daily News*, awarded the film three and a half stars, describing it as "a fine and deeply moving film."[66] The reviews triggered a party at the Woods apartment. Lorentz, de Kruif, and the staff were overwhelmed—the film's reception was much better than expected. The reviews would help them get a contract for national distribution.

Three months later, Lloyd Nosler, Lorentz's cutter, held a private screening in Hollywood for members of the Academy of Motion Picture Arts and Sciences, members of the Screen Directors Guild, and others. Louis Gruenberg directed an orchestra in parts of the score before the screening.[67]

By April 14, the government was ready to accept bids for national distribution of the film. Distributors reportedly thought that *The Fight for Life* was the first government-sponsored feature film to be commercially salable. On May 22, it was announced that Columbia Pictures was awarded the contract for national distribution. The contract stipulated that the film must be sold separately in key cities where it was to be shown and that the government was to share in the profits.[68] According to John E. Harley,[69] the contract was for five years, during which time the government was to receive 25 per cent of the gross. Requests for distribution rights came in from the United Kingdom, France, South America, Canada, and the Philippines.[70]

[64] "Pare Lorentz Goes to Fact for His Drama in His New Film, 'The Fight for Life,' at the Belmont," *New York Times*, March 7, 1940.

[65] *New York World Telegram*, March 7, 1940.

[66] "'Fight for Life' Proves Grim Dramatic Film," *New York Daily News*, March 7, 1940.

[67] Letter from Pare Lorentz, April 5, 1962. See also *Los Angeles Herald Express*, June 26, 1940. From the personal files of Pare Lorentz.

[68] *New York Times*, May 22, 1940. The first provision was probably in the contract to keep the film from being a part of block-booking pacts. Elements in Congress were trying to legislate against such pacts.

[69] *World-wide Influences of the Cinema*, 233.

[70] *Washington Star*, March 24, 1940. From the personal files of Pare Lorentz.

After the film was released, Dr. de Kruif, who had closely followed the production of the film, lashed out at the bureaucratic
red tape and other difficulties that had harassed Lorentz. He told
the press that the President had had to intervene three times to
save the film and that it was a miracle that the film was finished.[71]

Lorentz was satisfied with *The Fight for Life*. At one time he
believed that his best piece of film making was the "Day Walk" in
this film. In this sequence, Dr. O'Donnell, played by Myron Mc-
Cormick, leaves a tenement home after the successful delivery of
a baby. He walks through the filth of the slums and wonders why
he should bring a new life into such a world. As he walks, an
orchestra begins an accompaniment, "The Men of the City." Then,
as voice and music continue their theme and countertheme, Lorentz
completes the sequence with a succession of trucking shots of
tenements, poverty, and hopelessness.

> The thing that pleases me about this soliloquy sequence—and the
> earlier "Night Walk" of the interne—is that it has, I feel, a three-
> dimensional quality. The voice of the young interne expresses his
> personal feelings, the shots of those miserable tenements holler at you
> from the screen, but the music sings a ballad of people and tells the
> courageous story of those who live behind the ugly walls and to
> whom life is still important.[72]

No feature film had ever presented life in American cities so
realistically. Many critics were ready for the film and hailed
Lorentz's approach to the subject. It remained to be seen whether
audiences were ready for such a realistic presentation of unemployment, poverty, life in the slums, and childbirth. The reaction
of the medical profession to the film had also to be determined.

Lorentz anticipated that segments of the medical profession
might object to the film. Dr. De Lee believed that childbirth needed
close supervision and extreme sanitation. Even under the most
adverse conditions in slum homes, his doctors delivered more than
nine thousand babies without loss of life—a record no hospital

71 *New York World-Telegram*, May 19, 1940. From the personal files of Pare
Lorentz. Dr. de Kruif knew the President well and served as director of the March
of Dimes Foundation.
72 Bosley Crowther, "Lorentz Experiments," *New York Times*, March 10, 1940.

could equal.[73] Dr. De Lee's methods and his ideas on the importance of maternal care were, however, not universally accepted at the time.

For this reason Lorentz and Dr. de Kruif made several efforts to get critical approval of *The Fight for Life* from the medical profession. Screenings were held in Chicago at the Maternity Center, in New York at the New York Medical Academy, and in Baltimore at Johns Hopkins Medical School. Lorentz felt reassured by the reaction of the doctors at these screenings. He reported only two adverse comments: "You'll scare women to death," and "Why should the public know this?" After the New York Medical Academy voted approval of the film, Dr. James Alexander Miller, head of the academy, commented, "I have only one objection—there are no bad doctors in it."[74]

Lorentz and de Kruif believed that the statistics in the film were accurate because they had been checked and rechecked by the Office of the Surgeon General. An endorsement of the content came from Dr. Thomas M. Rivers, an official of the Hospital of the Rockefeller Institute:

> I told you yesterday afternoon after I had seen the picture, *Fight for Life*, how much I liked it; in fact, I like it so much that I must tell you again and in writing how thrilling and accurate it really is. From the medical and technical standpoint you should have no fear of criticism. You have put before the public in dramatic manner problems of social and economic importance that must be solved and the first step in the solution of a problem is the recognition of its existence.

Paul de Kruif arranged an important private screening in Dayton, Ohio, on January 30, 1940. It was attended by Charles F. Kettering, vice-president of General Motors, Dr. Walter M. Simpson, chief pathologist of the Miami Valley Hospital for Research, and many members of the staff of the hospital and the Miami County (Ohio) medical society—more than a hundred

[73] Lorentz, "Lorentz on Film," Program III.
[74] *Ibid.*

in all.[75] The approval was overwhelming. Dr. Simpson sent the following telegram to Lorentz:

> Practically all members of Dayton Obstetrical Society and their wives attended showing. All agree that there is no basis for comparison with other motion pictures and that *The Fight for Life* introduces new era in motion pictures. You and your assistants have done superb job in transporting story contained in book by my old friend and teacher, Dr. de Kruif, to screen, restraint, dignity and complete fidelity to spirit and facts contained in de Kruif's book. . . . Have heard only enthusiastic praise from every good obstetrician. Generally agreed that it will revolutionize obstetrical practice, save thousands of lives and help correct social conditions that contribute to present high maternal and infant morbidity rates.[76]

Later, Simpson sent a second telegram. He named those who saw the film in Dayton and described their enthusiastic reactions. His telegram added a statement attributed to Charles F. Kettering:

> *The Fight for Life* inaugurates a new era in the production of pictures dealing with scientists and scientific subjects. In this particular type of motion picture the story is the star rather than some glamorous actress. In addition to having strong popular appeal from an entertainment standpoint this picture will have a great beneficial influence on public health. Hope that Mr. Lorentz will make a score of similar pictures during the next decade.[77]

After *The Fight for Life* began its commercial run in New York, further endorsements came in. One came from the United Parents Associations of New York, whose motion picture chairman, A. M. Bush, wrote to Lorentz telling him that the organization intended to send out a special bulletin to all its affiliated parent-teacher associations urging their members to see the film.[78]

Following the opening in New York, a controversy over the accuracy of the film began in the press. One of the first attacks was made by Dorothy Bromley, a columnist for the *New York Post*. She questioned the statistics quoted in the film and presented a

---

[75] *Dayton Journal-Herald*, March 10, 1940.

[76] Telegram to Pare Lorentz from Dr. Walter M. Simpson, February 4, 1940.

[77] Telegram to Pare Lorentz from Dr. Walter M. Simpson, March 15, 1940.

[78] Letter from A. M. Bush to Pare Lorentz, March 27, 1940. The bulletin referred to is found in Appendix H.

117

much brighter picture concerning mortality connected with childbirth. She reported that the New York Maternity Center had kept the death rate at 1.9 per cent for home deliveries in tenements, and quoted a member of the staff of the center as saying that Lorentz's film would frighten mothers because it showed nothing but gloom. She quoted Dr. George Kosmak as being afraid of the same reaction among women.[79]

Dr. Harold B. Davidson, chairman of the Maternity Welfare Committee of the Medical Society of New York County, made a similar charge. He said, "The one fault of the picture is the inculcation of fear as the result of erroneous statistics,"[80] disagreeing with the statement that almost as many mothers died in childbirth in 1939 as had died twenty-five years before. He too provided statistics that disputed those in the film and that were supposedly endorsed by the United States Children's Bureau and the Medical Information Bureau of the Academy of Medicine.

Strangely enough, Dr. Paul de Kruif had foreseen the criticisms made by Dr. Kosmak and Dr. Davidson when he wrote the book. He had an answer to their charge before they made it: "Now in medical practice, a most amusing smoke-screen is laid down to cover childbed fever's scandal. It is the pious fear that mothers, told of childbed fever's threat, will dread to have children and actually stop having them. This is nothing but contempt for women's intelligence."[81]

The *New York Times* gave Lorentz the opportunity to answer some of the criticism directly. Dr. Max Schneider, secretary of the Special Committee on Maternal Welfare of the Medical Society of the County of New York, had written a letter to the editor of the *Times* in reply to the *Times* review of *The Fight for Life*. Dr. Schneider made three charges: that *hundreds* of thousands of mothers do not die needlessly each year as stated in the review— only *tens* of thousands; that there has been a decrease in the number of women dying as a result of childbirth and pregnancy,

[79] *New York Post*, March 15, 1940. From the personal files of Pare Lorentz.
[80] Rose A. Englander, " 'Fight for Life' Fails to Scare Women," *New York World-Telegram*, March 22, 1940. From the personal files of Pare Lorentz.
[81] *The Fight for Life*, 116.

a reduction in New York City alone of 30 per cent; and that doctors are better trained to handle delivery than the film indicates— "95 per cent of the cases delivered will take place spontaneously and not require the services of a trained obstetrician."[82]

Lorentz based part of his rebuttal on statistics he had obtained during the research for the film. He particularly attacked Dr. Schneider's final statement as being typical of the attitude responsible for many of the needless deaths: "As to his remark that 95 per cent of the cases will not require the services of a trained obstetrician, this is exactly the attitude of mind which has made obstetrics the lowest form of medical service in America today, the cause of so much unnecessary loss of maternal and infant life, of the crippling of thousands of mothers, and the chief reason why we made this picture."[83]

A famous maternity expert lined up behind Paul de Kruif, Pare Lorentz, and *The Fight for Life* when Dr. Allen Roy Defoe sent Lorentz his congratulations: "As one of the characters in it says, 'We can't learn too much about the business of bringing life into the world.' It seems to me that such a motion picture . . . can perform a great public service in making this more widely understood."[84] Dr. Defoe gave Lorentz permission to use his letter to promote the film. Dr. Defoe also praised the film in two columns in a series he was writing for the King Features Syndicate. He called *The Fight for Life* "the most eloquent advocate of greater and more scientific care of women in child-bearing that I have ever encountered in any form."[85] He referred to the seriousness of eclampsia and the reduction in the death rate resulting from the methods dramatized in the film.[86]

In spite of the controversy within the medical profession and reported in the press—or perhaps because of it—audiences con-

---

[82] Letter from Dr. Max Schneider to the editor, *New York Times*, March 17, 1940.

[83] Letter from Pare Lorentz to the editor, *New York Times*, March 17, 1940.

[84] Letter from Dr. Allen Roy Defoe to Pare Lorentz, April 2, 1940.

[85] Allen Roy Defoe, "Your Baby," *New York Journal American*, April 30, 1940. From the personal files of Pare Lorentz.

[86] Defoe, "Your Baby," *New York Journal American*, May 1, 1940.

tinued to attend the film at the Belmont, where it ran for more than two months.[87] Later, *The River* was added to the billing.[88]

Lorentz had considerable expert opinion on his side. The film had the endorsement of the Chicago Maternity Center, the surgeon general of the United States, Dr. Allen Roy Defoe, the staff of the Miami Valley Hospital, and the medical schools of the University of Chicago and Johns Hopkins University. What audience response is available indicates that doctors need not have worried about an adverse effect on women. Those questioned at the Belmont did not seem to be frightened about childbirth.

The film did not endorse specific programs of relief and housing; not once is WPA, PWA, or any other government agency mentioned. The problem of unemployment and poverty in industrial cities is central to the film. However, no special interest is designated as being responsible for the condition, nor is any specific federal program offered or implied as the solution. This aspect of the film should not have drawn partisan criticism, as it did in Congress.[89] The solution to the high maternity death rate offered by Dr. De Lee and his staff is careful scrutiny during the prenatal period, special training for doctors, and extreme sanitation during delivery. Can this solution be considered controversial?

One final note should be made about *The Fight for Life*. At the time of its release in 1940, it was banned in Chicago by the Police Department, which had censorship powers, because the film showed Chicago slums. It was not seen in the city of its setting until twenty-one years later, when WTTW, the Chicago educational television station, carried the NET series "Lorentz on Film."

[87] *New York Post*, April 23, 1940. From the personal files of Pare Lorentz.
[88] *New York Times*, May 3, 1940.
[89] Much of the congressional criticism of *The Fight for Life* is found in Chapter VII.

VI

OTHER PRODUCTIONS AND PROJECTS OF THE FILM SERVICE

THE success of *The Plow That Broke the Plains* made possible *The River*, which in turn led to the establishment of the United States Film Service. Lorentz believed that if the newly established service was to prove its own worth, the bulk of the proof must be furnished by new productions. The Film Service was given the responsibility "to produce motion pictures in conjunction with other federal agencies."[1] Not surprisingly, the first two agencies to contract with the Film Service for motion pictures were within the Department of Agriculture, the department that had given Lorentz his start.

Much of the preliminary work on *Power and the Land* was handled by Arch Mercey and Marion Ramsey, director of information and research for the Rural Electrification Administration (REA), sponsor of the film. The original objective of the film is outlined in a fragment of a letter in Lorentz's files:

> Problem: Our problem can be posed in the following manner: The *REA* program delivers a supply of cheap and abundant energy to the farm that the farmer is technically, physically, and psychologically unable to utilize in a manner that will greatly improve his standard of living.
>
> We believe an imaginatively produced, emotionally affecting film portrayal of the possibilities that are even now coming true is, if widely distributed, ideally suited to the job of making Americans conscious of the challenge and opportunity. *The River* and *Face of Britain* do the job as we want to see it done again—in terms of the electrification of agriculture, a bulwark of democracy.[2]

Two important points can be noted in the letter: the sponsor

[1] Letter from Lowell Mellett to Pare Lorentz, August 13, 1938. The complete letter is to be found in Appendix C.
[2] Letter, author unknown, n.d. From the personal files of Pare Lorentz.

seemed to want wide distribution of a film of merit; the sponsor recognized the high standard Lorentz had achieved in *The River*. The writer may have been John Carmody, the REA director, who had been greatly impressed by *The River* and who had made the initial arrangements with Lorentz about producing a film.

Initially, the negotiations to produce the film went smoothly. On April 22, 1939, Marion Ramsey wrote to Mercey that everything was "shaping up all right" because it seemed that the REA would be able to complete the financial arrangements with the Film Service. The REA had received word that "making the film is entirely in keeping with our authority and with our programs."[3]

However, by May 8 the REA seemed to have changed its mind about the project. Arch Mercey wrote to Lorentz, who was in Chicago filming *The Fight for Life*, that the REA was now considering three one-reel instructional films instead of a longer one, for financial reasons—that year the REA had about forty-six thousand dollars left that could not be used the next year. The REA told Mercey that pressure was being applied from outside the agency to produce some films quickly for use at meetings. The shorter films might take care of the problem and build support for a longer film. Mercey listed four possible actions the Film Service might take: it might withhold approval of the three short films through the Film Service authority to approve all scripts and contracts, recommend possible cameramen, suggest that the REA have another film unit make the film, or say nothing.[4] He felt that the second action would be best.

It is important to note that Mercey did not think it best to exercise the authority the Film Service had been given. The service could have refused to grant the REA permission to proceed on any film if it did not suit the wishes of the Film Service. Applying that authority could have been interpreted as co-ordinating government film activities, but it would serve to antagonize agencies and established production units.

The Film Service did not have to follow any of the recom-

[3] Letter from Marion Ramsey to Arch Mercey, April 22, 1939.

[4] Letter from Arch Mercey to Pare Lorentz, May 8, 1939.

mended actions. On May 11, 1939, Marion Ramsey wrote to Mercey to authorize the beginning of work on the original film, and to say that Charles Walker, who had done research on a variety of subjects for the REA, was coming to Washington on May 15 to begin work on a script outline for the film.

At the time the REA contracted with the Film Service for a motion picture, it was impossible for Lorentz to do any work on the film, although that was what John Carmody wanted. Lorentz was busy directing *The Fight for Life* in Chicago. There is evidence to indicate that the REA thought they had hired Lorentz.

Lorentz hired Joris Ivens, a documentary film maker of great reputation, to direct the REA film. His selection was in line with Lorentz's practice for hiring talent on the other films of merit—to get the best that the budget would allow. Ivens was hired in September, after his return from China, where he had made *The Four Hundred Million*, a documentary on the Japanese invasion.[5]

During the summer, Charles Walker developed the basic script from an outline Lorentz provided. Lorentz's outline, based on an old silent film *From Dawn to Dusk*, described two days, one without electricity, one with. After Ivens and the crew were hired, the next problem was to select a location. The site chosen was the Bill Parkinson farm near St. Clairsville, Ohio. Lorentz's maternal grandmother had come from this area, and he suggested it as a starting point because of its beauty.

The crew told the Parkinsons that they were looking for a typical, not a modern, farm, and a typical, not a modern, family.[6] The Parkinsons had a diversified dairy farm of average size with a small herd; they raised grain and did "a little of anything that could be done on any farm." The family consisted of the parents, four boys, and a girl. Contrary to general practice, the Parkinsons used mules rather than horses; a team of horses was rented for the appropriate scenes in the film.

The effect of the film would have been limited if an impover-

[5] Richard Griffith, "A Big Year for Fact Films," *New York Times*, September 17, 1939.

[6] Letter from Tom Parkinson, February 18, 1962.

123

ished family from the bottom third of the nation's farmers had been selected. One of the purposes of the film was to show what the coming of electricity meant to a typical farm family, a family the large power companies would not serve.

The Parkinson farm had been electrified in 1937. Ed Locke, script writer and assistant director, wrote to Pare Lorentz on October 6, 1939, describing the farm:

> The Parkinson farm consists of 175 acres devoted to pasture, wasteland, corn, and alfalfa in approximately that quantitative order. Parkinson's cash income comes from dairy cattle, of which he has twenty head. He raises hogs and some truck for family subsistence.
>
> When we arrived at the farm we found him using the following electrical equipment: 1. electric lights in house and barn, 2. electric motor attached to washing machine, 3. radio, 4. vacuum cleaner.[7]

The selection was made in part because of the electrification. Carmody had indicated the REA would provide further equipment as payment for use of the farm. As Tom Parkinson wrote, when the family learned that the sequences to be filmed after the changeover to electricity were to include a modern water system and plumbing for the house and barn, "We quickly got our heads together and told them we had no objection to tearing the place up to install such equipment, but it had to stay."[8] Locke listed in the letter to Lorentz what items the Parkinsons might use, and said that these items were needed in the last reel of the film. The REA was to install better lighting in the barn and plumbing in the house and barn, including a modern bathroom; but certain items, such as an electric milking machine and kitchen range, would only be lent.[9]

Locke provided justification for the installation of all the equipment:

[7] Letter from Ed Locke to Pare Lorentz, October 6, 1939. The electrification of the farm caused a few problems in the shooting. Lines leading to the house and barn were removed and the cables concealed in the ground. Occasionally, pictures and pieces of furniture were rearranged to conceal the evidence of electricity in the house. (Letter from Tom Parkinson, February 18, 1962.)

[8] Letter from Tom Parkinson, February 18, 1962. The family estimated they received about $900 worth of equipment.

[9] Letter from Ed Locke to Pare Lorentz, October 6, 1939.

124

. . . so that in the electrification quoted in the script we show the influence of electricity on health and work, both for the farmer and his wife, possible increase of income for the farmer by better care of his cattle and the dispelling of physical and cultural isolation by adequate lighting of the farm yard and radio.[10]

The crew that went to Ohio was small, consisting of Joris Ivens; Ed Locke; Arthur Ornitz, cameraman; an assistant for Ornitz; and Peter Sekaer, a still photographer for the REA. They lived in a hotel in St. Clairsville, six miles from the farm.

The presence of a motion picture crew in the valley provided excitement in many ways. For example, according to Floyd Crosby, Ivens wanted a scene of a burning barn, and arrangements were made to burn one. A strong wind was blowing on the day shooting was scheduled, but the fire was set anyway. Some burning tar paper from the roof blew into a nearby field and set it ablaze. Luckily, the crew and residents of the valley who had been watching the filming were able to contain it. One farmer at the scene had a heart attack from exertion, and the business manager for the crew (Locke?) was overcome by smoke.[11]

The shooting of a film on their own farm was a memorable event for the Parkinsons, and not merely because of the new equipment. They had known little but work all their lives, and each event in the shooting was new and many were humorous. As Tom Parkinson recalled, "Young boys don't mind eating supper two or three times so someone can get a 'reshot,' but when you milk the same cow five times I still laugh."[12] Ruth and her younger brother Bip disagreed constantly about going to school while the crew was shooting at the farm.[13]

Some of the rushes from Arthur Ornitz, the young cameraman, were not satisfactory. The crew was also inserting material in the original outline and shooting scenes not planned for—for example, Bip simply wandering around the farm, and the barn fire.

10 *Ibid.*
11 Letter from Floyd Crosby, September 6, 1962.
12 Letter from Tom Parkinson, February 18, 1962.
13 *Power and the Land* (exhibitor's campaign book), 2. From the files of the Museum of Modern Art.

For these reasons, Lorentz dispatched Floyd Crosby to Ohio with instructions to reshoot the unsatisfactory footage and to confine shooting to the original outline.[14]

According to Crosby, Ivens was also worried about the ability of his cameraman, and the unsatisfactory footage was distracting Ivens from his directing. It was hoped that Crosby's presence would stabilize the crew and Ivens. Crosby was on location several days before he could see any of his own rushes—thus disturbing both Crosby and Ivens.

Crosby's first rushes were almost lost. The wrappings had disappeared by the time the film cans arrived at the REA office in Wheeling. The REA staff sent the cans on to Eastman Kodak. Eventually, the film was returned to Crosby, but only because his name was on the enclosed camera report and Eastman Kodak knew that he was shooting in Ohio.[15]

Once Crosby's rushes were viewed, Ivens' direction picked up immediately.[16] Crosby received a great deal of credit from Lorentz for getting the film back on the right track. Lorentz had confidence in Crosby's technical ability and his ability to follow instructions.[17] Even the Parkinsons were aware of the improvement in the work after Crosby arrived.

Because Lorentz's own time was being devoted to finishing *The Fight for Life*, he transferred supervision of *Power and the Land* to Tommy Atkins, a member of the Washington staff of the Film Service. Atkins then wrote to Ivens, praised him for his work on the film to date, and asked him to concentrate now on shooting material that would be in direct contrast to the electrification of the farm. Atkins told Ivens that the Washington staff, including Lorentz and the REA officials, were very pleased with Crosby's rushes.[18]

---

[14] Interview with Pare Lorentz, July 28, 1961. Two sequences shot by Ornitz before Crosby arrived were highly effective: the sequence of Bip walking through the fields with a cornflower and the sequence of the horses in the fog. Crosby thought that the latter sequence was one of the most beautiful in the picture. (Letter from Floyd Crosby, September 6, 1962.)

[15] Letter from Philip Martin to Frank Lee, St. Clairsville, Ohio, October 21, 1939.

[16] Recorded interview with Floyd Crosby, February, 1962.

[17] Letter from Pare Lorentz, April 5, 1962.

In November, Lorentz once again took over supervision, because of various problems in the script and the final form of the film. A misunderstanding arose between Lorentz and Ivens. Lorentz wrote Ivens that he had tried without success to interest John Steinbeck in writing the narration. Lorentz then decided to write the narration himself. He wrote Ivens that his plans had been

> ... to have as little to do with the direction of the work of the people of well-established reputation who are working for us as is humanly possible. I also told you, however, that it is obligatory for me to translate the wishes of these government departments who wish films made.
>
> ... but one point we must be clear on: while I am perfectly willing to agree that you might make a very exciting documentary film from the material you have, unless that film is specifically enough like the original outline approved by the men who gave me the money and who trust me to see that such a picture is made, I feel it would be an unfortunate thing for both of us.[19]

Ivens wanted to make the film longer, but Lorentz explained that this would not be possible because funds were not available for a longer film and because it would be easier to get distribution if it was no more than three reels long.

Time was getting short for the Film Service to be saved. Lorentz had to get the film finished in the manner intended as quickly as possible. In six months the budget of the service was scheduled for reconsideration. Ivens had already run beyond November 14, the date assigned for him to finish shooting. Soon there would be no funds from which to pay Ivens and his crew. Lorentz had to prod him along.[20]

Lorentz's comments to Ivens on film length and distribution were echoed in a memorandum from Mercey to Marion Ramsey a week later. Mercey wrote that he could not provide an estimate of

[18] Letter from Tommy Atkins to Joris Ivens, October 25, 1939.

[19] Letter from Pare Lorentz to Joris Ivens, November 20, 1939.

[20] In spite of the difficulties, Lorentz retained his respect for Ivens and recommended him to Hallie Flanagan Davis, director of the Federal Theatre Project, to direct a one-reel film she wanted to produce. (Letter from Pare Lorentz to Hallie Flanagan Davis, April 1, 1940.) Ivens has also remarked recently on his admiration for Lorentz and the pleasure he had working for him. (Letter from Joris Ivens, August 1, 1962.)

127

the costs of distribution, because distribution would depend on the quality of the film, "the final result in terms of professional movie-making."[21] Another point that Mercey believed would affect distribution was the availability of other short subjects. Mercey indicated also that Hollywood's attitude toward the treatment of electrical power might have some effect on distribution. Because of the experience with *The Plow* and *The River*, he recommended that the film be two reels long so that it could be scheduled more easily with commercial programs.

Mercey recommended two possibilities for commercial distribution: to enter into a contract with a national distributor to handle the film and pay for the prints, or to have the Film Service handle commercial distribution, with the REA paying for the prints. He believed that the Film Service had the best setup for any educational distribution; again, the REA would pay for the prints. Mercey thought the service charge would probably be paid by the organization requesting the film.[22]

By November 30, the financial situation of the film had become acute for the REA. Ramsey called several facts to the attention of Mercey, who passed them on to Atkins:

1. The REA general budget on expenditures is tight at best.
2. The Film Service agreed to do a picture for so much money and the figure threatens to exceed the agreement by a large percentage.
3. Ivens spoke to Ramsey in the field, requesting $3,000 or $4,000, no more than $5,000. An earlier request for $8,000 floored them.
4. After production they need funds for distribution out of this year's budget.[23]

Mercey added a penciled note to the effect that the REA installation of new equipment was to have been completed in five days but had taken twenty-three, delaying shooting a great deal. Not all the increased expense and delay were caused by the Film Service.

Ramsey had suggested in his letter to Mercey that it might help

[21] Memorandum from Arch Mercey to Marion Ramsey, November 28, 1939.
[22] *Ibid.*
[23] Letter from Arch Mercey to Tommy Atkins, November 30, 1939. This is another indication of the trouble Ivens was causing.

if Lorentz would call Harry Slattery, REA administrator, and ask for more funds. Ramsey thought that Slattery would do nothing until he heard from Lorentz. There was great concern at the REA over whether this was an Ivens or a Lorentz film. They thought they had arranged to have a film produced by Lorentz. Their concern made it necessary for Lorentz to maintain supervision over the film.

Shooting was completed in November. Early in 1940, preliminary editing was done by Ivens and his wife, Helen van Dongen.[24] After the rough cut, Lorentz put his crew to work on polishing and cutting it to length. Lorentz wrote to Mercey that the rough-cut version looked like a "swell film."[25]

Shortly before the Senate hearings began in the spring of 1940, Slattery wrote to Lorentz urging him to finish *Power and the Land* as soon as possible. Slattery was worried about his own fiscal problems within the REA, but he thought that if the film could be exhibited to Congress, it would show what the Film Service could do. He wrote:

> I can say with utmost sincerity that I believe that your interests have suffered somewhat for lack of the rural electrification film, because its availability would have made it possible to show Senators and members of Congress a tangible and arresting product growing out of and relating directly and exclusively to the work of a specific government agency, with a program that is very generally rated sound and popular. Such a film would help you even now in this respect.[26]

But the film was months away from completion, and the production efforts of the Film Service were destined to last only two more months. A memorandum from Philip Martin reported that the work print was completed and shipped to Washington on May 21, 1940.

The film still lacked music and narration. Douglas Moore was

---

24 She cut his earlier films and later worked with Flaherty. This cutting was probably done between January 15 and February 1, 1940, when Ivens was back on the REA payroll.

25 Letter from Pare Lorentz to Arch Mercey, February 12, 1940.

26 Letter from Harry Slattery, administrator, REA, to Pare Lorentz, April 30, 1940.

129

hired to compose the music, and Stephen Vincent Benét was selected to write the narration. The two had collaborated on the score and libretto of the opera *The Devil and Daniel Webster*, which had been well received in New York in 1939. Both were hired by William Phillips, head of graphics for the REA.[27] Their choice parallels Lorentz's choice of Thomson and Gruenberg.

The film had been completely cut and edited before Ivens first showed it to Moore and Benét. Moore made notes after several viewings and obtained timings of the sequences. Ivens was very co-operative, offering to make small cuts or to enlarge scenes if they did not fit the soundtrack; later, during recording, Moore's music fit the timing of the scenes exactly.

One problem in working on the score was that Moore and Benét were drawn to the same high points in the script. A compromise was reached. When voice and music reached a climax at the same time, the music was "discreetly tuned down." An example of this procedure is found in the family dinner scene. Moore did not anticipate any narration here, but Benét wrote an effective invocation, "which although quite right and very moving, tuned out the part of the music I liked best."[28] Moore's music for the scene of cutting the corn inspired Benét to write a verse to fit the music. Unlike Thomson's music for *The Plow* and *The River*, all the themes are original—there are no quotations.

Before resigning from the Film Service, Lorentz made an arrangement with the REA by which Film Service personnel would see that the picture was completed as planned. The final assembly was done by members of his crew in Washington.

Power and the Land had its world premiere at St. Clairsville, Ohio, on August 31, 1940. Its New York opening was at the Rialto Theatre on December 10, 1940, where it shared billing with *Trail of the Vigilantes*.[29] It was distributed nationally by RKO Radio Pictures.[30]

[27] Letter from Douglas Moore, December 6, 1961. Moore received five hundred dollars for the score and also received money to hire an assistant, Henry Brant, to do the scoring, the same man who scored *The Plow* and *The River* for Virgil Thomson.

[28] *Ibid.*

[29] *New York Post*, December 11, 1940. From the files of the Museum of Modern

The Land was the other motion picture that the Film Service was able to get under way before losing its production powers. Like *Power and the Land*, it was contracted for by a branch of the Department of Agriculture. As in *Power and the Land*, shooting began in the second half of 1939; the film was not finished by the time Lorentz resigned. Unlike *Power and the Land*, it was not finished by Lorentz's crew but by its director.

The course of negotiations leading to production of *The Land* was not smooth. As in all the other films, clearing finances was a part of the problem. Another major difficulty was to get an acceptable script in time. General agricultural conditions changed before the film was completed, and official agricultural policy was in a state of flux as well.

Negotiations began on May 9, 1939, when R. M. Evans, AAA administrator, wrote to Lowell Mellett to inform him that the AAA wanted the Film Service to produce a three-reel sound motion picture dramatizing the agricultural conservation program.[31] His letter contained three provisions:

1. That a satisfactory script can be written;
2. Assurance can be given of completion of the picture by November 1;
3. The Comptroller General will approve transfer of the funds for this purpose to the National Emergency Council.[32]

Evans noted that they would have forty thousand dollars for such a film and hoped that the fifty thousand dollar figure that they had been given by the Film Service could be reduced by using some footage that was already available. Evans also told Mellett that the film was to be directed by Lorentz, although Lorentz was just beginning *The Fight for Life*.

Art. History was repeating itself in that this was the same theater at which *The Plow That Broke the Plains* had had its New York premiere.

[30] Although it was the last picture to be finished by the Film Service, no mention is made of Pare Lorentz or the Film Service in the credits.

[31] Letter from R. M. Evans to Lowell Mellett, May 9, 1939. Lorentz had apparently proved the value of his approach to some people in government because Evans's letter specifically stated that the film was to be "of a professional standard comparable to *The River*."

[32] *Ibid.*

Evans offered to put a script writer on the AAA payroll immediately in order to facilitate matters until the transfer of funds was approved, he also offered research assistance to the script writer.[33]

Mercey forwarded a copy of Evans' letter to Lorentz in Chicago. It seems from Mercey's accompanying letter that Lorentz had at one time suggested to the AAA the possibility of two scripts, with John Steinbeck doing one. Mercey wrote that the AAA was now interested in only one. Mercey thought that the project was secured, and urged the hiring of a writer as soon as possible so that the script would be ready in four or five weeks. He explained that the November 1 deadline was set so that the film could be distributed commercially between then and January 15, when the AAA wanted to start using the film at farm meetings.[34]

A few days later, Mercey again wrote Lorentz, this time to outline recommendations for the script. He noted that the AAA wanted to avoid controversy, and recommended that the film not be an "exposition of a device or series of devices [meaning particular mechanical and administrative means of coping with the farm problem]."[35] Mercey recommended the following highlights for the film:

     I. Land is a basic resource.
    II. Agriculture is changing.
   III. Relationship between town and country, agriculture, and industry is more apparent.
   IV. General remedies—better farm use, raise income.
    V. Government is attacking farm problems on many fronts.

The film would be challenging to produce, in Mercey's opinion, because of the specific nature of its proposed distribution. As he wrote, "The task becomes not one of doing an educational film for the AAA, but that of doing an exciting picture which will have

33 *Ibid.*

34 Letter from Arch Mercey to Pare Lorentz, May 9, 1939.

35 Letter from Arch Mercey to Pare Lorentz, May 15, 1939. These devices might be changed or discarded by the time the picture was finished—an accurate forecast indeed.

theatrical use followed by field use in farm meetings throughout the country."[36]

Mercey wisely recommended not setting a deadline until the script was ready and it would be possible to foresee some of the production problems. He did not believe that November 1 would be a final date, although he knew that the AAA would want some commercial distribution before January 15.[37]

A few days later, Mercey reported to Lorentz that the AAA was excited by the proposed script and general idea. The AAA had forty thousand dollars for the film and wanted to put a writer to work as soon as possible.[38] Lorentz approved a script outline and the cost of forty thousand dollars, although he indicated it could be done better for fifty thousand dollars.[39] He did, however, set the deadline for the film as December 1, if the script and money were ready by July 1. The outline now read:

Farming as a Way of Life
America Is a Farm Land
The Machine and the Farm
The Machines and the World
Men, Machines and Land
The Answer[40]

Russell Lord, well known as a writer on agriculture, was selected to develop the script outline. In late May, Mercey drove out to Lord's farm in Maryland to hire him. Lord described his interpretation to Lorentz on July 25, 1939, suggesting that "the picture could show an upbuilding of farms and people in a new design."[41] He noted that the major problems to be depicted were soil mismanagement, machine displacement, and migrants. He recommended that the film present a number of approaches to the solution, ranging from the changes on the face of the land and

[36] *Ibid.*
[37] *Ibid.*
[38] Letter from Arch Mercey to Pare Lorentz, May 22, 1939.
[39] Letter prepared for the signature of Pare Lorentz by Arch Mercey, May 22, 1939.
[40] *Ibid.*
[41] "Flaherty Rediscovers America," *Land*, Vol. I, No. 1 (1941), 68. This was past the deadline Lorentz set for the script.

in agricultural practice to the programs of the AAA. However, the picture had to do more than present what the AAA was and what it was doing. Lord ended the letter by saying that he thought it was fundamentally "a rather simple picture."[42]

By August 24, 1939, a few changes had been made in the basic outline that Lorentz had approved in May. The first point was deleted, and the last point was changed to "America Starts Over."[43] The new outline described in detail the basic sequence of shots for each part as well as suggestions for specific locations, and contained a scene-by-scene analysis of the content.[44]

When the AAA decided to proceed with the picture, Lorentz told them that he would be unable to direct it because of his work on *The Fight for Life* and his plans to return to *Ecce Homo!* and said that the Film Service was more than willing to produce the film and would hire an outstanding director.

Lorentz hired another famous documentarian, Robert Flaherty, to direct the film. It had been more than a year since the two had met in England, where Flaherty had told Lorentz he would like to work for the United States government if they were sponsoring films like *The River*.[45]

Lorentz told Mercey to wire Flaherty in London to inquire if he was available. Flaherty replied something to this effect: "Deposit 2,000 pounds to my account Chase National Bank."[46] Mercey then wrote him explaining some of the facts about government employment and mentioning the salary. Flaherty accepted the offer.[47]

[42] By 1941, two years later, he was admitting that he did not know what he was talking about, because it had not been simple at all.

[43] U.S. Film Service, script outline, *The Land*, August 24, 1939. From the personal files of Pare Lorentz.

[44] The mystery becomes, whatever happened to this outline? Did Flaherty ever see it?

[45] See p. 71. Flaherty had not directed a film since *Elephant Boy* (1937).

[46] Letter from Arch Mercey, March 22, 1962.

[47] Frances Flaherty, the director's wife, had returned to this country and purchased a farm in Vermont. The pressure of the approaching war had made them both uneasy. Even though England had become a second home to them, they were eager to return to the United States. When Mrs. Flaherty learned that her husband was going to work for the Film Service, she was overjoyed. "I only remember how glad I was that here was an opportunity I had been hoping for that would bring Bob back to this country." (Letter from Frances Flaherty, December 29, 1961.) She was thank-

Film critics were happy to note Flaherty's return to his home-land. Richard Griffith, later Flaherty's biographer, said that his return to production was another sign that 1939 was an important year for documentary films. Griffith was fascinated by the pos-sible results of a collaboration between Flaherty and Lorentz. He wrote: "Flaherty has dealt mainly with the far places of the earth; Lorentz has made films about our lives here and now. The result of their joint work may well be the mature film of American life for which many of us have been waiting."[48] But there was no collaboration intended in the Film Service plans.

In August, Flaherty went to Washington and met with AAA officials. Russell Lord arrived from Maryland to discuss the script and written commentary.[49] Lord wrote that at the time the story line was left to Flaherty but that there was "a general suggestion that something be done in the line of ground-line reconstruction of soil and man in this country during the few years since Lorentz's two films."[50]

Shooting for *The Land* began in the vicinity of Des Moines, Iowa, on August 28, 1939. The crew included Irving Lerner, as-sistant cameraman and general assistant to Flaherty; Key Hart, assigned by the AAA as liaison man between the crew and govern-ment agencies; Arthur Rothstein, sent by Roy Stryker to be still photographer and photographic assistant to Flaherty; Vernon Kelly and Douglas Baker, from the Film Service staff, as drivers and handymen; E. K. Allison, fiscal agent; and George Gercke, who kept Lorentz and Mercey posted on the progress of the crew.[51]

In a lengthy letter from Des Moines, Gercke described to Lorentz the first week's work. The crew went out to shoot about

ful that a place had been found for her husband in his own country, "made possible by a film-maker of his own stature under a sponsorship that recognized the value of their work." (*Ibid.*)

[48] "A Big Year for Fact Films," *New York Times*, September 17, 1939.

[49] This was probably no later than August 24, the date of the previously mentioned scenario, and possibly even before, since Flaherty lined up a crew and began shooting in Iowa on August 28.

[50] Lord, "Flaherty Rediscovers America," *Land*, Vol. I, No. 1 (1941) 67. This does not fit with the previous discussions between the AAA and the Film Service and with the fact that Flaherty was working directly for the Film Service, not the AAA.

[51] Letter from George Gercke to Pare Lorentz, September 3, 1939.

7:30 each morning, traveling some thirty-five miles, and returned in the evening. They found that they had to do most of the shooting in the morning or late afternoon because the midday light was unsatisfactory and seemed to flatten everything. They had shot tests on Monday and about 1,500 feet a day on Tuesday, Wednesday, and Thursday. Bad weather on Friday prevented any shooting on that day, and they shot only a few hundred feet on Saturday. All tests and rushes were air-expressed to New York.

According to Gercke, they were now going to leave Des Moines and travel to St. Paul because Flaherty thought that he had all the footage of corn farming he could get at the moment. "The corn picking and harvesting, mechanical and otherwise, cannot be had until at least a month from now."[52] Their plans were to shoot for a few days in dairy country and then go north to Duluth and Superior for footage of grain elevators and grain ships. Later, they planned to come back down through Iowa, go on to Kansas City to film the stockyards and large rail shipping yards, then to Muskogee, Oklahoma, to shoot a large Soil Conservation Service conservation area that Russell Lord had told them would provide them with much material. Later, they would move on to Dalhart, Amarillo, and the Panhandle in Texas and then go south to the Rio Grande Valley and film the cotton and tobacco areas along the way.

Gercke expressed concern about two matters: the leadership of the group, and the absence of Russell Lord. Gercke did not plan to be with the crew full time, and thought that the crew would lack leadership after he left. Matters disturbing him and the crew were the January 1, 1940, deadline, which caused three crew members to threaten to quit; the effect the war in Europe would have on agricultural policy by January 1; the most disturbing matter, the lack of a story to work from (he enclosed the one they had, which was upsetting Flaherty); and the absence of Russell Lord, who was supposed to have joined the crew with the completed story. Gercke described his understanding of Lord's role as follows:

I do not know what to think but that Lord has co-operated the way
[52] *Ibid.*

136

I understood he was to do. I had thought of him as the buffer, the man with the agricultural knowledge and also a story sense, who was to stand between the agricultural scientists and officials on the one hand, and Flaherty, the artist and director, on the other. I thought he was going to be available July 1 to work on this story, as he told Arch and me in June, and now it is after September 1. I do not say of my own authority that there is no story; I am simply saying that Flaherty feels he has not got one.[53]

He told Lorentz that what the group needed was "a dynamic mind which knows both the problem and how to convert it into a motion picture." The only such leader Gercke could think of was Lorentz himself. He did emphasize to Lorentz that he was reassured about Flaherty, who had not yet wanted to bother Lorentz. Gercke interpreted this as meaning that "he is still trying to soak himself in the material and shoot as he goes along."[54]

Gercke noted that Flaherty was being distracted by the progress of the war: "His brother, his friends, still live there. He is terribly upset by the war news. Only rarely, in the evenings, does he talk about anything else. He sits and listens to all the radio bulletins and buys all the papers. (In this he does not differ much from the rest of us.) But it is hard to penetrate his mind."[55]

The troubles for Flaherty's crew and the film were just beginning. On September 11, Mercey wrote Lorentz that he had been trying to get the AAA and the Department of Agriculture to indicate what effect the war crisis would have on agriculture. He enclosed two press releases by Wallace and AAA chief R. M. Evans announcing that the policy was to be that farmers were to proceed as if there were no war.[56] The AAA wanted to prevent overexpansion in planting and to encourage the continued importance of conservation.

Russell Lord wrote to Lorentz on the same day to say he believed the war situation and its effect on agricultural policy would

[53] *Ibid.*
[54] Flaherty was working at a disadvantage. He had been out of the country for nine years, the whole period Roosevelt had been in office putting the ideas and policies of the New Deal to work. He had been back in the United States less than a month.
[55] Letter from George Gercke to Pare Lorentz, September 3, 1939.
[56] Letter from Arch Mercey to Pare Lorentz, September 11, 1939.

help the film by assuring its strong support from top officials in Washington. He wrote also to Flaherty on the same day, enclosing a copy to Lorentz. Lord told Flaherty that Henry Wallace was excited about a book called *Vanishing Lands* and was planning a "save our soil" campaign. Lord did not think that Wallace's new campaign would change the theme and projected date for Flaherty's film. He wrote: "What he is now thinking would seem to accentuate the picture of America, with an upturn of land use and human security at the other end, which you, Pare, and I have projected."[57]

At this time Lord confused Flaherty even further by sending him another script treatment, this time for a conservation theme. It too was in five parts, restating some of the points of the previous outlines. No wonder that Richard Griffith wrote that Flaherty discarded the script, took to the road, and filmed what he wanted.[58]

Russell Lord provided a detailed account of Flaherty on the road, describing him as "like a little boy revisiting, rediscovering his homeland, marvelling at its beauty, friendliness, and power."[59] Flaherty was attracted to everything he saw and encountered—farms, hotels, pinball machines, apple pie, broadcasts of prize fights. Lord described Flaherty's great gifts as a traveler—his ability to eat anything, sleep anywhere, and get along with people. Lord wrote that in the beginning the mood of the crew was robust and cheerful but that it changed as they turned south. The weather grew hot, hotels were unbearable, and the food was no longer as good as it had been. Not only was the war having an effect on Flaherty, but he could not believe the deplorable conditions he found among the migrant workers in the cotton fields, with whom he spent a great deal of time talking.[60]

Flaherty and the crew were on location into the next spring, filming irrigated and mechanized farms as well as those in several eastern states. There had also been, by Flaherty's own account, endless conferences with Wayne Darrow, head of the Division of

[57] Letter from Russell Lord to Robert Flaherty, September 11, 1939.
[58] *The World of Robert Flaherty*, 140.
[59] Lord, "Flaherty Rediscovers America," *Land*, Vol. I, No. 1 (1941), 74.
[60] *Ibid.*, 74–75.

Information of the Department of Agriculture. Darrow told Flaherty, "Take your time and don't pull any punches."[61] Apparently, the deadline was being waived. Griffith assessed the Flaherty efforts as follows: "They covered the American agricultural story as no reporter had covered it, on film or in print, but they returned to Washington with a sense of insecurity."[62]

Early in 1940, Flaherty wrote to Jay Leyda in London: "The truth is that I am sweating pretty hard over the film I am trying to finish for the government. I never tackled a tougher or more confusing job and there are many times when I don't know whether I am standing on my head or not."[63]

Flaherty was now working past the January 1 deadline. The film would not be ready for the agricultural meetings beginning on January 12. However, contrary to Mercey's earlier fears, the AAA was still interested in the film.[64]

Early in 1940, Flaherty and Lorentz met in New York to view Flaherty's footage. Arch Mercey invited Willard Lanphere of the Division of Information of the AAA to join them. The screening was set for March 1, with a conference to follow.[65]

Clearly, *The Land* was getting beyond the control of the Film Service. The footage was for a film different from the one originally agreed upon with the AAA, the sponsor. Through his own efforts and after discussions with the AAA, Flaherty was turning the picture into something else. He and Lorentz had an agreeable discussion about their differing points of view about the film. Lorentz gave Flaherty a choice: either Lorentz's cutting crew would edit, with Flaherty and Lorentz as partners in the decisions, or Flaherty would take over the whole picture himself, directly under the AAA. If Flaherty did take it over, Lorentz thought that Flaherty

[61] Theodore Strauss, "The Giant Shimmies down the Beanstalk," *New York Times*, October 12, 1941.

[62] *Op. cit.*, 40.

[63] *Ibid.*, 140.

[64] It may have been a mistake to expect Flaherty to be finished in time. He never worked in a hurry or according to deadlines. His whole approach to film making was contrary to what he had agreed to do.

[65] Letter from Arch Mercey to Willard Lanphere, February 28, 1940.

could develop his own ideas for assembling the film without being inhibited by Lorentz and the original plans.[66]

Flaherty's decision—to assume responsibility himself under AAA auspices—was made sometime between March 13, 1940, and the end of the month. Tommy Atkins wrote to Flaherty on March 13 requesting certain information about *The Land*: the present status of the film, Flaherty's idea of the film and how it should be cut, and his ideas about the narration and the score.[67] Atkins asked him to provide this information quickly so as not to delay the film.

On April 1, Atkins received a letter from J. H. McCormick, of the Department of Agriculture's Division of Information, saying that McCormick would soon be coming to New York to pick up the remaining negative for *The Land* at Deluxe Laboratories.[68] Transfer of the film to McCormick had begun on March 28.[69]

Thus ended the responsibility of the Film Service for *The Land*. Flaherty worked on the film through the summer of 1941, using facilities provided by the Department of Agriculture. The premiere was at the Museum of Modern Art on April 9, 1942.[70] It has been shown only nontheatrically and has never been seen by the public at large.[71]

The Film Service had responsibilities other than producing films. It served as a distribution center, cataloguing, publicizing,

[66] Letter from Pare Lorentz, April 5, 1962.

[67] Letter from Tommy Atkins to Robert Flaherty, March 13, 1940.

[68] Letter from J. H. McCormick to Tommy Atkins, April 1, 1940.

[69] Letter from Philip Martin, Jr., to Tommy Atkins, n.d.

[70] Griffith, *op. cit.*, 141.

[71] Mrs. Flaherty has written of her personal disappointment in the outcome of a project for which she and her husband had had such great hopes:

"I naturally dreamed of great things to come from the association and this sponsorship.

"I cannot tell you how deep my own feelings are about this film and about our whole experience of working it out there in the basement of the AAA, with the good, the earnest, but propagandist and myopic people of the Agriculture Department.

"Without the U.S. Film Service and Lorentz behind it, Bob was left again to fight his battles alone. This is the measure of my deep unhappiness when the U.S. Film Service broke down."

(Letter from Frances Flaherty, December 29, 1961.)

and distributing government films. In 1940, its work was being performed by sixty-eight employees, thirty-nine in distribution and twenty-nine in field production work.[72]

While the Film Service was in the NEC, study guides for both *The Plow That Broke the Plains* and *The River* were produced to accompany educational screenings of the films. Prints of *The Plow* and *The River* were available for sale or loan. Listings of other available government films were compiled and printed. In May, 1939, Mercey reported to the House Appropriations Subcommittee that the Film Service had cleared 2,847 films from twenty-six agencies for distribution in 1938–39.[73]

Among the most popular films that the Film Service distributed were *The Plow* and *The River*. Lowell Mellett reported to the House subcommittee that *The Plow* had been available for educational distribution since August, 1938, and had had 3,060 bookings for 375,000 persons. In March, 1939, the first month *The River* was available for educational distribution, this film had 193 bookings for an audience estimated at 112,000.[74] About a year later, the Film Service report to the Senate Appropriations Committee listed 5,694 bookings for *The Plow* and 5,476 for *The River*.[75]

The major project of the Film Service, not specifically listed among its duties at the time of its creation, was to produce films about the United States for Latin America, and films about Latin America for the United States.[76] The proposal for the Latin American film program was presented to an interdepartmental committee on Latin American affairs in 1938 and again in August, 1939. On August 16, 1939, George Gercke wrote Lorentz that the

[72] U.S. House of Representatives, Appropriations Subcommittee, *Hearings on Department of Labor–Federal Security Agency Appropriations Bill, 1941*, 76 Cong., 3 sess., 1940, 286.

[73] U.S. House of Representatives, Appropriations Subcommittee, *Hearings on Work Relief Appropriations Act, 1940*, 76 Cong., 1 sess., 1939, 306–307.

[74] *Ibid.*, 295.

[75] U.S., Senate, Appropriations Committee, *Hearings on Department of Labor–Federal Security Agency Appropriations Bill, 1941*, 76 Cong., 3 sess., 1940, 235.

[76] This project grew out of Lorentz's discussion with Sumner Welles on entering *The River* in the Venice International Film Festival.

141

program for 1939 would be the same basic program offered in 1938. He enclosed a copy of the proposal.[77] The total cost of the recommended program was to be $180,000. The sum of fifty thousand dollars was proposed for a new film on the Latin American republics for distribution in the United States; the same amount was to be spent on a new film on the United States for Latin America. The balance was for distribution.

Two months later, Gercke wrote Lorentz of the problems they were experiencing with the interdepartmental committee. The program was about to come up for final consideration. First of all, Gercke wanted to be sure that Undersecretary of State Sumner Welles was firmly committed to the program and would guide it through the committee—the program had been criticized by the State Department. Gercke wrote that such support by Welles would indicate that the President was for it and would make it easier for the program to get through the Budget Bureau. In Gercke's opinion, the program could be carried on by the Film Service whether the committee approved it or not, because the State Department could exercise supervisory powers over any government program that affected foreign policy. Obviously, Welles's support was essential.

Gercke was greatly concerned by the fact that the film program had been placed in the hands of the Subcommittee on Motion Pictures of the Interdepartmental Committee on Cooperation with Other American Republics, some of whose members were representatives of Hollywood corporations. "This is an absolutely untenable position. Either the Film Service is the consultant to the Committee on motion picture activity or the Subcommittee is," Gercke wrote.[78]

Plans for the program were more ambitious than Gercke's letter indicated, and may account for Hollywood's sudden interest in government films. The purpose of the program was to translate the State Department's Good Neighbor Policy into "films about us

[77] Letter from George Gercke to Pare Lorentz, August 16, 1939. For the complete proposal, see Appendix I.

[78] Letter from George Gercke to Pare Lorentz, October 13, 1939.

for them and films about them for us."[79] Of major importance was the plan to produce new films and record Portuguese and Spanish sound tracks for half a dozen of the government's best films, to serve as the nucleus of a Pan-American film library that would also contain films from the Latin American countries. This library would be an extension of the distribution activities of the Film Service. The Axis powers, particularly Germany, were flooding South America with propaganda films, causing concern in the State Department.

Lorentz and Gercke hoped to send a scout to South America to study production and distribution problems and to line up outstanding writers, musicians, and actors. It was intended that the films about Latin America should preserve the purity of their popular and folk music. It was learned that the wife of the Argentine ambassador was a musicologist and had an extensive collection of Latin American folk music. Elizabeth Meyer, a staff member of the Film Service, who had been part of the advance crew in Chicago for *The Fight for Life*, began the compilation of music through the Argentine and other embassies.[80]

The project was doomed when Congress did not approve the necessary funds. As Mercey noted, "We made recommendations which were some years ahead of their time and which, for the most part, were carried out under different auspices and somewhat different approaches."[81]

Another problem the Film Service attacked was the difficulty the government had been having in procuring raw film and getting good developing and printing. Before Lorentz left the Film Service, an attempt was made to standardize these procedures. A merit clause was put into contracts with printers and developers that stated that any mechanical work done for the federal government had to meet commercial standards.[82]

Toward the end of his tenure, Lorentz called on several government officials to explain the Film Service and to solicit support, in

[79] Philip Sterling, "Following *The River*," *New York Times*, October 15, 1939.
[80] Interview with Pare Lorentz, July 27, 1961.
[81] Letter from Arch Mercey, March 22, 1962.
[82] Letter from Arch Mercey, February 4, 1964.

143

an attempt to keep the government producing informational films for commercial distribution. He described the need for the program: "If *Time* magazine has the *March of Time* once a month, this is the voice of Henry Luce. The United States Government deserves to have at least thirty minutes a month to explain in film the major problems which affect the whole country, Republicans and Democrats alike."[83] Lorentz drew up a proposed maximum program for the Film Service, presupposing that it would have all the money and men that it needed. He listed subjects that lent themselves to film, such as Surgeon General Parran's proposed mass attack on the five basic killers. He also wanted to make films about Hawaii, Alaska, Puerto Rico, the Virgin Islands, and other areas of the United States that were not well known to the population of the great cities. No one was interested.

The final accomplishment of the Film Service was to obtain a clarification of all law pertaining to government information, researching law that related to all governmental information activities, from the Government Printing Office to the Geodetic Survey. Through this clarification, the Film Service was placed within a legal framework.[84]

[83] Interview with Pare Lorentz, July 27, 1961.
[84] *Ibid.*

144

VII

THE END OF THE FILMS OF MERIT

In February, 1940, the activity and anxiety of those working for the Film Service must have been intense. Lorentz and his New York staff were completing arrangements for the opening of *The Fight for Life*. Lorentz was considering writing the narration for Ivens' *Power and the Land* himself or hiring someone else to do it. He wanted that film, which was in rough-cut form, finished as soon as possible. In addition, Lorentz was concerned about the delays plaguing the production of Flaherty's *The Land*. In Washington, Mercey and his administrative staff were preparing a request for what everyone hoped would become a permanent appropriation for the operation of the Film Service as part of the Office of Education.

Lowell Mellett, as director of the National Emergency Council, had been very helpful before and during the hearings the year before. However, Film Service affairs were not going so agreeably in the Office of Education—the personalities of Pare Lorentz and Commissioner of Education John W. Studebaker clashed.

Also in 1940, Hollywood was still displeased with the government's motion picture activities, the displeasure being heightened by the artistic success of *The Fight for Life*: "Uncle Sam's invasion of the motion picture field is giving Hollywood's producers, including James Roosevelt, a pain in the neck. The insignificant amounts which the government spends in filming and distributing admittedly remarkable pictures threaten to show up professional production costs."[1] Evidence of Hollywood displeasure also came directly from the motion picture industry. Delegates to the first

[1] Ray Tucker, "News behind the News," *New London Day*, March 23, 1940. From the personal files of Pare Lorentz.

145

annual convention of the Pacific Coast Conference of Independent Theatre Owners were urged to "combat the unjustified and unneeded entrance of the government into our movies"[2]—obviously a direct slap at the Film Service.

The Film Service decided to stress its centralizing activities at the upcoming hearings of the House Appropriations Subcommittee. Since no funds were earmarked for production in the new budget, attention should be focused on the benefits to be derived from such centralizing activities as cataloguing and distributing films and providing consultation services. The first budget hearings in 1939 had stressed the accomplishments made and proposed through production, which had seemed very costly. The new budget would look less formidable. It included the following items:

Personal Services	$71,880
Supplies and Materials	3,500
Communication Service	3,000
Travel Expenses	5,000
Transportation of Things	1,200
Printing and Binding	5,000
Rent	3,700
Equipment	13,120
Total	$106,400[3]

Studebaker called attention to the fact that no money was being requested for the production of films, although the Film Service thought they should be making some films.

Mercey detailed the source of funds for operation in the past year. The WPA initially provided $75,900, the same amount came from the PWA, and $16,700 came from the FSA—a total of $168,500. Later, the WPA provided an additional $162,500,

[2] "Government Films under Fire," *Los Angeles Examiner*, May 10, 1940. From the personal files of Pare Lorentz.

[3] U.S. House of Representatives, Appropriations Subcommittee, *Hearings on Department of Labor–Federal Security Agency Appropriations Bill, 1941*, 76 Cong., 3 sess., 1940, 282. The budget for the Radio Service was being examined at the same time by the subcommittee. An item of testimony was brought out early in the hearing that reflected on a later statement by Mercey. The Radio Service used a number of people from relief rolls in various capacities.

which was used to finish *The Fight for Life*, do work on *Ecce Homo!* and maintain the distribution and educational picture consultation services.[4]

Only four films were mentioned in the testimony in 1940 as opposed to the long list of potential productions presented the year before. This is another indication of the attempt to emphasize the money-saving benefits of centralizing film activities of the government as proposed by the Film Service.

Some of the attitudes of the subcommittee members toward the Film Service can be determined from what happened the first time Mercey mentioned *The Fight for Life*. Representative Albert J. Engel asked for details about the cost of the film and whether the garbage-can scene had been cut out yet. Mercey told him it remained in the film.[5]

Next, the subcommittee considered the employees of the Film Service. When asked where they came from, Mercey replied that from the beginning the Film Service had tried to hire only topflight professional persons. When asked by Chairman Malcolm Tarver how they were selected, Mercey answered: "We select them on a merit basis. Practically all of our employees, we feel, have an excellent record of merit behind them."[6] They were selected upon the recommendation and opinion of the production consultant and other technical persons on the staff.

Studebaker and Mercey were then asked to submit the expenditures for the various activities of the Film Service for the current year. These figures were:

Distribution (39 Employees)	$56,320
Production Staff	34,400
The Fight for Life (Fiscal 1940)	22,041
R. E. A. Picture (Fiscal 1940)	7,452
A. A. A. Picture (Fiscal 1940)	13,680
Ecce Homo!	1,020[7]

4 *Ibid.*, 284.

5 *Ibid.*, 284–85.

6 *Ibid.*, 286.

7 *Ibid.*, 294. Several employees were paid for working on more than one production.

147

The following schedule of salaries was offered for 1941:

Director's Staff	$ 9,500
Assistant Director's Staff	10,000
Script and Research Section	16,860
Distribution Section	28,060
Assistance in Business Administration	7,460
Total	$71,880[8]

Because the new request was for only one-third as much as the budget for the previous year, Chairman Tarver asked Mercey if they expected to receive any further funds from the WPA. Mercey's answer was, "That remains to be seen." He then pointed out that the new request included no funds for production but would support a film-distribution program. He stated that this request "for the first time establishes a film division as a regular appropriation in the government framework."[9]

Representative John Huston asked if there had been any complaints from private producers because of competition from the Film Service. Mercey replied that there had been fears in 1935 that there might be competition, that these fears continued when *The Plow* was released, but that the attitude changed when *The River* was released. "The private producers felt that the government was in a position to make pictures of this general character, which Hollywood was not in a position to make; and therefore they felt that we were filling a certain niche in movie making which no other source filled."[10] Mercey was right, but only in part. The Film Service *was* producing films that no other source— notably Hollywood—was making, but whether Hollywood's attitude toward the Film Service had changed was another matter.[11]

At this point, Mercey placed in the record an excerpt from T. R. Adam's *Motion Pictures in Adult Education*, which stressed

[8] *Ibid.*, 288–93. Mercey predicted that Lorentz probably would resign because the budget provided only $7,500 for his salary as opposed to the $10,000 he had received in 1940. His salary was being cut because there had been a complete reallocation of salaries consistent with standards in the Office of Education.

[9] *Ibid.*

[10] *Ibid.*, 298.

[11] See p. 145.

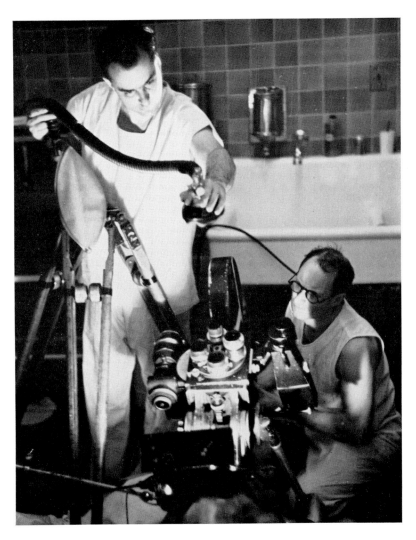

Pare Lorentz and Floyd Crosby checking shot in Chicago Maternity Hospital. *The Fight for Life.*

The Fight for Life: Pare Lorentz, author and director; Louis Gruenberg, composer; Alexander Smallens, conductor.

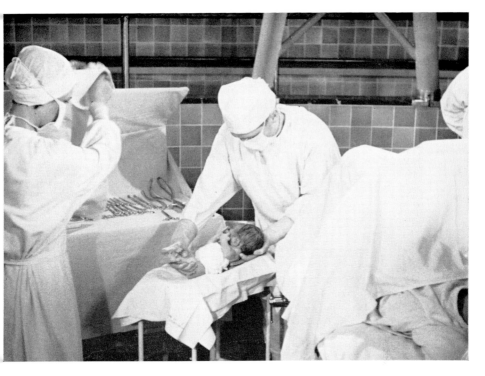

Birth. From *The Fight for Life*.

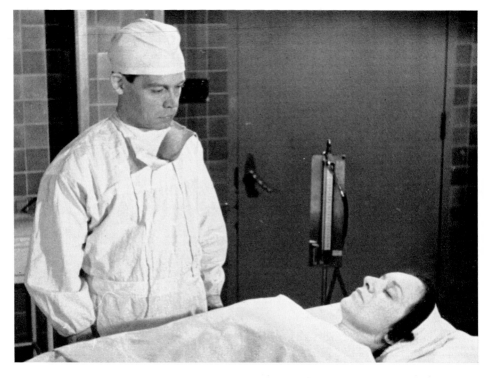

Death. Myron McCormick as Dr. O'Donnell and "patient," a graduate of the Chicago Maternity Center and a doctor on the staff. From *The Fight for Life*.

Lecture scene. "You came to the Maternity Center because you wished to learn more about obstetrics." Storrs Haynes and Will Geer. From *The Fight for Life*.

Will Geer, followed by a Chicago Maternity Center staff nurse and Myron McCormick, enters a tenement to deliver a baby. From *The Fight for Life*.

Chicago slums. "They brought them into all our great cities from
the hills and fields to build their machines and roll their steel . . .
and left them in these shacks." Left to right: Chicago Maternity
Center staff nurse, Storrs Haynes, and Myron McCormick. From
The Fight for Life.

Chicago slums. "Here are ruined teeth and tainted blood and in-
fected lungs. . . . Here are men who want decent clothes and homes
and medical care for their women and children. How can they
keep alive in these places?" From *The Fight for Life.*

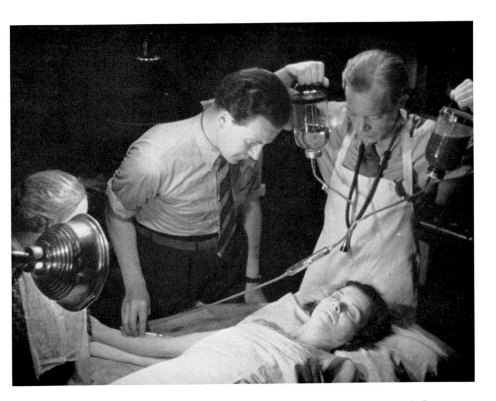

"The blood is the life." Left to right: Dorothy Urban (behind the light), Will Geer, Myron McCormick, and Dorothy Adams. From *The Fight for Life.*

The Parkinson farm. "Heat the water, carry the water, pour it in the tub. Every week, just like cleaning the lamp." (Stephen Vincent Benét) From *Power and the Land*.

Washday. "There is a machine to do the wash, but it runs by electricity. . . . Here on the farm where it is needed most, electricity is hard to get." (Stephen Vincent Benét) From *Power and the Land*.

RURAL ELECTRIFICATION ADMINISTRATION

Mending by the light of a coal-oil lamp. "She doesn't care so much about her own eyes but her children's." (Stephen Vincent Benét) From *Power and the Land*.

Farm family. "Good people of the solid, old stock who settled in this country 300 years ago." (Robert Flaherty) From *The Land*.

Farm migrants. "The land had played out on them he said. . . .
Most of our migrants are young people with young children."
(Robert Flaherty) From *The Land*.

Contour plowing. "A change has come over the land in the last few years. Farmers have turned to a new way of working it . . . new pattern, new furrow lines, new terrace lines, to hold the rain where it falls." (Robert Flaherty) From *The Land*.

Plowed fields. "It is a pattern that will always hold the soil, no matter what the slash of winds or the wash of rains. . . . It's a new design." (Robert Flaherty) From *The Land*.

the importance to adult education of the Film Service and its work in producing, cataloguing, and distributing government films: "If the United States Film Service were granted the necessary funds and freedom to prepare suitable printed matter to accompany the distribution of existing government films, a major development might take place in visual education for adult groups."[12] Adam said, further, that individual film units were jealous over the rights to their own films, that the government should adopt uniform production procedures, and that agencies should not "obstruct the unifying influence of the new Film Service in production techniques."[13]

From this point in the hearings, the congressmen seemed hostile toward the Film Service. The main cause of the hostility appears to have been the fact that the Film Service and Lorentz's previous production unit had miraculously existed for five years on relief funds without any money specifically appropriated by Congress. The only funds they had used that had not been earmarked for relief were those from the REA for *Power and the Land* and from the AAA for *The Land*. Thus, it was quickly established that none of the $331,000 being spent during fiscal 1940 was being spent for the purpose for which it had been appropriated—no WPA workers were used. Mercey was given an opportunity to justify the use of the money in this manner. He said:

> It was used for the purpose of furthering the express wishes of the President that the several departments and agencies engaged in carrying out the relief and work relief programs should produce motion pictures illustrating the physical and human problems confronting the country and the methods adopted by the government for their solution. To carry out this work the Film Service employed as many people as possible through the Replacement Service; but for actual movie-making it was necessary to hire competent technicians and to pay them on a per diem basis, that is when actually employed.[14]

[12] P. 49.

[13] *Ibid.*, 50.

[14] U.S. House of Representatives, Appropriations Subcommittee, *Hearings on Department of Labor–Federal Security Agency Appropriations Bill, 1941*, 76 Cong., 3 sess., 1940, 299.

Representative Engel returned to the matter of the garbage-can scene in *The Fight for Life* to close the hearings on a note of hostility. He wanted to know whether the scenes of bad housing conditions were taken from real life:

> MR. ENGEL: For instance, you have in that picture a scene of people going to a garbage can and taking out food. Were these people actually going there, or were they actors playing that part?
>
> MR. MERCEY: I will have to ask our production manager, Mr. Atkins.
>
> MR. ATKINS: They are actual documentary scenes. They were not staged.
>
> MR. ENGEL: They were not staged? The people actually went out there and got that food out of the garbage can?
>
> MR. ATKINS: That is true.
>
> MR. HUSTON: I have seen that right here in Washington in the last eighteen months.
>
> MR. ENGEL: I am amazed to learn that after seven years of the abundant life under the New Deal we still have people eating out of cans.[15]

The irony in this questioning is depressing. Lorentz had successfully accomplished what he had set out to do in *The Fight for Life*—he focused attention on human erosion in our cities. The congressmen did not seem to be really concerned about, or even aware of, the poverty and starvation—even in Washington—until they were shown it in a motion picture.

Following questioning about the new equipment requested, Chairman Tarver asked Studebaker to present evidence that would establish the legality of appropriations for the Radio Service and the Film Service. Studebaker presented the legal opinion of Fowler V. Harper, general counsel of the Federal Security Agency, who stressed material in the law of 1867, which had created the Office of Education, as being fully adequate to cover these services. He referred particularly to the following:

> ... and to diffuse such information respecting the organization and management of schools and school systems and methods of teaching, as shall aid the people of the United States in the establishment and

[15] *Ibid.*, 300.

150

maintenance of different school systems, and otherwise promote the cause of education throughout the country.[16]

The subcommittee did not accept Harper's interpretation and turned down the request for funds. Its recommendations were released on March 21, 1940:

> Two estimates, one in the amount of $40,000 and one in the amount of $106,400, were before the committee, involving the establishment, on a permanent basis, of a radio service and a film service, respectively. The authorities have concluded that there is at the present time no existing law that would authorize the carrying on of these services. The sums named have, therefore, been eliminated from the bill. The committee reserves judgment on the merit of the two activities and in the event enabling legislation is passed, will review the estimate of needs for funds to carry on any work under these heads in the light of the existing conditions.[17]

Lorentz went to Washington as quickly as possible after the House report was released. There he told the press that General Counsel Foley of the Treasury Department had issued a memorandum in July, 1939, "approving statutory foundation of the Film Service, and the memo was approved in turn by the General Accounting Office."[18] Why Harper had not referred to this is not known. Perhaps he had not because the Radio Service was not included in Foley's memorandum and because he wanted to justify both in one interpretation.

The issue of the Film Service was widely discussed in the press. Drew Pearson wrote:

> The famous *Plow That Broke the Plains* is headed for the junk heap.
> It was put on the skids when the House Appropriations Committee scuttled the $106,000 budget of the United States Film Service on a parliamentary technicality. The only hope for the agency is the Senate, which can restore the fund.

[16] *Ibid.*, 301.

[17] U.S. House of Representatives, Appropriations Subcommittee, *Department of Labor–Federal Security Agency Appropriations Bill, 1941*, 76 Cong., 3 sess., 1940, 48, *Report 1822*.

[18] *Washington Star*, March 24, 1940.

The United States Film Service is one of the least expensive and most widely acclaimed activities of the government.[19]

Editorials in the *Dayton News* and the *Louisville Courier-Journal* are further examples of the kind of support the Film Service was receiving in the press. The editorial in the *Dayton News* was written to accompany Pearson's column just quoted. Both editorials praised the past record of the Film Service and urged the Senate to restore the appropriation. Their final comments bear repeating:

> Even with that doubtful assurance abandonment of the Federal Film Service would be tragic. Here is an instance in which the Senate may restore a House cut and not be criticized for selfish extravagance, instead praised for assuring continuance of a highly deserving public service. It should without question provide the $106,000 drop in the bucket which the Film Service needs—and if it is to go, must have.[20]

> The United States Film Service can yet be salvaged by the Senate. Those who believe that democracy, to be successful, requires a clearer understanding of fundamental problems of the Nation by the great masses of citizens, should demand that the Senate save this service.[21]

Not all the press comment was so favorable. A writer for the *Lafayette* (Indiana) *Journal and Courier* accepted Engel's estimate of the cost of *The Fight for Life* as $178,000, although Mercey had testified that it was $150,000.[22]

Studebaker, Lorentz, and Mercey appeared before the Senate Appropriations Subcommittee on April 17, 1940. Senator James Byrnes, who had offered the Film Service some hope the previous year, was not there. Senator Kenneth McKellar was probably not favorably disposed to the Film Service because of his opposition to the TVA, which Lorentz had praised and endorsed in *The River*.

[19] Drew Pearson, "Washington Merry-Go-Round," *Worcester Gazette and Post*, April 13, 1940. From the personal files of Pare Lorentz.

[20] "Keep the Film Service," *Dayton News*, April 3, 1940. From the personal files of Pare Lorentz.

[21] "We Need the United States Film Service," *Louisville Courier-Journal*, April 2, 1940. From the personal files of Pare Lorentz.

[22] "Fakery Exposed," *Lafayette* (Indiana) *Journal and Courier*, April 2, 1940. From the personal files of Pare Lorentz.

Studebaker submitted to the Senate subcommittee the same budget he had submitted to the House: $71,880 for salaries and $34,520 for general expenses, a total of $106,400.[23] At the very beginning of the hearings, Studebaker pointed out to Senator McKellar and Senator Richard B. Russell that there was some question about the legality of the Film Service. Studebaker reminded McKellar that the senator thought the basic law establishing the Office of Education was adequate to permit the office to carry on library work, and that Studebaker thought it was also adequate to cover the Radio Service and the Film services.[24]

McKellar quickly made clear his basic stand on the Film and Radio Services. First of all, he was doubtful about the wisdom of using radio and films for education. Second, there was no provision in the Constitution for educational activities by the federal government. Educational activities could be carried on only by setting up an "organization to help the states. . . . That is the underlying basis of the Department of Education or the Bureau of Education."[25] McKellar doubted that radio and film activities could legally be set up; and, if they were, how would they help the states?

Studebaker placed in the record a statement of services rendered the states by the two agencies. Emphasis was given to the activities that offered the states co-operation and services through radio and films. The statement included several references to requests from the states for various kinds of service. Studebaker said that many activities of the Film Service other than production provided visual aids, research programs, consultation and co-operation with state and federal agencies, a clearinghouse and relay service for federal films, and distribution.[26]

Studebaker's statement on production activities also reflected the change in policy. He said that films would be produced on a

23 U.S. Senate, Appropriations Committee, *Hearings on Department of Labor–Federal Security Agency Appropriations Bill, 1941*, 76 Cong., 3 sess., 1940, 229.

24 *Ibid.* Studebaker was relying on Harper's opinion based on the law of 1867, an interpretation that the House had already ruled was inadequate.

25 *Ibid.*, 230.

26 *Ibid.*, 230–36.

reimbursable basis, as had been done in *Power and the Land*—the only film Studebaker referred to in his statement.[27]

McKellar, ignoring Studebaker's defense, charged that Studebaker and Mercey had said little or nothing in previous reports about helping the states. McKellar then read a section of the *Report of the President of the United States to the Congress Showing the Status of Funds and Operations under the Emergency Relief Appropriations Acts of 1935, 1936, 1937, 1938, and 1939, as of December 31, 1939, Dated January 15, 1940.* In this section, nothing pertaining to the purposes of the Film Service referred to the states; in the list of accomplishments of the Film Service, only brief reference was made to the states. Studebaker had never seen the report, and was unable to answer the charge immediately.

Then Studebaker attempted to show the relationship between radio, films, and education by pointing out that the Office of Education helped the states by improving means of communication:

> For example, we think it would not be disputed that we should be of assistance to the States in improving ways of using printed matter for educational purposes.
> How are we going to deal with the improvement of education, unless we can deal with its techniques? The techniques are communication; in person by voice, teacher and pupil relationships, as we say. Later, we got the printed matter into education. Then, we illustrated the printed matter. Later, the pictures were made to move, and now—[28]

McKellar interrupted at this point to stress the importance of cooperating with the states, but said that the country was opposed to activities by the federal government in the field of education.

Following this exchange, Studebaker and W. D. Boutwell, head of the Radio Service, explained the past program of the Radio Service to Senators McKellar and Russell. Studebaker then introduced Pare Lorentz, who told the committee about his brief history with government motion pictures. He told them he had come to Washington at the invitation of a cabinet official to sug-

27 *Ibid.*, 236.
28 *Ibid.*, 237–38.

gest ways and means to improve government films. The feeling at the time, he thought, was that the government might be making too many movies. Following questions about government motion picture activities in the past, McKellar read aloud a list of the activities and objectives of the Film Service. *The River* was mentioned twice in the list of objectives and three times in the list of activities. McKellar asked if theaters charged for these films and how the films were distributed. When Lorentz started to answer, McKellar cut him off curtly and went back to reading the report.[29] When McKellar finished reading the report, Lorentz again attempted to answer the senator's question about distribution, but the senator cut him off again and asked whether appropriations had ever been made for films. Arch Mercey quoted from an appropriations act of February 25, 1913, for the Bureau of Mines, and from the act appropriating funds for the Housing Authority. Neither act specifically used the word "films," but each had been interpreted to include them. Studebaker quoted from the 1927 Appropriations Act for the Office of Education, which did refer specifically to motion pictures. Each appropriations act for the office since 1927 had used the same terminology, "for purchase, distribution, and exchange of educational documents, motion picture films."[30] Appropriations *had* been made for motion pictures within the Office of Education since 1927—these were *not* new expenditures.

McKellar then asked about the amount of money and personnel involved in government motion picture work. Mercey and Studebaker had been unable to secure the information from the various agencies, and so they could not answer the question. McKellar countered by criticizing them for making films with money appropriated for other purposes. Lorentz tried to mollify McKellar by referring to the changing philosophy of the Film Service. He pointed out that they were not asking for funds to produce pictures in the new budget: "Actually I, myself, would like to see less movies made in the government. We felt it was the intent of the

29 *Ibid.*, 245.
30 *Ibid.*, 247.

President when he set us up under Executive Order in 1938, that we should examine film-making and see whether it was not overlapping."[31] He said he came to Washington, examined the program, and recommended that the government make one picture but make it meritorious enough to get it into commercial theaters. He presented capsule histories of *The Plow* and *The River*. McKellar interrupted to ask what happened to the money earned by those two films. Lorentz told him that they had been made available without charge. McKellar wanted to know the cost of the films and the source of the money, since there was no appropriation for them.[32] Lorentz said that Comptroller General McCarl had given the required interpretation and provided the legal basis for the work in producing films. Lorentz again stressed the "new look" of the Film Service and its value in consolidating motion picture activities across agencies and departments to give the government as large a return as possible on its investment in motion pictures. To McKellar's query about the source of funds for operation the previous year, Mercey replied that almost all the funds had come from relief agencies. McKellar then sprang the same trap that Representative Engel had used several weeks before.

> SEN. McKELLAR: Just let me read you something. You gentlemen are law-abiding citizens, are you not?
> You look so. You have got fine faces, and you look like you are.
> The act approved June 30, 1939 provides this—this is the W. P. A.:
> "Sec. 10(b) the funds made available by this joint resolution shall be used only for relief or work for persons in need except as otherwise provided herein."
> No provision is made for making moving pictures, or spending this money for moving pictures, and whoever give you that relief money for that purpose undoubtedly violated the law, and you gentlemen in accepting it have undoubtedly violated this law.[33]

No serious attempt was made to justify the violation of the law, as Mercey had tried to do before the House subcommittee, by re-

[31] *Ibid.*, 248.
[32] *Ibid.*, 249.
[33] *Ibid.*, 251.

ferring to the President. Lorentz tried to explain, but McKellar was adamant. "No funds are provided for films or radio," he said.

Following Mercey's accounting of the money received from the REA and the AAA, Lorentz tried to explain the complexity of the motion picture business. Perhaps because he was upset by the charge of violating the law, or because he had been constantly interrupted by McKellar, Lorentz got off to a poor and confused start. In his attempt to draw on his background as motion picture critic and to acquaint McKellar with the workings of the motion picture industry, his choice of words was faulty. McKellar interrupted him twice to challenge his ability or right to "represent the motion picture industry."[34] Lorentz seemed to pull himself together briefly after the second challenge, and made a clear, simple statement about the value of fewer and better films and the idea behind films of merit.

Studebaker attempted to present the case for making films and radio programs. Senator McKellar replied that he would need time to study the matter but that he probably would not approve such activities, which he considered outside the scope of duties of the Office of Education. In his opinion, he thought it was "utterly futile" from a practical point of view. Studebaker replied, "Whether it is futile or not is another question."[35]

In answer to McKellar's basic objection, Studebaker presented evidence to show that the Radio Service was helping the states improve educational radio service to the public, but McKellar rejected his claims. Studebaker tried to present further evidence along this line, but McKellar cut him down with the pronouncement, "If you established a radio or film office here in the department, I think it would be unwise and would not be justified by the law, in my judgment."[36]

It was impossible to counter such an attitude. Every argument the witnesses advanced was rejected.

Arch Mercey made one final point for the Film Service before

34 *Ibid.*, 252.
35 *Ibid.*, 253.
36 *Ibid.*, 254.

157

adjournment. He got McKellar to admit that the committee was concerned with trying to save the taxpayers' money. Mercey attempted to show how the budget for the Film Service would do that: the service would see to it that the films would be of high quality and that fewer films would be made.

Lorentz's final statement before the subcommittee underscored his attitude toward the Film Service and what he thought was the true nature of its accomplishments:

> If the United States Film Service disappears from the government, in the Office of Education, I would not feel that any calamity, any great catastrophe, would happen in the country. I feel this—that we have pioneered, we have learned how to do this work within the government. We have a group of trained men who have been trained over a great number of years in the development of these films. It is not easy to step out and find men who are trained in the recording of facts. There is a great deal of difference between recording facts and recording fiction and drama. We feel that if we disappear from the government, it will return to the lackadaisical method of film-making that existed when we started in 1935.[37]

In his final remarks, McKellar was highly critical of the use of funds for motion picture production which had been appropriated for other purposes. He referred to a motion picture industry built up with the use of relief funds, and said that films should be made only by direct appropriation.[38]

Studebaker did not help the chances of the Film Service when he told McKellar at the end of the hearing that the House had decided that the Office of Education had no right to undertake a motion picture program. He reminded McKellar that it was the opinion of the general counsel of the Federal Security Agency that McKellar's statement approving a library program in the Office of Education also gave the office authority for a film program. But Studebaker qualified the statement and limited whatever effectiveness it might have had when he said, "I am not sure that your expression applies to this."[39] He did not mention the legal ap-

[37] *Ibid.*, 261.
[38] *Ibid.*, 262–63.
[39] *Ibid.*, 263.

proval Lorentz had secured from the General Accounting Office in 1939.[40]

When the appropriations bill for the Department of Labor and the Federal Security Agency came out of the Senate committee, it contained no mention of the Film Service, thus concurring with the decision of the House.[41] In addition, the House Subcommittee on Appropriations approved a restriction on the Film Service and the Radio Service to prevent the transfer of relief funds to these two services.

> The joint resolution [Sec. 12c] as does the present law, prohibits allocations of funds to agencies unless specifically authorized. The committee recommends a specific prohibition on allocation of funds to the Radio Division or the United States Film Service or for carrying out the functions of such agencies transferred to the Office of Education. While such prohibition may be unnecessary because the general language prohibits such an allocation, since the provision in existing law was ignored in such a case specific prohibition is written in.[42]

The House and Senate bills went into conference committee several times, but the specific prohibition in Section 12c remained when they were finally approved. The Federal Security Agency appropriation contained an old provision of twenty-six thousand dollars as part of its budget for general office and travel expenses, which provided for "purchase, distribution, and exchange of educational documents, motion picture films, and lantern slides."[43] The Film Service was given nothing on which to operate.

[40] At the close of the hearing, Studebaker filed several exhibits for the record on behalf of the Film Service. These included comments on *The Fight for Life* in the form of newspaper, magazine, and trade-press articles, as well as the special tributes by Kettering and Dr. Defoe, comments by educators in the form of articles about *The River*, the letter from President Roosevelt to Studebaker transferring the Film Service to the Office of Education, excerpts from T. R. Adam's book *Motion Pictures in Adult Education*, and two editorials in defense of the Film Service.

[41] U.S. Senate, Appropriations Committee, *Hearings on Department of Labor–Federal Security Agency Appropriations Bill, 1941,* 76 Cong., 3 sess., 1940, 18, *Report 1487.*

[42] U.S. House of Representatives, Appropriations Subcommittee, *Department of Labor–Federal Security Agency Appropriations Bill, 1941,* 76 Cong., 3 sess., 1940, 21, *House Report 2186.* The resolution referred to in the report is *Public Resolution 88,* 76 Cong., 3 sess., 1940.

[43] U.S. Congress, *Public Law 665,* 76 Cong., 3 sess., June 26, 1940.

The day after Lorentz, Mercey, and Studebaker appeared before Senator McKellar, the support of the President was finally obtained. The President had received a letter, dated April 10, 1940, from Sumner Welles in which he expressed concern over the failure of the House Appropriations Subcommittee to provide funds for the continuance of the Film Service. Welles hoped that in another year it would be possible to put into effect the projects recommended to the Interdepartmental Committee on Cooperation with Other American Republics. On April 18, President Roosevelt wrote to Senator Carter Glass, chairman of the Senate Appropriations Committee, and enclosed the letter from Welles. The President encouraged Senator Glass to reconsider the budget for the Film Service because

> The continuance of such services in the Office of Education is of particular importance, in order to provide for the proper coordination of these activities [distribution, consultation, etc.]. The continuance of the Film Service is of importance to the State Department at this time as indicated in the attached letter of the Undersecretary, dated April 10, 1940.
>
> I, therefore, urgently request that those items which were eliminated by the House be restored.[44]

Fortunately, there were still some who thought the Film Service and its projects had merit and deserved a place within the government. On April 26, Senator Elmer Thomas presented an amendment to the Department of Labor–Federal Security Agency Appropriations Bill adding $106,400 for the operations of the Film Service.

Senator Thomas presented the original budget for the Film Service, as submitted to the House and Senate subcommittees, and gave a brief history of the Film Service and its request for funds. He used the same interpretation of the general clause in the 1867 law creating the Office of Education that had been used in the hearings.

Thomas turned the floor over to McKellar so that he could ex-

[44] Letter from President Franklin D. Roosevelt to Senator Carter Glass, April 18, 1940.

plain why the Film Service was singled out for elimination and not the other units, which continued to produce films. McKellar centered his attack on his amazement that a motion picture industry, built up secretly through the misuse of funds, existed in the federal government. He continued by quoting from the hearings the exchange between himself and Arch Mercey that showed that the REA and the AAA had transferred funds to the Film Service. In his opinion, it was "monstrous" to do so because of the prohibition of the WPA law against using the appropriated money for anything other than work relief.[45] However, REA and AAA money was *not* WPA money.

Senator Arthur Vandenberg asked Thomas if he could state the appropriations being spent by the other agencies and departments. Thomas apologized for not being able to provide the information, explaining that the practice was widespread and often concealed.[46] McKellar stated that the committee had adopted a resolution asking each department to list all funds being spent on films. This prompted Senator William H. King to offer to present an amendment "that none of the appropriations herein contained shall be used for the manufacture or distribution or utilization of films."[47] The amendment was withdrawn because many of the appropriations were in other bills already approved.

The argument presented by McKellar was opposed by Thomas, who set out to prove that government motion picture activities were old, common, and acceptable. After saying that the government had been making films for at least twenty-five years, Thomas pointed out that the manner in which funds appropriated for information were spent was left to the discretion of the departments. He presented a list of some of the films produced by the Department of the Interior, separately from the Film Service, to show that film making was a common activity. This list indicated also that many of the films had scientific utility and were useful to the

45 U.S. *Congressional Record*, 76 Cong., 3 sess., April 26, 1940, LXXXVI, Pt. 5, 5088.
    46 This information was closely guarded by the agencies themselves, and they had not divulged it to Studebaker and Mercey during the hearings.
    47 U.S. *Congressional Record*, 76 Cong., 3 sess., LXXXVI, Pt. 5, 5089.

states.[48] Thomas listed also the agencies that had film units and mentioned films made by many other agencies. Thus he showed that film making was extensive and common, and had been going on for some time. Thomas contended also that a central agency could be of help in distributing the films made by other agencies with their own appropriations.

In a quick exchange with Thomas, Senator Robert Taft tended to minimize the value of this activity, pointing out that each agency had distributed its own films before 1938.[49] Thomas described the distribution activities of the Film Service, and went on to read reviews of *The Fight for Life* and an article referring to such other Film Service projects as *Power and the Land* and *Ecce Homo!* He returned to the point that reflected the changed philosophy of the Film Service—the emphasis on its distribution activities.[50]

At this point in the debate, Senator Taft began a lengthy and incisive attack on the Film Service in particular and motion picture activities by the federal government in general.[51] The length and depth of his statement seemed to indicate that it might have been prepared as an argument against Senator Thomas' amendment. Taft's statement was widely reported. Because it tended to represent conservative opposition, it should be summarized.

There were, apparently, only a limited number of government films that Taft found acceptable. These had to be strictly informative scientific and health films, specialized and not dramatized. As far as he was concerned, films for general education were beyond the responsibility of the federal government. He was particularly opposed to the documentary film. In connection with his attack on documentary films, he raised the specter of Russian Communists and their films. *The Fight for Life*, to which he referred, did not mention or endorse *any* program for the correction of the two social evils it presented, although Taft implied that it did. Taft used two other arguments against government documentary films. He saw no need for telling the people about such

[48] *Ibid.*
[49] *Ibid.*, 5092.
[50] *Ibid.*
[51] *Ibid.*, 5095.

activities as the national parks—whether they knew or *did not* know anything about them, and he did not want such films stirring up the public to lobby with their representatives about the problems presented in the films. Both arguments seem shortsighted. First, no one could possibly be hurt or offended if the public became interested in national parks through films. Second, the films of merit were actually intended originally to tell the public what the problems facing the government were and how the government intended to solve them.

No one challenged any of the arguments offered by Taft. In fact, the next to gain the floor was Senator McKellar, who supported Taft by attacking the purposes of the Film Service one by one, as presented at the hearings, and commenting on them in a sarcastic manner. For example:

> "3. To continue distribution of the documentary films, *The Plow That Broke the Plains* and *The River.*"
> These two films have been seen by the entire country, and I doubt whether there is any reason for continuing their distribution.
> "5. To provide a central information office on all government film activities."
> This is the first time films were ever known to be made of government activities. No money was appropriated for that purpose. Such moneys as have been used for it were secretly used under appropriations made for other purposes. The money appropriated for these purposes was transferred to the film industry.[52]

These arguments are also shortsighted. As long as Americans continued to misuse the Great Plains and as long as floods continued unabated, there was need for both films. Congressmen knew that films of merit had been produced with federal funds. Money had been appropriated to agencies for information purposes in the past, and motion pictures were a means of communicating information, as Senator Thomas had pointed out.

Senator Sherman Minton gained the floor next and wondered whether perhaps Taft was worried about government propaganda movies because they would be competition for the Republican

52 *Ibid.*, 5096.

163

movies that had been recently publicized. He got no answer from Taft.

McKellar, after a brief statement of hope that the debate would remain on a nonpartisan level, said that only one department—the Department of Agriculture—had ever openly asked for an appropriation for films. He stated that he was opposed to Thomas' amendment because "it has now for the first time come out in the open; and it comes out for the purpose of consolidating all the other agencies that have grown up secretly, without specific appropriations."[53] McKellar said that if the government passed a law that it could make movies and carry on a motion picture service, then he thought the Appropriations Committee would approve the funds requested.

At this point, the debate took a strange detour. Senator Henry Ashurst took the floor to say that he had been greatly upset by a letter from Secretary of the Interior Ickes that stated that anyone, other than amateurs and newsreel photographers, who wanted to make motion pictures of any area under the jurisdiction of the Department of the Interior would, with certain exceptions, have to get authority in writing and pay a fee. Ashurst felt that Secretary Ickes had usurped power in charging fees for filming on public lands. He went on at some length, taking time out to discuss the secretary's character with humorous effect. He introduced an amendment to ban such fee charging by the Department of Interior but withdrew it since it was out of order.[54]

At the close of the debate, Senate Majority Leader Alben Barkley lent his support to the Film Service:

> However, it has always been my understanding that these films have been used to advise the people of the activities of agencies of the government. . . . I have always derived considerable information and inspiration from such pictures. As a rule, I think no American citizen can observe one of these pictures without feeling somewhat proud of the activities of the government. It may be more enlightening and more entertaining than merely reading about it in a book, pamphlet, or newspaper.

[53] *Ibid.*
[54] *Ibid.*, 5097.

I think there is much to be said for the suggestion that the Congress ought to know more about what is being done with the money it appropriates. It may be our fault, and probably is our fault, that that matter had not been inquired into heretofore; but it is a little difficult for me to make up my mind to hit at this one agency, which, so far, is the only one that has come out into the open by asking for an appropriation. The appropriation is recommended by the Budget Bureau, and is requested by the President, who has approved the Budget and sent it to Congress. If we could overhaul all the film agencies at one time in one bill so as to know what is going on, it might be a good thing to do; but I hesitate to do it with respect to this particular agency, especially when it is designed to coordinate all the activities of all the film-producing agencies of the government.

For that reason I feel very much inclined to support the Senator's amendment.[55]

Following Senator Barkley's final statement, which emphasized that the money to be appropriated was to be spent on distribution, Senator Thomas read the letter President Roosevelt had written Senator Glass on April 18. The vote was called for, the amendment was defeated, twenty-four in favor, thirty-six opposed, and twenty-four not voting. Of those voting for it, all were Democrats except Senator Alexander Wiley.

Response to the failure to provide funds to carry the Film Service beyond June 30, 1940, followed quickly. Bosley Crowther wrote in the *New York Times*:

This column cannot permit the week to pass without taking note of the regrettable fact that the United States Senate has permitted the United States Film Service to expire, as of June 30, by failing to place in the Federal Security supply bill an appropriation for its continuance.

We wouldn't know a thing about the political aspects of the case nor would we rashly conclude that this means the end of Mr. Lorentz's productivity. But it does seem a pitiful shame that the government, so long as it intends to make pictures, refuses to hire a man with such proven capabilities as Mr. Lorentz for the job.[56]

President Roosevelt did not remain silent. He was interviewed

[55] *Ibid.*, 5100.
[56] May 5, 1940.

165

while returning to Washington from Hyde Park. The *New York Times* reported his reaction:

> By inference the President denounced failure of the Senate and House Appropriation Committees to provide an appropriation of $106,000 for the United States Film Service. When told that the agency faced extinction unless the money was forthcoming, Mr. Roosevelt said that although Congress had a right to refuse to appropriate for the purpose, it was deplorable to witness abolition of the agency which produced such films as *The Plow That Broke the Plains*, *The River* and *The Fight for Life*.
>
> To devote public funds to financing the operation of the film agency was about as useful an application of money that could be imagined, the President said.[57]

The *New York Herald Tribune*, in covering the same interview, added a few more comments. The President was reported to have said that the Film Service "had been a great success with the public, was of great educational value and had the approval of private film producers."[58] The President also indicated that it might be possible to continue the Film Service with a subsidy from some governmental department.

Time presented a brief factual account of the findings of the House committee and complimented Senator Elmer Thomas for his effort to save the service. *Time*'s final remark was appropriate though brief: "It looked like a fade-out for the United States Film Service."[59]

Under the headline "Government Films under Fire," the *Los Angeles Examiner* reported on the first annual convention of the Pacific Coast Conference of Independent Theatre Owners. The principal speaker, William G. Ripley, an exhibitor and trustee of the organization, urged motion picture exhibitors, distributors, and producers to organize for the following purpose: "To combat the unjustified and unneeded entrance of government into our business.... Contaminating our business—or any business—with

[57] May 7, 1940.

[58] *New York Herald Tribune*, May 7, 1940. From the personal files of Pare Lorentz.

[59] May 6, 1940, 15.

166

politics is destructive of the sound and fundamental principles of free government."[60] Clearly, elements in the commercial film industry were still opposed to Lorentz's films.

Late in May, 1940, Lorentz gave William O. Player, Jr., his own summary of what had happened to the Film Service:

> It boils down to this. We spent five years trying to show that we were on the level—fighting for, and finally winning, the right to produce and show our pictures on a sole basis of merit.
>
> But we didn't take time out to build any political fences. Merit was the only selling point we had—and they've never learned to understand that down in Washington. We finally sold our point to Hollywood and to the theatre owners, but in the meantime . . . .[61]

Could a way have been found to keep the Film Service going, as President Roosevelt intimated? Pare Lorentz thinks so, if it had not been for events in Europe and the changing attitude here in the United States. About finishing *The Land*, he wrote:

> However, the important thing is not what happened to the movie, but what happened to the world. Given a peaceful world, we all could have managed working together on that production, but given the fact that France fell in June 1940, all peaceful activities were winding up in the United States, good, bad or indifferent.[62]

Because of the changing world, the government was soon to need films to explain the defense-mobilization program to the people. The government ignored the accomplishments of Pare Lorentz, the lessons learned by his crews about producing factual films, and the talents of expert and recognized documentary film makers. Instead:

> . . . the government turned to commercial producers for documentary films on such subjects as lend-lease, increased defense production, and the necessity for closer cooperation with Latin-American countries. Some of these films were produced in Hollywood, others by

[60] May 10, 1940. From the personal files of Pare Lorentz. The rest of the speech contains several factual errors about *The Fight for Life*.

[61] Player, "Cut," *New York Post*, May 23, 1940. From the personal files of Pare Lorentz.

[62] Letter from Pare Lorentz, April 5, 1962.

167

studio people who offered their services to the emergency organizations set up in Washington.[63]

Like the films of merit, these were seen in commercial theaters, but, unlike them, they were controlled from start to finish by Hollywood, and Hollywood reaped whatever profits they made.

The experiment of producing films of merit by and for the federal government ended, in one sense, on June 30, 1940, when all available funds had been expended. In another sense, it did not end until *Power and the Land* had its premiere on August 31, 1940. In a third sense, it may be said that the experiment never really ended, because some of the films—notably *Power and the Land, The River,* and *The Plow That Broke the Plains*—are still available for distribution and purchase from the Department of Agriculture.

Several points should be emphasized from the two sets of congressional hearings that concerned themselves with appropriations for the Film Service.

Congressmen questioned the legality of a motion picture production service in the government, particularly since it was housed within an agency established in 1867—the Office of Education—and was basing its legality on rather general phraseology from the enabling act.

In addition, members of the Appropriations Committee were upset by the use of relief funds for the production of films. What was especially disturbing to them was that the Relief Acts of 1939 specifically contained language barring transfer of funds to the Film Service. Mercey and Lorentz had, however, received the approval of the General Accounting Office in 1939.

The Film Service did not furnish the committee with convincing evidence that it would bring about any savings in government motion picture activities. Its production plans in 1939 were extensive. Unfortunately, most congressmen thought that making films required an exorbitant amount of money. In 1940, Film Service representatives were unable to report specifically what the

[63] Arthur Knight, *The Liveliest Art: A Panoramic History of the Movies,* 252.

financial effect of their consolidation program would be. Other film units refused to co-operate.

Certain congressmen objected to *The Fight for Life* as having no value for the government. Because this film was the only one in commercial circulation at the time of the hearings in 1940, it was the one most closely associated with the Film Service. If *Power and the Land* could have been released in the spring of 1940, some congressmen might have seen more value in movie making.

In 1940, the Film Service had the misfortune of pleading its case before Senator McKellar. McKellar was opposed to the TVA, one of President Roosevelt's favorite programs. *The River*, distributed by the Film Service, was about the TVA; the Film Service was another of the President's favorite activities. Here was a chance for McKellar to strike at both. The President had run into trouble with Congress at this time for a variety of reasons, and it was easy for congressmen to strike back at the executive branch by denying funds to one of the President's projects.

The Film Service, unfortunately, had its ancestry in an unpopular New Deal agency, the Resettlement Administration. Neither the agency nor its administrator, Rexford G. Tugwell, had been popular with Congress, and its information activities had come in for considerable attack.[64] From there the film unit (not yet called the Film Service) was moved to the Farm Security Administration, where it was sustained by relief funds. When the Film Service itself was created officially, it was housed in the National Emergency Council and then transferred to the Federal Security Agency as part of the Office of Education. All of these, except the Office of Education, were New Deal creations. The distrust of, or distaste for, these New Deal structures could be indirectly passed on to the Film Service, and probably was—as may have been true of Senator McKellar's attitude toward the TVA and, indirectly, the Film Service.

Strangely enough, there seems to have been little value in the honest approach of the Film Service to Congress for funds. Several

[64] MacCann, *op. cit.*, 163–73.

other agencies had their own production units, to which the congressmen also objected, but their funds were concealed in information budgets and were not cut back. The Film Service was eliminated. Perhaps if the Film Service had stayed hidden and not sought a separate budget, Lorentz could have produced further films for the government.

It should also be remembered that rising international tension in Europe and the Far East was drawing attention away from domestic problems and toward foreign affairs. Lorentz thought that the German invasion of Poland, followed by the entry of England and France into the war against Germany, marked the end of the Film Service.[65] Even the President seemed to be caught up in the change. Perhaps this is why there is little evidence of efforts on his part to intervene in behalf of the Film Service.

It can be gathered from the hearings that several congressmen believed that the government should not be making pictures. This conviction, added to the unfavorable attitude of Congress toward information activities by the executive branch—which exists to this day—did not help the cause of the Film Service.

Lorentz made little effort to endear himself to congressmen. He set out to prove the value of his belief in communicating information to the public by making the best films possible within the funds available. If he had been more of a producer or executive director and less of a film maker, things might have been different. Unfortunately, he was wrong in believing that he could make his point to a hostile or, at best, unconcerned Congress.

In Lorentz's drive to prove his point by making outstanding motion pictures and to prove the value of the Film Service by setting up a distribution center, there had not been time to make enough friends in Congress who had the right kind of influence. Most of the time, Lorentz was away from Washington on location or on the road trying to get distribution. He assumed that the support of the President would be enough. All these liabilities were much more than the merit of the films could overcome.

The preceding points are generally based on the reaction of

[65] Interview with Pare Lorentz, April 25, 1961.

congressmen as reported in the hearings.[66] Two other factors should be considered, although for various reasons their direct influence on the Film Service cannot be established as clearly as the preceding points.

It is unfortunate that friend and foe alike referred to these films as propaganda films. The popular attitude toward propaganda in the United States at the time was unfavorable. Propaganda seemed to be something the enemy used and was a term democracies usually avoided.[67]

Ralph D. Casey has written of the public's highly unfavorable attitude toward propaganda at the time of the hearings.[68] It could be inferred, by those suspicious of the New Deal or of propaganda, that the government was engaging in an un-American activity by making such films.

Interested persons in the executive branch reacted to the charge of propaganda in Lorentz's films. Margaret Farrand Thorp wrote that the government at that time thought that it was one of the important duties of the representatives of any democratic people to give accounting of their stewardship; that the American people had always expected and desired this; that, for years, federal agencies had issued reports, furnished information, and sent speakers around the country. Washington officials also countered with the fact that the films were inexpensive. According to Mrs. Thorp, the government assessed public suspicion of government motion pictures as follows: " 'People are suspicious of the government's use of the motion picture,' says the government, 'only because it is more effective than other media, easier to pay attention to, harder to disregard.' "[69]

The government of the United States is still opposed to engaging in certain propaganda activities. For example, William Albig noted that "Voice of America" programs that contained anything

66 For Roosevelt's own conflict with Congress at this time, see Rexford G. Tugwell, *The Democratic Roosevelt*, 404–406, 410–12, 460 ff.

67 William Albig, *Modern Public Opinion*, 29.

68 "The Press, Propaganda and Pressure Groups," in Wilbur Schramm (ed.), *Mass Communication* (Urbana, University of Illinois Press, 1960), 227.

69 *America at the Movies*, 165.

but straight newscasts invariably involved that agency in contro-versy with Congress and other administrative agencies.[70] The United States Information Agency makes motion pictures, but none can be shown in the United States.[71]

An additional factor that probably operated against the Film Service is that not all the opposition to the service and Lorentz's efforts was to be found in Washington. The commercial motion picture industry centered in Hollywood seems to have been hostile toward the program from the start.

This opposition first became apparent when Lorentz went to Hollywood to purchase stock footage for *The Plow* and found that he was locked out of the studios. The opposition could again be noted when Lorentz was unsuccessful in securing bookings through any distributor or exhibitor in spite of the good reviews resulting from the premiere.[72]

Hollywood would have been happier if production was com-pletely stopped in Washington, because then questions of exhi-bition and distribution blockades could not be raised again. Lorentz's continued presence in Washington was likely to be obnoxious to Hollywood for several reasons. First, when the Film Service was established, its executive director, Pare Lorentz, was given the option of approving all use of government property and personnel in commercial films. By 1938, Hollywood was inter-ested in making greater use of such property and personnel, as will be shown, and Lorentz stood in the way. If he held any animosity toward the commercial industry because of their efforts to thwart him, he could withhold approval of their requests.

Second, Hollywood resented any competition in making and exhibiting motion pictures. King Vidor, one of the directors who helped Lorentz get the needed stock footage, recently wrote that he could offer no accurate information on whether it might have been the motion picture industry that was responsible for the closing of the Film Service. He added:

[70] *Op. cit.*, 314.

[71] Letter from Anthony Guarco, deputy director, Motion Picture Service, United States Information Agency, February 14, 1964.

[72] See Chapter II, pp. 42–48.

I would believe, however, that it could be apropos of the mood and attitude of those times and therefore would be inclined to accept the information as true. There was a great reaction or resistance to an activity of production in other localities and this would apply, I would suppose, more strongly with the government than any other place. I mean to infer that the autocratic tendencies and domination and power of the movie-moguls of that period would be against any governmental activity as a form of competition.[73]

Floyd Crosby, Lorentz's cameraman and still active in Hollywood, voiced a similar opinion: "The Film Service was closed down largely because Hollywood was becoming worried about the fact that the government was making good pictures, and brought a good deal of pressure to bear."[74]

Paul Rotha and Richard Griffith[75] have written that the commercial motion picture industry resented competition from outside its own circle. According to them, exhibitors and renters have opposed the showing of anything except entertainment films on commercial screens, because anything else might keep the audience away. For this reason, commercial exhibitors and renters have resisted the development of the nontheatrical field. Rotha and Griffith wrote that the powers in Hollywood have suppressed creative efforts because of their desire to keep studio and screen space filled or face the prospect of losing money. It has been extremely difficult for independent film makers to exist in that atmosphere. Those who have succeeded were the exception and not the rule.[76]

Finally, Pare Lorentz and Sumner Welles began actively working for an exchange program with the Latin American republics at a time when Hollywood was becoming interested in Latin America as a market. Foreign markets have been an important source of income for Hollywood. "Since 1920, the industry has received from 25% to over 40% of its gross income from abroad."[77] Any threat to this income, such as the plans proposed

---

[73] Letter from King Vidor, March 22, 1962.
[74] Taped interview with Floyd Crosby, February, 1962.
[75] *The Film till Now*, 22.
[76] *Ibid.*, 33–34.
[77] Albig, *op. cit.*, 412.

by Lorentz and Sumner Welles to exchange films with Latin America, would certainly be cause for rapid action. It will be recalled that as soon as possible the industry had representatives on the committee considering the program, and George Gercke expressed concern over their presence.[78]

Ever since the formation of the Motion Picture Producers and Distributors of America and the arrival in Hollywood of Will Hays to head that group, the industry had developed a policy toward the federal government. Part of this policy was to do whatever was necessary to keep motion pictures free from government interference or regulation.[79] Later the Hays Office developed an "enlightened concern with the foreign relations of an industry which serves all the nations of the world."[80] This part of their policy toward the federal government was threatened by Lorentz's plans.

Lorentz's and Welles's proposal offered a serious threat to plans by the industry to expand distribution in Latin America. No wonder Margaret Thorp wrote that the motion picture industry was "delighted" to assist in the program. Even though the industry had a policy against "selfish propaganda" in films, they saw nothing wrong with producing films "spreading information about the American way of life,"[81] especially if they were paid to make the films and could distribute their regular offerings as well, it might be added.

Hays and his representatives were successful with both parts of their policy. In 1945, Raymond Moley wrote, "The overall good will that exists in legislative halls toward the motion picture industry confirms the wisdom of Hays's early plans."[82] For example, in 1938, there was concrete evidence of government co-operation with the industry when the State Department worked closely with the industry through the Hays Office in negotiating contracts for sending American films to foreign countries. This

[78] See Chapter VI, p. 142.
[79] Raymond Moley, *The Hays Office*, 44.
[80] *Ibid.*
[81] Thorp, *op. cit.*, 164.
[82] *Op. cit.*, 49.

co-operation was particularly important in negotiating the Cinematograph Films Act with Great Britain in that year.[83] In 1945, the International Department of the Motion Picture Producers and Distributors of America was still working closely with the State Department.

Late in Roosevelt's second term in office, Hollywood started making films on subjects of interest to the government.[84] With the exception of the Warner Brothers exposés, films on crime, and a few isolated films like King Vidor's *Our Daily Bread,* Hollywood had avoided films of social or political content. When Roosevelt announced his policy of naval expansion on January 28, 1939, and met unexpected opposition in Congress and elsewhere, Hollywood went to work. Previously, motion picture companies had co-operated in the production of newsreels about the sinking of the *Panay* by the Japanese.[85] Charles A. and Mary R. Beard quote *Variety* and the *International News Service* as saying that the Administration was extremely pleased by this co-operation.[86]

The Film Service had originally come into being partly because Hollywood had not been interested in subjects that were of concern to the Administration. The combined evidence of a son of the President working in Hollywood and of the industry's new-found desire to produce films of interest to the Administration indicates that the Film Service was becoming less necessary.

A noticeable change took place in Hollywood's official attitude toward propaganda at this time. In his report to the industry on March 28, 1938, Will Hays praised the producers for turning out films devoted to entertainment and avoiding "the lure of propaganda."[87] A year later, his report to the industry on March 27, 1939, represented a striking reversal: he lauded film makers for turning out films that dared do what he had warned against the

---

[83] *Ibid.,* 174–76.

[84] Thorp, *op. cit.* Production began on such films just before a threatened monopoly investigation of Hollywood by Congress.

[85] *America in Midpassage,* 597–98, 605.

[86] By this date James Roosevelt was at work for Samuel Goldwyn. (*New York Times,* December 5, 1938.)

[87] Thorp, *op. cit.,* 160–61.

year before—that is, do something other than just entertain the millions. He acknowledged that the screen had a social function and responsibility.[88] In this way he gave official sanction to producing films that would please the government. This is another indication that the Film Service was becoming superfluous through Hollywood's actions.

And so, even though no direct evidence can be found of action against Lorentz's work after the release of *The Plow*, there is circumstantial evidence that the Film Service could be considered a threat to the commercial motion picture industry and that the industry undertook action to make the Film Service unnecessary.

When the Film Service was stripped of its budget by Congress in 1940, an irritating prick was removed from Hollywood's conscience. Now there was no one to show the commercial producers what they should be doing as part of their offering.

These are the reasons the United States Film Service was stripped of its production budget in 1940, in spite of the merit of its productions: antagonism and antipathy in Congress, a lack of support from the executive branch, opposition by the public and Congress to propaganda activities by the government, and opposition from Hollywood.

[88] *Ibid.*, 161–62.

VIII

AN EVALUATION OF THE FILMS OF MERIT

LORENTZ did not win the support of Congress for his work in the films of merit.[1] From the time of the release of *The Plow That Broke the Plains* in 1936, he did have the support of many of the critics; the public also supported his work by going to see the films. Three of the films—*The Plow That Broke the Plains, The River*, and *Power and the Land*—are still available from the Department of Agriculture.

All three of Lorentz's films discussed here, *The Plow That Broke the Plains, The River*, and *The Fight for Life*, plus *The Nuremberg Trials*, can be seen in the NET series "Lorentz on Film," which has played on educational television stations around the country a number of times. Virgil Thomson's suites based on the music for *The Plow That Broke the Plains* and *The River* have been recorded several times and are currently available in a recording by Leopold Stokowski and the Symphony of the Air.

When each film was released, it received good reviews from the critics.[2] All but one of the reviews of *The Plow That Broke the Plains*, from the time of its premiere at the Mayflower Theatre in Washington, were favorable.[3] That one review, although designed to criticize the film severely, did state that Lorentz and his crew

---

[1] The evaluation is limited to a discussion of the four films actually completed by Lorentz and the Film Service, *The Plow that Broke the Plains, The River, The Fight for Life*, and *Power and the Land*. It does not include *The Land*, which Flaherty finished, under the auspices of the AAA, or *Ecce Homo!* which was never finished.

[2] I do not mean to imply that the critics were unanimous; there were dissenters. A study of all the reviews available, including the material in the personal files of Pare Lorentz and the clipping file for each film at the Museum of Modern Art, indicates that more critics reacted favorably toward each film than reacted unfavorably.

[3] See p. 41.

did a "splendid job technically."[4] Reviews that appeared in the press and periodicals after the release of the film were also favorable. For example, the review in *Literary Digest* stated that the United States now led all European nations in the results of documentary film making.[5] The reviewer for the *National Board of Review Magazine* praised the film for its "surprising artistic skill."[6]

The River also fared well at the hands of the critics. Of Lorentz's three productions and the other film produced by the Film Service, *The River* is the most praised and most discussed. The initial reviews of the film, particularly those resulting from the river-city premieres, were all highly favorable.[7] Reviews following the Washington premiere on December 7, 1937, were also filled with praise.[8] The film was hailed as a masterpiece of epic stature. For example, V. F. Calverton wrote: "The cinema, simple and plain as a photograph, yet inspired by imaginative shots and scenes suggestive of the life of the river, has a quality about it which is epical. ... *The River* is a masterpiece of social documentation and cinematic dramatization."[9] Howard Barnes ranked the film with the greatest of sociological film studies.[10] Others rated it as among the finest cultural contributions of the New Deal.[11]

Much of the reaction to *The Fight for Life* was also favorable.[12] The film received excellent national publicity when *Look* and *Life* both presented picture stories on the film and featured it as Movie of the Week.[13] Franz Hoellering, writing in the *Nation*, said that Lorentz and the Film Service had made motion picture history

[4] Folliard, "Tugwell's Farmer's Lot Is Sad Compared to Soviet Film Idyll," *Washington Post*, May 11, 1936.

[5] "Dust Storm Film," *Literary Digest*, May 16, 1936, 32.

[6] June, 1936. From the files of the Museum of Modern Art.

[7] *Ibid.*, 112–13.

[8] *Ibid.*, 114–15.

[9] "Cultural Barometer," *Current History*, April, 1938, 55.

[10] *New York Herald Tribune*, February 6, 1938. From the files of the Museum of Modern Art.

[11] Calverton, "Cultural Barometer," *Current History*, April, 1938, 55. See also Meyer Levin, "The Candid Cameraman," *Esquire*, January, 1938, 177.

[12] See p. 113 for reaction of critics to the premiere.

[13] *Look*, March 12, 1940; *Life*, March 18, 1940, 98.

with *The Fight for Life*, a picture filled with memorable moments.[14] William Boehnel wrote that the film was both a "bitter indictment of slum conditions" and a "gripping plea for greater medical knowledge among obstetricians."[15] Frank Nugent called the film "as dramatic as life itself."[16] The reviews for *Power and the Land* were mixed—that is, it was a good film, but it had certain faults. Reviewers indicated that the subject lacked the controversy and excitement that Pare Lorentz's films had contained but that there were other points to its credit. For example, the reviewer for the *Magazine of Art* wrote that Ivens "has produced a film which is straightforward, unpretentious, able, and suitable."[17] The first half of the film, which shows life on the Parkinson farm before electricity, especially impressed critics. Philip T. Hartung wrote: "It is, however, particularly brilliant in its documentary aspects in the first half which has a nostalgic, back-to-the-land quality. Joris Ivens has done a fine job of portraying a preelectrification farm."[18]

Complimentary reviews following the release of each film were gratifying to Lorentz and his staff. He had set out to make films for the government that would be good enough to show on commercial screens. The reviews show that he succeeded in his goal. In the first two films, the complimentary reviews helped get the commercial distribution he sought.

Recognition of the films continued. *The River* won the J. Emanuel Plaque as the best short feature of the year. It also won first prize as best documentary at the Venice International Film Festival in 1938.[19] Lorentz's script for *The Fight for Life* was selected for inclusion in *Twenty Best Film Plays*.[20] William

14 March 16, 1940, 372.

15 *New York World-Telegram*, March 7, 1940. From the personal files of Pare Lorentz.

16 "Pare Lorentz Again Goes to Fact for His Drama in His New Film, 'The Fight for Life,' at the Belmont," *New York Times*, March 7, 1940.

17 January, 1941, 43.

18 *Commonweal*, December 20, 1940, 232. From the files of the Museum of Modern Art.

19 See pp. 73ff.

20 John Gassner and Dudley Nichols, *Twenty Best Film Plays*.

Boehnel ranked it as the best documentary of the year,[21] as did the National Board of Review, which gave honorable mention to *Power and the Land*.[22]

Historians and students of motion pictures have described the stature of each of the films. In 1939, Lewis Jacobs wrote of the first two films: "The documentaries of Pare Lorentz have pointed the way to a lyrical blending of narration and music, and to a contrapuntal relation of sound and image."[23] He listed both films as among those "prominent in the educational realm for their attempts to project esthetic values as well as information."[24] In 1957, Arthur Knight analyzed the style, approach, and effect of the two films. His summary was: "These two films are classics and pioneers in American documentary and serve as the recruiting ground for many of our leading documentary film-makers. They also began to focus public attention upon the form itself."[25] Recently, A. R. Fulton called *The River* "a great documentary, if not the greatest that the art of the motion picture has produced."[26]

Paul Rotha assessed the value of *The Fight for Life* ten years after its release and described it as a masterpiece. He granted that the film had shortcomings, but thought that these were unimportant when one considered Lorentz's major accomplishment in the film. He wrote, "Lorentz attacked and solved a problem which documentary makers had been evading for a decade: how to make dramatic and emotional use of real people in their everyday surroundings."[27]

Richard Griffith believed that *Power and the Land* would have usefulness beyond its original purpose—to show the need for rural electrification. He wrote that the film was "an argument for rural cooperatives . . . and, deeply, an emotional impression of

---

[21] "Best Films," *New York World-Telegram*, December 28, 1940. From the personal files of Pare Lorentz.

[22] *Mobile Register*, December 23, 1940. From the personal files of Pare Lorentz.

[23] *The Rise of the American Film*, 442.

[24] *Ibid.*

[25] *The Liveliest Art: A Panoramic History of the Movies*, 250–51.

[26] *Motion Pictures: The Development of an Art from Silent Films to the Age of Television*, 200.

[27] *Documentary Film*, 317.

farm life."[28] In 1946, Jean Benoit-Lévy called *Power and the Land* one of Ivens' finest works, "an impression of actuality which the author has drawn from his subconscious and filtered across his temperament."[29]

An examination of the films and the reviews shows that most of the same elements in each film were responsible for the praise the film received. These elements are the photography, the musical score, and the narration.

A study of Lorentz's films reveals a highly developed contrapuntal relationship between pictures and sound track. There is also a change in dramatic structure from a presentation of man in conflict with nature to man in conflict with society. This change is accompanied by a change from a symbolic presentation to a realistic one.

The photography in each film drew praise from the reviewers. Frank Nugent described *The Plow* as "photographically exceptional,"[30] and thought the photography in *The River* was even better.[31] Study of the two films supports the evaluation by Nugent. Lorentz knew better what he wanted in the second film, and the photographers knew more about shooting on location. Lorentz, relying less on stock footage in the second film, had greater control of the pictorial sequences.

The reviewer for *Variety* noted that Crosby's camera work in *The Fight for Life* brought out "the life-like quality of the subject."[32] Crosby's footage of the slums and of the "Day Walk" and "Night Walk" sequences are unforgettable, leaving an impression of the city as a living desert. Footage of a comparable nature is to be found only in the best newsreel footage of the bombed cities of Europe taken during World War II.

Photography of a different sort is to be found in *Power and the*

28 Rotha and Griffith, *The Film till Now*, 612.

29 *The Art of the Motion Picture* (trans. by T. R. Jaeckel), (New York, Coward-McCann, Inc., 1946), 92.

30 "Raw Deal for the New Deal," *New York Times*, May 24, 1936.

31 *New York Times*, February 5, 1938.

32 March 6, 1940. From the files of the Museum of Modern Art.

Land. The footage is just as realistic, but the emotional tone is not so somber. Philip T. Hartung praised the photography, particularly its appropriateness, in his review in *Commonweal.*[33]

It is significant that Floyd Crosby was the photographer on three of the four films of merit. He filmed parts of *The River* and *Power and the Land* and was completely responsible for the camera work in *The Fight for Life.* He brought a high degree of technical skill to the three films, and justifies Lorentz's insistence on hiring the best possible people for the production of each film in order to make films of merit. Lorentz placed a high value on Crosby's ability, and had Crosby work with him in the special Air Corps photographic unit.[34]

Three outstanding contemporary composers were selected for the film scores for the four films of merit. The praise their scores received further supports Lorentz's insistence on highly talented co-workers. Only Gruenberg had ever composed a motion picture score before, but through their own skills as composers and their willingness to work closely with the film makers, all three developed outstanding and appropriate scores.

The reviewer for the *National Board of Review Magazine* described Thomson's score for *The Plow* as "remarkably eloquent."[35] Thomson's score for *The River* was also described by Frank Nugent as eloquent. Nugent went on to say, "Virgil Thomson's score, a symphonic blend of old spirituals, folk ballads, and original music, has matched the images perfectly."[36] When reviewing *The Fight for Life*, Nugent rated Louis Gruenberg's score more highly than he did Thomson's earlier scores.[37] The reviewer for the *Magazine of Art* thought that the *The Fight for Life* had something of the qualities of a symphony and that Gruenberg's score contributed highly to this effect.[38] Reviewers pointed out that

[33] December 20, 1940, 232.
[34] Interview with Pare Lorentz, April 25, 1961.
[35] June, 1936.
[36] *New York Times*, February 5, 1938.
[37] "Pare Lorentz Again Goes to Fact for His Drama in His New Film, 'The Fight for Life,' at the Belmont," *New York Times*, March 7, 1940.
[38] April, 1940, 323–24.

Douglas Moore's score for *Power and the Land* was in character with the film—brilliant, yet simple and earthy. Philip T. Hartung and the reviewer for *Variety* both made comments along this line.[39]

The scores for Lorentz's films grew in complexity. Thomson's score for *The Plow That Broke the Plains* was very effective in its use of familiar themes and its development of such themes, their use for counterpoint and ironic comment. In the score for *The River*, Thomson, in his collaboration with Lorentz, developed these techniques to a greater degree of effectiveness. The original motifs he developed, such as the "River Theme," are particularly effective and memorable. The score for *The River* is the epitome of a score that integrates refreshing original themes and the skillful development of familiar themes.

For his third film, Lorentz obtained a score from Louis Gruenberg that was comprised entirely of original music. The emotional impact of the film was generally enhanced by this score, the longest ever composed for a dramatic film to that time. It is difficult to imagine the scenes of childbirth without the orchestrated heartbeat, the "Day Walk" without the theme of "Men of the City," or the "Night Walk" without the emotional thrust of Joe Sullivan's improvised blues. Gruenberg's themes have charm, vitality, and affirmation. All the films would be lesser productions without their distinctive musical scores. As important as the contributions of these composers are, it should be remembered that the scores were developed under Lorentz's supervision. He knew the type of music he needed for each film, and he got it.

The narration or script for each of the films received praise from the reviewers. Margaret Taselaar, reviewing *The Plow That Broke the Plains* in the *New York Herald Tribune*, spoke well of its narration.[40] Lorentz's skill as a writer of narration for documentary films improved rapidly. V. F. Calverton compared his narration for the second film to Walt Whitman's *Leaves of Grass*.[41] James Joyce was quoted as describing it as "the most beautiful

39 *Commonweal*, December 20, 1940, 232; *Variety*, March 6, 1940.
40 May 26, 1936. From the files of the Museum of Modern Art.
41 "Cultural Barometer," *Current History*, April, 1938, 55.

prose I have heard in ten years."[42] Carl Sandburg wrote to Lorentz's publishers after reading the narration in book form and said, "It is among the greatest of the psalms of America's greatest river."[43]

In *The Fight for Life*, Lorentz moved away from the poetic narration used in *The River* and wrote effective, natural dialogue for his characters. The reviewer for *Scholastic* described Lorentz's script as "a powerful piece of film-writing."[44] As mentioned earlier, the script was selected for inclusion in Gassner and Nichols' *Twenty Best Film Plays*.[45] The narration for *Power and the Land*, written by Stephen Vincent Benét, impressed both the reviewer for *Time* and Philip T. Hartung.[46]

The work of the narrators and the actors was also praised. A number of reviewers commented on Thomas Chalmers' reading of the narrations for *The Plow* and *The River*.[47] Nugent was impressed by the performances of the professional actors in *The Fight for Life*,[48] and the reviewer for *Variety* complimented the hospital patients for retaining their naturalness.[49] William P. Adams, the narrator for *Power and the Land*, received compliments from Hartung and the reviewer for *Variety*.[50]

One of the outstanding qualities of the three films produced, directed, and written by Lorentz is the contrapuntal relationship between sound track and pictures. The use of the technique developed from one picture to the next.

The most effective sequences in *The Plow That Broke the Plains*, "War" and "Dust Storm," both made use of counterpoint. In "War," Lorentz skillfully intercuts scenes of farming with

[42] White, "Pare Lorentz," *Scribner's*, January, 1939, 10.
[43] Postcard from Carl Sandburg to William Sorkin, n.d. From the personal files of Pare Lorentz.
[44] April 1, 1940, 34.
[45] Gassner and Nichols, *op. cit.*
[46] October 14, 1940, 114; *Commonweal*, December 20, 1940, 232.
[47] "The Plow That Broke the Plains," *National Board of Review Magazine*, June, 1936; "The River," *National Board of Review Magazine*, November, 1937.
[48] "Pare Lorentz Again Goes to Fact for His Drama in His New Film, 'The Fight for Life,' at the Belmont," *New York Times*, March 7, 1940.
[49] March 6, 1940. From the files of the Museum of Modern Art.
[50] *Commonweal*, December 20, 1940, 232; *Variety*, October 2, 1940.

scenes of military maneuvers. Throughout the sequence, music reminiscent of World War I, particularly "Mademoiselle from Armentières," is heard. The music is light and gay when first heard, but becomes progressively more intense and militaristic as the sequence builds. In this way Lorentz makes of farming a military, regimented activity. A minimum of narration is used in the sequence to develop the idea that "wheat will win the war!" Counterpoint is used toward the end of "Dust Storm" when the strains of "Old Hundred" are heard as dust sifts through a home on the prairie. The ironic comment made in this manner is highly effective.

There is more use of counterpoint between sound track and pictures in *The River*. For example, the "River Theme" is heard first as we see the tree-covered hills of the North. It is repeated, though altered in mood, as we see these hills stripped of their foliage. As the lumbering crews strip the hills, we hear "There'll Be a Hot Time in the Old Town Tonight." As the industrial sequence develops, Thomson interpolates "The Eagles They Fly High in Mobile" into the score to make further comment. Hymn tunes are skillfully used in *The River*, as they were in *The Plow*: "Yes, Jesus Loves Me" is heard during the scene of sharecroppers picking cotton; "When Gabriel's Awful Trumpet Shall Sound," during the flood. Further comment is made by the plaintive treatment of "Go Tell Aunt Rhody the Old Gray Goose Is Dead" during the scenes of eroded land. Lorentz uses the narration in *The River* also in a contrapuntal style. The roll call of rivers is spoken during the opening sequence of the growth of the river and again later as the flood moves down the river. The roll call of trees is used in the same way as we see the lumbering sequence and then the stripped hills. A roll call of cities is similarly used in the industrial sequence and in the flood.

Much of the effect of the counterpoint in *The Plow* and *The River* comes from the use of familiar musical themes placed against contrasting pictorial sequences. The counterpoint in *The Fight for Life* is a result of original music, narration expressing the doubts of the leading character, and realistic footage of the

185

city of Chicago. Both the "Day Walk" and the "Night Walk" sequences also make use of counterpoint.

In the "Day Walk," Dr. O'Donnell moves through the slums of Chicago and expresses his doubts about the value of bringing life into such surroundings. As we hear him voice his doubts, we see shots of the slums, row upon row of tenements, poor people scrabbling through refuse heaps for scraps of food, children playing in the streets. Gruenberg composed the "Men of the City" theme to accompany the sequence. The purpose of the music, in Lorentz's words, was "to get across the sense that there are decent human beings behind some of those buildings."

In *The Fight for Life*, changes can be noted in the dramatic structure. The first two films presented man in conflict with nature, showing what man had done to nature and how nature had retaliated and concluded with a presentation of how man was trying to repair what he had done to nature. In *The Fight for Life*, we see man in conflict with society. We are shown what society has done to man in the form of slums. We see how man tries to help others through techniques used at the Chicago Maternity Center in the heart of the slums.

As Lorentz moved toward a character-centered type of dramatic structure, he also changed from a symbolic to a realistic presentation. Much of the content of the first two films is symbolic, whereas it is realistic in *The Fight for Life*. In *The Plow*, a bleached skull is used as a symbol of the drought. One farmer looking to the sky for rain symbolizes all farmers in the Dust Bowl. A Negro jazz drummer beating away at his drums and a ticker madly dispensing tape are used to symbolize the wild speculation of the twenties. A horse circling wildly in the face of the dust storm symbolizes the desperation the storms provoked. Not a single person or place is identified in the film. The same is true of *The River*. The effect of the sequence of the sharecroppers is that they symbolize all sharecroppers, not a single family. The people we see displaced by the flood symbolize thousands of the homeless. The warning whistles, the flashes of lightning, the footage indicators—all are symbols of the rising flood. The pictures of nine or ten city skylines

186

symbolize hundreds of cities in the valley. One of the values of the first two films is that Lorentz effectively converted hundreds of years of history and thousands of miles of territory into meaningful symbols.

In *The Fight for Life* the emphasis is less on the symbolic representation of a problem and the forces that caused the problem than it is on one man, one maternity center, and the slums of one city. Dr. O'Donnell is more than an uncertain young intern; he is a doctor with doubts and fears. All the locales are clearly identified, and most of the characters, even some of the patients, are given names. The only character who is a symbol is the receptionist who, nameless, represents the organization and constant activity of the maternity center. The presentation of material in *The Fight for Life* is realistic and straightforward. It is not necessary for Lorentz to develop concepts through the careful selection and arrangement of pictorial material and the use of counterpoint. When counterpoint is employed, it is used to help us understand the problems Dr. O'Donnell faces within himself and sees around him in, first, the "Night Walk" and, second, the "Day Walk."

A further indication of the shift in emphasis toward a more realistic presentation can be seen in comparing the central characters in *Ecce Homo!* and *The Fight for Life*. Both films are character-centered films. The central character of *Ecce Homo!* symbolizes the unemployed. He has no name, only a number—#7790. He is able to do any kind of work. The central character of *The Fight for Life*, Dr. O'Donnell, is a much more carefully delineated character. He has a profession. We are told where he works and lives, whereas #7790 works his way from one unidentified city to another.

The four films of merit succeeded as films of high artistic quality. They impressed critics by the way in which they were made. They earned their way onto commercial motion picture screens. They are worthy of study by anyone interested in the art of the informational film.

187

The films of merit were created with two goals in mind. One was to make them worthy of being seen on commercial motion picture screens. This goal was achieved. The second was to use them to inform the public about problems that existed in the United States and about government solutions to the problems. It was hoped that the films would create a favorable attitude within the general public toward the various government programs. Unfortunately, the government never attempted to measure a change in attitude within the public toward the programs described in the films. Lloyd Ramseyer used *The Plow* and *The River* in an experiment to measure the influence of documentary films on social attitudes. He reports that both films produced attitude change, particularly with older groups.[51]

The films could not be effective in producing an attitude change unless they were widely seen. In this they succeeded. *The River* was distributed commercially by Paramount Pictures; *The Fight for Life*, by Columbia Pictures; and *Power and the Land*, by RKO Radio Pictures. *The Plow That Broke the Plains* was distributed independently by the Resettlement Administration and the Farm Security Administration. Figures on the commercial distribution of the films are unavailable.

These films were also distributed by the government on an educational basis to schools and other interested groups. As evidence of its continuing merit, *The River* has become one of the most widely seen short features of all time. Department of Agriculture records show attendance figures of far more than six million from the time of its release to the present day, and those records are incomplete. C. A. Carello, chief of the Motion Picture Service, Department of Agriculture, wrote: "We know that this figure is incomplete in several ways. The figure represents only the recorded non-theatrical distribution from this office and from our cooperating Film Libraries, and does not include commercial distribution by Hollywood or circulation of privately-owned prints."[52]

[51] "A Study of the Influence of Documentary Films on Social Attitudes" (unpublished Ph.D. dissertation, Ohio State University, 1938), 92, 125.

A report from the Department of Agriculture provided the following statistics for the distribution of *The River* in one year, 1961. The film had 2,064 showings, with an attendance of 131,754. The department had 254 prints available for circulation. Seventy-two prints were sold of *The River*, more than any other Department of Agriculture film in that year.[53] According to the same report, *Power and the Land* was shown 259 times to a total of 25,532 persons in 1961.

During the centennial of the Department of Agriculture, the government recognized the importance of Lorentz's work. On January 28, 1963, a special program was held in Washington, during which Lorentz received a gold medal from Secretary of Agriculture Orville L. Freeman. As a part of the program, *The River* was shown.

Study of the films reveals that they were designed to effect a change in attitude. Care was given to the pattern of organization of each film to aid the viewer in following the exposition of the material. Skillful use is made of repetition, parallel structure, and irony. Considerable use is also made of identification.

Three of the films follow the basic pattern of problem solution. In the original version of *The Plow That Broke the Plains*, Lorentz presented first the development of the Dust Bowl and then the government plan to aid those stricken by resettling them on land suitable for agriculture. In *The River*, Lorentz presented the problem of the misuse of natural resources that led to the flood and then the government plan as typified by the Tennessee Valley Authority, to stem floods and reclaim the land. In *Power and the Land*, we see the need for electricity on farms as Ivens presents the endless drudgery of farm labor for men and women; the last section of the film shows the electrification of the farm and its effect on lightening the work.

The one film that is not so clearly oriented to problem solution is *The Fight for Life*. There are two problems in the film, and they

52 Letter from C. A. Carello, October 31, 1963.

53 U.S. Department of Agriculture, *Report of the Distribution of Department of Agriculture 16mm Motion Pictures for Fiscal 1961.*

are skillfully interwoven in Lorentz's story. However, the causes and solution are set forth for only one of the problems—that of the loss of life in childbirth. The causes and solution of unemployment and city slums are not offered, although, interestingly enough, both were presented in the radio script for *Ecce Homo!* the film that Lorentz set aside in order to make *The Fight for Life.* The problem of unemployment and poverty moves as an undercurrent throughout most of the film, and comes to the surface on several occasions to assail the viewer with some of the most realistic and depressing footage ever used in a motion picture to that time.

Each of the films has a tight degree of organization because each is structured in time sequence. *The Plow* begins with the Great Plains in their natural state. Lorentz first shows the coming of the cattle industry, then the coming of the sodbuster, the war, overplanting, land speculation, rising prices, the drought, and then the Dust Bowl, followed by the exodus of many of the farmers and the resettlement program. Lorentz compressed one hundred years of misuse into less than thirty minutes of screen time by following a symbolic presentation of history. He accomplished the same thing in *The River*, compressing more than two hundred years of man's abuse of the Mississippi River Valley into a brief film. Again the presentation of the causes of the problem is presented symbolically in time sequence. The two problems in *The Fight for Life* are unified in the chronological presentation of part of the career of Dr. O'Donnell. The film traces the life of the doctor from the moment in the hospital when a patient dies after childbirth, through his decision to learn more about maternal care and obstetrics at the Chicago Maternity Center, his internship there, including trips through the Chicago slums, and his revived dedication after he saves a woman following delivery. *Power and the Land* also has a tightly structured time sequence. The need for rural electrification is presented by following the members of a farm family through their labors on a single day from sunrise to sunset. The decision to seek a rural co-operative and the coming of electricity to the farm follow in time sequence.

190

Two criticisms arise out of the problem-solution organization. In the three films, the problems are presented much more excitingly than the solutions and receive more time in the development. Lorentz's scripts for the first two films, the photography, the cutting and pictorial content, the music—all are more imaginative in the problem sections than in the solution sequences. This is also true to a great degree in *Power and the Land*.

My own interpretation of this emphasis is that Lorentz was personally more concerned with the problems that the country faced in the depression years. He accepted the solutions put into operation by the government. His task was to make the country see the need to spend money for these solutions. He believed that he could make the audience see the need by showing the problem as powerfully as possible. Interestingly enough, the same approach to balance and the treatment of problem and solution can be seen in the scenario Lorentz wrote for *The City*, directed by Ralph Steiner and Willard Van Dyke, both former cameramen with Lorentz.

The danger in the approach Lorentz used is that the problem may be presented so powerfully that the solutions advanced by the government seem almost feeble by comparison. At least one critic made this criticism at the time of the release of *The River*.[54] The criticism is a just one only if the programs shown are the only solutions. The government was doing more, particularly through the Soil Conservation Service and other reclamation projects. More was needed to solve the problems, but it was not within Lorentz's power or was it the responsibility of the sponsoring agencies to indicate what else was needed. Before anything further could be done, the support of an aroused public was needed. Lorentz helped arouse opinion through the two films. The implication of much of the final sequence for *The River* is that the TVA was only the beginning, only part of the solution. A motion picture service, co-ordinating the motion picture activities of a number of government agencies, as Lorentz hoped the Film Serv-

[54] White, "Pare Lorentz," *Scribner's*, January, 1939, 10.

ice would do, could have presented solutions of greater strength and scope.

The other criticism arising out of the use of problem-solution structure for the films is based on the third film, *Power and the Land*. In this film, the solution is too pat. The Parkinson family is suddenly seen using a large number of electrical appliances that they could not possibly afford. At least one reviewer commented on this problem in the film.[55]

The two outstanding techniques for handling the content in the films are repetition and parallel structure. Both techniques contribute to the effectiveness of the messages conveyed by the films. There is little repetition of visual images in the four films. However, lines or phrases of dialogue are repeated, as are musical themes. Several key phrases are repeated in *The Plow That Broke the Plains*. For example, such lines as "High winds and sun, high winds and sun," "without rivers, without streams, with little rain"; "Wheat will win the war"; "Baked out, blown out, and broke"; are all repeated after other lines have intervened. The melodies of "Mademoiselle from Armentières" and "Old Hundred" are both repeated in Thomson's score; the second time each melody is used, it serves to make ironic comment on the pictures it accompanies.

Long portions of the sound track of *The River* are repeated: the roll call of rivers, the roll call of trees, the roll call of cities. The second time the sets of narration are used, they make ironic comment on the pictorial content. Lorentz even repeats the factory whistles for ironic effect. A. R. Fulton has called attention to the ironic effect of the repetition in *The River*.[56] Skillful use is also made of the repetition of certain musical themes in *The River*. The "River Theme" is repeated at the beginning of the flood sequence with ironic effect. "How Firm a Foundation" is used at the opening of the film and again at the beginning of the sequence describing the work of the TVA.

[55] New York Post, December 11, 1940. From the files of the Museum of Modern Art.

[56] *Op. cit.*, 199.

The technique of repetition can also be found in *The Fight for Life*. In order to indicate how the maternity center carried on its work twenty-four hours a day, seven days a week, Lorentz frequently used shots of the receptionist repeatedly asking, "Has she had a baby, or is she having a baby?" and other questions in an endless pattern. Repetition is found in the continuous lines of expectant mothers entering the center, in the groups seated in the waiting rooms, and in the visits by the doctors to the slums to deliver babies. Numerous references to blood provide a repetitive framework. Another repetitive device used throughout the film is the line of dialogue by O'Donnell about getting a cup of coffee. When themes of Gruenberg's score are repeated, they are used for suspense or for affirmation. The orchestrated heartbeat is used repeatedly throughout the film to create suspense in the delivery scenes. Every time a child is safely delivered, a particular melody —the "Theme of Life," I call it—is heard. The "Men of the City" theme is repeated at the end of the film to help affirm O'Donnell's sense of satisfaction after saving the woman's life.

There is no use of repetition as a technique for handling content in *Power and the Land*. However, Charles Walker, the script writer on the film, used a technique that Lorentz developed to a high degree of perfection in *The River*—the technique of parallel structure. In *Power and the Land*, the problem and the solution are presented in parallel—that is, every task pictured in the first part of the film is repeated in the second half. In the first half, the tasks are difficult and often disappointing in their outcome, such as the spoiled milk being returned from the creamery. In the second half, the tasks are all done with the aid of electrical power. The tasks are easier to perform and bring obvious satisfaction and relief to the farmer and his family. The desire to make the structure as parallel as possible led to the criticism of the second half of the film referred to above.

In *The River*, three of the major sequences are developed in parallel. These three sequences reveal two of the most striking qualities of *The River*—its unity, and the artistic relationship between the visual and aural elements of the film.

193

The opening sequence, which traces the course of the river from its minute beginnings in an upland forest to the Gulf of Mexico, accompanied by the roll call of rivers and Thomson's music, is one of the unforgettable moments in films. The sequence begins with the musical river motif, a simple trumpet call, and shots of clouds. Mists break, first to reveal the Rockies and then the Appalachians, with appropriate descriptive words by the narrator. The river is built from close-ups of its dripping beginnings on the side of a hill through ever expanding shots of larger and larger streams of water. The movement of water is from top to bottom and usually from left to right. When the river itself is reached, the left-to-right flow of water is continued as the boat on which the camera is mounted moves to the left against the flow. Throughout the sequence, Thomson's music builds on the river motif and takes on a hymnlike quality. Chalmers intones the roll call of rivers as the river is built, visually and aurally.

There seem to be at least two variations on this basic sequence in the film, one more obvious than the other. The lumbering sequence parallels the opening sequence in several ways. Just as the narrator chants the roll call of rivers in the opening sequence, he chants a brief roll call of trees of the North and some of the cities to which they were shipped. Musically, the sequence begins with the river motif. However, the mood of the music is developed in a different way. The music for the first sequence treats the river reverently, with its hymn-like theme and voicings. The music for the lumbering sequence reflects feverish excitement and activity with an agitated and lively interpolation of "There'll Be a Hot Time in the Old Town Tonight."

Visually, the similarity of the opening sequence to the lumbering sequence is even more apparent. The lumbering sequence starts with panning shots of the tree-shrouded hills in the mist, much like the opening shots of the film. Larger and larger trees are felled into larger and larger bodies of water. Just as the river moved faster and broadened across the screen, so the tree-filled streams move more and more rapidly until the screen is filled by a lake covered with logs. Most of the movement is, again, from left to right. The three elements of the sequence build quickly and powerfully to the industrial footage that follows.

The flood sequence is a more obvious parallel of the opening sequence, visually and aurally. The film begins with shots of clouds and mists breaking over mountaintops as the trumpet call sounds. So does the flood sequence, but then stripped, charred, and denuded hills are seen through the mists, and Chalmers intones the roll call of trees. Fulton has noted the irony of this technique.[57] The panning of the hillsides is usually from left to right. As if to emphasize the danger lurking in the barren, burned-over hillsides, the hills are shown in silhouette in increasingly steeper angles.

The close-up of the dripping icicle is akin to the close-up of the freshet at the source of the river. The development of the river is paraphrased ironically in the build-up of the flood as trickles of water and bits of mud begin to slide downhill. As rain begins to fall, the water moves downhill and through streams in increasing volume and speed. More mud moves out. The movement on the screen is almost all from top to bottom and from left to right, as in the first sequence. The shots expand in width, and the flood races on until, instead of moving placidly on down to the gulf, the river is roaring across roads and fields, tearing at bridges and dikes. To increase the tension, close-ups of turbulent, tumbling torrents of muddy water are intercut. The narrator repeats long portions of his opening, including the list of states and part of the roll call of rivers. The roll call of cities in the dike-building sequence is also recalled. In fact, large sections of all the previous narration are reused as the flood builds to a crescendo, making the flood a powerful, reiterative, dramatic climax.

Thomson varies the development of the "River Theme" considerably in the flood sequence. He uses a French horn, instead of a trumpet, to state it mournfully, to begin the sequence. The theme is repeated, echoed, and re-echoed, and finally stated in discord. The music that follows, although based on a different hymn tune, is similar in tone until the factory whistles of the industrial

[57] *Ibid.*

195

sequence are parroted by the alarm blasts for the flood. The score becomes more emotional in tone—the agitated music of the industrial sequence punctuates the rescue efforts and frenzied dike building.

Much of the persuasive force of *The River* is due to the parallel structure of these three sequences. Lorentz unified his message aurally and visually for greater strength. The parallel structure also makes possible much of the irony in the opening sections of the film. It is the completeness of the parallel structure that helps to make *The River* one of the finest documentaries of all times.

Lorentz made use of another technique in the first two films, which may help to explain their effectiveness in arousing public opinion. Both *The Plow That Broke the Plains* and *The River* rely on the technique of identification for much of their effectiveness in appealing to the audience. A marked increase in the amount of identification used can be noted in the later film, and may be another reason why *The River* is one of the most effective documentary films ever made.

The first device used in *The Plow* to get viewer identification is the map of the United States. The effect is to make the viewer feel immediately that the Dust Bowl is an American problem, his problem. The identification is continued when animation is used to insert the first shot of the Great Plains within the designated area on the map. Other visual symbols are used throughout the film to reinforce identification: an American cowboy, a covered wagon, reapers pulled by horses, a parade with many American flags, the Negro jazz drummer, a windmill, "flivvers." The musical themes Thomson selected add identification to the process—he used many hymns, familiar cowboy songs, and popular music.

In *The River*, Lorentz added a barrage of identification in his narration to the visual and aural impressions. This was done through the roll calls of rivers, cities, and trees. The viewer is almost powerless to resist identifying with the problem being portrayed, because the technique is used incessantly.

Lorentz's treatment of the two problems in *The Fight for Life* effectively arouses the sympathy of the viewer for those who live

196

in the slums and for those who give birth. It is with the child-bearing situation that most viewers would identify. Lorentz wanted the audience to know that it was possible to have children much more safely than national statistics quoted in the film indicated. By identifying with the patients and their families in the film, the viewer would want the same kind of medical care during childbirth—that is, skilled obstetricians, complete sanitation, and thorough examinations.

However, the realistic presentation of the slums prevents identification with the conditions in that footage. It is possible that Lorentz wanted to do no more than make the public aware of the slums and arouse sympathy for those who lived there. After all, he intended to return to *Ecce Homo!* which, judging from the radio script, was a much more detailed and symbolic treatment of the problem of unemployment reflected in the slums of *The Fight for Life*. The radio script contained identification in the narration and musical accompaniment, as did the first two films, and could have been an effective instrument for arousing public opinion on unemployment.

The second goal of the films of merit led to charges of propaganda by reviewers and congressmen. In several instances, the intent was to discredit the films.[58] The reviewer for the *National Board of Review Magazine* noted that the propaganda charge was being used to keep *The Plow That Broke the Plains* off commercial screens.[59] Bernard De Voto objected to the final section of *The River* because it was propaganda making a special plea.[60] *The Fight for Life* was criticized by Senator Robert Taft because it was propaganda for housing and medical legislation, even though no federal programs or legislation are mentioned in the film.[61]

It should be emphasized again that during this period the word "propaganda" had a popular meaning completely different from its original meaning—it was a technique used by the dictatorships to mislead and enslave their subjects. Democratic governments

---

[58] For example, see p. 42.
[59] June, 1936. From the files of the Museum of Modern Art.
[60] *Saturday Review of Literature*, April 9, 1938, 8.
[61] U.S. *Congressional Record*, 76 Cong., 3 sess., 1940, 5095.

usually avoided referring to the fact that they used propaganda because of the unsavory character the word had assumed.[62]

The charge of propaganda was unfair. The purpose of the films was not to mislead the public into advocating any legislation. For the problems presented in the first two and the last film of merit, legislation had already been approved by the public through their representatives. In the third film, Lorentz deliberately avoided any reference to proposed legislation. The problems portrayed existed, as did the solutions. In the first film, the public might have been misled about the scope of the problem and some of its causes, but they were not misled about the purpose of the film—to make them aware that the Dust Bowl was serious and that the government was taking steps to correct the problem and assist those affected by it.

However, as some reviewers correctly noted, the films were "propaganda" in the larger, original sense of the word. The films were made for specific educational purposes, and were part of an organized effort by the government to acquaint the public with the existence of certain problems and to gain support for the programs advocated to correct them.

It should also be pointed out that the content of each of these films was developed independently by Lorentz, with little or no pressure from government sponsors. When Secretary Wallace said that there was no corn in *The River*, Lorentz did not add corn. When President Roosevelt asked him to change one of the opening lines in *The River* to "From as far east as New York" instead of "Pennsylvania," Lorentz resisted because he knew from his research that the tributaries of the Allegheny River in Pennsylvania were farther east than those in New York. He submitted his films to his sponsors only when they were finished, and never changed a line or a scene. His work was treated with respect and understanding by cabinet and White House officials.

Lorentz's achievement in the films of merit is outstanding. He

[62] Albig, *op. cit.*, 291. For a detailed examination of the problem with regard to the films, see pp. 171–72.

pioneered in techniques and goals for government motion pictures. He showed that, even on the limited budgets provided by government agencies, it was possible to produce motion pictures worthy of commercial distribution. Since the time of his productions, the only government documentary films to be shown on commercial screens were those produced during World War II, and most of these films were made by the armed forces with professional talent obtained from the commercial motion picture industry. After Lorentz left the Film Service, the REA followed his policies in hiring persons of recognized talent to write the script, compose the music, and read the narration for *Power and the Land*. The REA wanted a motion picture comparable to *The River*, and followed standards established by Lorentz in order to get such a picture.[63]

James McCamy has written that Lorentz's use of talented persons in all phases of production is responsible for setting his motion pictures above all other government productions.[64] But this is only one of the reasons for the success of the films of merit. Other factors in their success include the intrinsic excellence of the films, achieved through Lorentz's enormous talent as a motion picture director and writer, his determined efforts to get the films distributed, and, last but not least, efforts upon the parts of his friends in the motion picture industry. Also of great importance are the contributions made by those who worked with Lorentz in the production of the films and that made by Arch Mercey in the administration of affairs in Washington.

Lorentz succeeded in making excellent motion pictures even though he had had no prior experience as a film producer, director, or writer. These films are important in documentary film history. *The Plow That Broke the Plains* was the first documentary film produced by the federal government, and earned its place on commercial screens at a time when commercial interests were hostile to government motion picture activities. *The River* is

---

[63] See p. 121.
[64] *Government Publicity*, 49–50.

recognized as one of the finest documentary films ever produced. *The Fight for Life* pioneered in the so-called semidocumentary techniques of motion picture production.

These films are antecedents of the documentary films made in the United States today. When a documentary film maker commissions original music for a production, he is following Lorentz's lead. When he shows what man has done to nature and what nature does to man in retaliation, he is moving in the Lorentz tradition. When he combines a dramatized story with factual material, he is following the trail Lorentz blazed in the first semidocumentary. These films served to focus the attention of film makers on form. A number of persons gained experience in making documentary films as members of Lorentz's crew; others have studied the films to learn how to make documentaries.

Lorentz produced these motion pictures in spite of a number of obstacles, particularly the difficulty in clearing and obtaining funds. If it had been possible for Lorentz to find sponsorship for his projects outside relief agencies, it might have been possible for him to continue making motion pictures without establishing the United States Film Service. However, the Film Service was marked for cancellation by Congress as soon as it requested funds.

Congress has not looked with favor on requests for money to propagandize the public or perpetuate power in the executive branch, as was seen in the hearings on the Film Service budget. It can be seen in the attitude of Congress at the present time, as revealed in congressional bans on commercial screenings of the productions of the United States Information Agency. The agency had to obtain special authority from Congress before commercial showing of *Years of Lightning—Days of Drums* (1965), a documentary about the late President John F. Kennedy. Two charges, familiar to those who have studied the attacks on Lorentz's films, were made in the House debate on granting this special authority: (1) Americans should not be propagandized, and (2) Democrats would use the Kennedy film as a campaign weapon.[65]

Until Congress recognizes the need for the federal government

[65] "House Votes to Show Kennedy Film in U.S.," *New York Times*, June 10, 1965.

to communicate directly with the public about problems and programs, or until the time of another national emergency, no one will be able to pursue the goal Pare Lorentz established for government motion pictures in 1935—the goal of films of merit.

Today the dissemination of information in the United States can best be described as a paradox. The citizen is beseiged by more information through more media than ever before, and yet information that concerns him as a citizen often fails to reach him. Through his films Lorentz proved that quality documentaries could break through the mass of messages and communicate to the viewer a real understanding of, and involvement in, the subject.

The films of merit are classics in documentary film making. They are classics because their themes are important and because talented, dedicated men shaped them with artistry, imagination, and—ultimately—truth.

APPENDICES

LETTER from Comptroller General McCarl to the Administrator, Resettlement Administration, August 19, 1935, including copy of letter from Rexford G. Tugwell to Comptroller General McCord, August 12, 1935

Comptroller General McCarl to the Administrator,
Resettlement Administration,
August 19, 1935:

There has been received your letter of August 12, 1935, as follows:

The RA proposes to have a motion picture with sound accompaniment made at an estimated expense of $6,000, which will have for its subject matter the extent and richness of the western plain lands before their abuse, the settlements thereon, the beginning of misuse, such as overgrazing, overproduction, mechanized farming by absentee owners, etc., and the results thereof, such as wind and soil erosion, drought, dust storms, floods, worn land and poverty. There will also be animated maps showing the area of lands now unfit for profitable farming, and the areas where farmers must be supported, rehabilitated or moved, and animation showing soil areas which can be farmed scientifically and profitably.

In carrying out its function of dealing with soil erosion and other similar problems mentioned in the Executive Order creating the RA, the Administrator is faced with the necessity of educating its employees and the employees of cooperating agencies of the government with respect to these problems. The Administration's own employees consist not only of its employees in Washington but of a large staff in the field. The employees of the cooperating agencies (among which are the N. E. C., the A. A. A., the Department of Agriculture, the Agricultural Extension Service, the Indian Service, the C. C. C., the F. E. R. A., and the P. W. A.) are likewise located in the field as well as in Washington. A moving picture of the character described above will be one of the most effective, quick, and inexpensive means of explaining some of these problems of the Administration to its employees and to the employees of these agencies.

The work of the Administration necessarily requires scientific approach and technique. Technicians, scientists, and scholars of the land problems can give the Administration the benefit of their study, advice, and suggestions, and the picture will also aid in giving these people, located in various parts of the country, an understanding of our problems.

In short, the primary object of the motion picture is to help the Resettlement Administration and its employees to visualize and understand better the problems confronting them, and to aid them in the prevention of the results of soil erosion and related problems. The expense is a necessary one to the accomplishment of the objectives of the Emergency Relief Appropriations Act of 1935.

Section 3 of the E. R. A. A. of 1935 provides:

"In carrying out the provisions of this join resolution the President may (a) authorize expenditures for . . .: and such other expense as he may determine necessary to the accomplishment of the objectives of this joint resolution: . . ."

Executive Order #7027, dated April 30, 1935, establishes the Resettlement Administration and authorizes the Administrator in the performance of his duties and functions "to employ the services and means mentioned in subdivision (a) of Section 3 . . . to the extent therein provided. . . ." On June 15, 1935, the President allocated $1,000,000 "for administrative expenses in the District of Columbia and elsewhere as authorized by Executive Order #7027, of April 30, 1935."

In view of the facts above set forth and in view of the further fact that the motion picture will clearly reduce the need for sending people into the field to explain the work of the Resettlement Administration and the need for calling people from the field to Washington to receive explanations, the proposed expenditure for the motion picture appears to be a necessary incident to the effective and economical functioning of the Resettlement Administration.

Your opinion is requested as to whether funds in the allocation for administrative expenses in the District of Columbia and elsewhere, as authorized by Executive Order #7027, authorizing the Administrator to employ the services and means mentioned in subdivision (a) of Section 3 of the E. R. A. A. of 1935, will be available for the making of a motion picture such as herein described.

In view of your explanation as to the objectives proposed to be ac-

203

complished by the motion picture, this office is not required to object to the use of funds under the allocation for administrative expenses of your Agency for such purpose.

APPENDIX B

LETTER from President Franklin D. Roosevelt to Lowell Mellett, director, National Emergency Council, August 13, 1938

August 13, 1938

MY DEAR MR. DIRECTOR:

In accordance with the provisions of Executive Orders No. 6889-A of Oct. 29, 1934, No. 7034 of May 6, 1935, and subsequent Executive Orders prescribing the duties and functions of the National Emergency Council, I desire that the National Emergency Council undertake the coordination of certain activities of the several departments and agencies engaged in carrying out the relief and work relief programs.

It has been found advantageous for these agencies to produce motion pictures, sometimes with sound accompaniment, illustrating the physical and human problems confronting the country and the methods adopted by the Government for their solution. Such pictures serve a double purpose. For the people as a whole they make understandable the basic causes of present conditions. For the government employees in the relief and work relief programs, there is provided, not only the invaluable aid that results from this understanding by the general public, but the clarification of the purposes of the relief statutes which they are engaged in administering.

Two such motion pictures have been produced by the Farm Security Administration—*The Plow That Broke the Plains* and *The River*. In addition, several departments and agencies have produced and are producing shorter films dealing with various aspects of their programs. I desire that in the future the distribution and the exhibition of these films be coordinated by the National Emergency Council in order that they may most effectively and economically serve the purpose for which they were produced.

I have been informed that the Works Progress Administration, the Public Works Administration and the Farm Security Administration feel that further pictures are needed to effectuate their programs in dealing with the problems of unemployment. It seems to me that this can best be done through the production of one picture illustrating the problems of all three agencies and that such a project can best be administered by the National Emergency Council, which was established to coordinate interagency activities, and I am, therefore, directing that you undertake the production and distribution of this picture.

For this project I am approving the expenditure of $265,000 of the funds appropriated by the Emergency Relief Appropriations Act of 1938, to be made available by the Secretary of Agriculture, the Works Progress Administration and the Federal Emergency Administrator of Public Works in the following amounts: Secretary of Agriculture, $35,000, Works Progress Administration, $120,000, Federal Emergency Administrator of Public Works, $110,000.

This project shall be subject to all the restrictions and limitations of said Act.

Sincerely yours,

FRANKLIN D. ROOSEVELT

APPENDIX C

LETTER from President Franklin D. Roosevelt to Henry A. Wallace, secretary of agriculture, August 13, 1938

August 13, 1938

MY DEAR MR. SECRETARY

I have today signed a letter to the Executive Director of the National Emergency Council, requesting him to coordinate the activities of the Farm Security Administration, U.S. Department of Agriculture, the Works Progress Administration and the Public Works Administration in the distribution and exhibition of motion picture films produced by those agencies dealing with various problems relating to their work relief and relief programs.

I have also directed the National Emergency Council to undertake the production and distribution of a motion picture dealing with the problems of unemployment and of the programs of the three named agencies in meeting those problems. By my letter No. 2300 to the Secretary of the Treasury, I have approved for this project the expenditure of $265,000 out of funds appropriated by the Emergency Relief Appropriations Act of 1938, approved June 21, 1938.

I desire that $35,000 of this amount be transferred by you from the amount appropriated to you by said Act to the National Emergency Council and be charged to the $25,000,000 I have heretofore authorized you to use for administrative expenses.

Sincerely yours,

FRANKLIN D. ROOSEVELT

APPENDIX D

LETTER and enclosure from Lowell Mellett, director, National Emergency Council, to Pare Lorentz, director, United States Film Service, August 13, 1938

August 13, 1938

To: The Director of the United States Film Service
From: The Executive Director
The attached provides for the creation of the United States Film Service and prescribes rules and regulations for its administration.

LOWELL MELLETT
The Executive Director

The United States Film Service

Under authority of Executive Orders No. 6889-A of October 29, 1934, No. 7034 of May 6, 1935, No. 7073 of June 13, 1935 and subsequent Executive Orders prescribing the duties and functions of the National Emergency Council, and Executive Order 7906 of June 6, 1938, providing for the continuance of the National Emergency Council, and by direction of the President as of August 13, 1938, there is hereby created as a division of the National Emergency Council, the United States Film Service.

Rules and Regulations

The following rules and regulations for the United States Film Service are hereby prescribed:
1. The functions and duties of the United States Film Service shall be to coordinate the activities of the several departments and agencies which relate to the production or distribution of motion picture films; to maintain a film library of governmental and other film subjects of interest and educational value to educational and institutional organizations and other groups, and to exchange films with such organizations and groups; to distribute and exhibit such motion picture films; to act as consultants to governmental, educational and foundation organizations on motion pictures; and to produce motion pictures in conjunction with other Federal agencies at the direction and with the approval of the Executive Director of the National Emergency Council.
2. The Director of the United States Film Service shall be responsible for the performance of the aforesaid duties and functions and shall render monthly reports to the Executive Director of the National Emergency

Council, summarizing the activities and operations of the United States Film Service.

3. All appointments of personnel in the United States Film Service shall be approved by the Executive Director of the National Emergency Council, or in his absence by the Executive Officer.

4. All salaries in the United States Film Service shall be fixed in accordance with the classifications under Executive Order No. 6746 insofar as practicable and shall be subject to the approval of the Executive Director of the National Emergency Council.

5. The locations of the offices and physical equipment of the United States Film Service shall be designated by the Executive Director of the National Emergency Council and changes in location shall be approved by the Executive Director.

6. The personnel of the United States Film Service shall be governed by the same regulations as to hours of work, sick and annual leave and other employment conditions as have been promulgated for the administration of the National Emergency Council.

7. In accordance with the existing rules and regulations of the National Emergency Council, all outgoing official mail of the United States Film Service shall be subject to the approval of the Executive Director.

8. All information which is to be printed or mimeographed for distribution by the United States Film Service shall be approved by the Executive Director of the National Emergency Council or his designated subordinate.

9. After approval by the Director of the United States Film Service, all requests for supplies and equipment, travel authorizations, and other expenditures shall be submitted in writing to the Executive Officer of the National Emergency Council for his approval. The existing procurement facilities of the National Emergency Council shall be utilized.

Approved August 13, 1938.

LOWELL MELLETT
The Executive Director

APPENDIX E

LETTER from President Franklin D. Roosevelt to Lowell Mellett, director, National Emergency Council, September 20, 1938

September 20, 1938
MY DEAR DIRECTOR:

I am gratified by your advice that the United States Film Service has been established as a division of the National Emergency Council under the authority of my letter of August 13, 1938, and that it already has

207

begun the coordination of the motion picture activities of the Federal Government.

In the furtherance of this work I am sure you will receive the complete cooperation of the heads of the several departments and agencies. In my judgment this cooperation should develop a system of minimum standards of quality in the motion pictures which the Federal Government produces, exhibits and distributes.

In this connection, it is desirable that certain minimum requirements be included in all of the motion picture contracts into which the Federal Government may enter. The United States Film Service should examine all such contracts prior to their signing and provide the contracting representatives of the Government with a clearing approval of the many technical points involved.

Likewise, it seems to me desirable that the scripts for all motion pictures to be produced by the various agencies of the Federal Government should be examined by the United States Film Service and the agencies given the benefit of its constructive and technical criticism. A clearance of these scripts through the United States Film Service should tend to improve the pictures, prevent wastage, and effect very real economies in production.

On many occasions, Federal Government personnel and property are used in the production of commercial motion pictures. It would seem desirable that the United States Film Service, in advance of production of such pictures, should examine the parts of the scenarios that involve Government participation and give motion picture producers the benefit of expert Government consultation.

I know you always will bear in mind that the production, exhibition and distribution of pictures by the Federal Government is in no way to compete with commercial films. It is, however, a legitimate function of the Government to give information about the work of the Government which otherwise would not be available to the public. This bears, in effect, the same relationship in films to private producers as the publishing of informational pamphlets and reports bears to private publishers of books, magazines and newspapers.

Sincerely yours,

FRANKLIN D. ROOSEVELT

APPENDIX F

LETTER from President Franklin D. Roosevelt to John Studebaker, commissioner of education, July 1, 1939

July 1, 1939

MY DEAR COMMISSIONER:

On August 13, 1938, I directed the Executive Director of the National

Emergency Council to coordinate the production, distribution and exhibition of motion pictures dramatizing certain aspects of the work relief program, in order that those functions might most effectively and economically serve the purposes for which the functions were instituted. Under the authority of that letter, and of my letter dated September 20, 1938, the United States Film Service was established as a division of the National Emergency Council for the purpose of coordinating the Motion Picture Activities of the Federal Government.

The Film Service was instructed (in order that all proposed pictures to be produced by departments or establishments of the Government might be improved, wastage prevented, and real economies in production effected) to develop a system of minimum standards of quality in motion pictures produced, exhibited and distributed by the Federal Government; to see to it that these requirements were included in all motion picture contracts into which establishments of the Government might desire to enter; to examine all such contracts prior to their execution, and provide the contacting representatives of the Government with a clearing approval of the many technical points involved; and to examine all scripts (which should be cleared through it) for such proposed motion pictures and provide the several establishments with the benefit of constructive technical and professional criticism. It is my further desire, as indicated in my letter of September 20, 1938, that the Film Service examine in advance of production, scripts or portions thereof which may be used by private commercial producers who in connection with such scripts, are utilizing Federal property or the services of Federal personnel. Such examination is desirable in order to furnish such producers with the benefit of Government consultation.

During the past year, the Film Service has instituted a clearance service for films produced by the Government, whereby users of such films can write to one agency and receive information and bookings for classroom, educational and informational use. The Film Service has prepared a directory of United States Films and other material advising and informing schools and the public concerning the production, distribution and use of Government Motion Pictures; and, pursuant to its original objectives, has acted as a consultative agency to the various Government departments and establishments, and to non-Federal organizations interested in the production of motion pictures which involved the use of Federal property or personnel. At this time, the Film Service has in production four motion pictures, two of which are closely related to the work relief program, and two of which deal with separate product phases of American agriculture.

By Section 201 (a) of Reorganization Plan, No. II, prepared under the provisions of the Reorganization Act of 1939, I transferred the functions of the United States Film Service to the Federal Security Agency, to be administered therefore in the Office of Education. This transfer was made in view of the fact that the functions of the Film Service appeared clearly to be a part of the educational activities of the Government, and should, therefore, be consolidated with similar activities being carried on in the Office of Education. It is my desire that the functions of the Film Service specified above should be continued. I direct, therefore, that there be established in the Federal Security Agency, effective July 1, 1939, a division to be known as the United States Film Service, to be administered in the Office of Education under the direction and supervision of the Administrator of the Federal Security Agency. All the powers, functions and duties specified in this letter will hereafter be exercised by the United States Film Service; and there is hereby transferred to it all the personnel, property, records, contracts and equipment of the United States Film Service of the National Emergency Council.

I have been informed that the Administrator of the Federal Works Administration and the Secretary of Agriculture feel that the completion and distribution by the Film Service of the two motion pictures related to the work relief program which it now has in production are necessary to help effectuate their programs in dealing with the problem of unemployment. I direct, therefore, that the program of production and distribution of these pictures be continued. For this project I am approving an expenditure of $168,500 (Federal Works Agency: WPA, $91,800; Federal Emergency Administrator of Public Works, $60,000, and Department of Agriculture: Farm Security Administration, $16,700.) This project shall be subject to the restrictions and limitations of the Acts from which the funds are derived.

I know that you will always bear in mind that the production, distribution and exhibition of pictures of the Federal Government are in no way to compete with commercial films. It is my belief, however, that it is a legitimate function of the Government to furnish information which would otherwise not be made available to the public, concerning the work of the Government. In effect, the exercise of this function will bear the same relationship to commercial film producers as the publication of informational pamphlets and reports of the Government bears to commercial publishers of books, magazines and newspapers.

Sincerely yours,

Franklin D. Roosevelt

APPENDIX G

PORTION of a letter from Pare Lorentz to Louis Gruenberg containing instructions for the musical score for *The Fight for Life*

. . . .

Every scene was directed to metronome and for the dramatic effect the music must start exactly with the film. From the moment we see the city hospital until the baby is born the beat of the music must not vary and there must be no change in instrumentation sufficient enough to be noticeable. The conception in direction was that we would have the mother's heartbeat two beats in one with the accent on the first one with the echo exactly one and a half times as fast and without an accent. Factually a beat of one hundred a minute with a fetal heartbeat of exactly one hundred fifty a minute. The picture will not be cut with this precision, but the music must have this precision, inasmuch as the nurses and doctors were directed within these tempos. Then we have a transition. The minute the child is born the baby's fluttering heart dominates the beat, so this transition, except for any passage you may like, a trumpet cry, a crescendo, any device you may wish to use for the birth pain, is merely a cue for a different beat. Within half a minute the doctor discovers the woman is dying. Again the film is directed and cut to a specific time. The heart is pounding to hang on, the dramatic change in the score is that suddenly the mother's heart again takes over. The slower beat surges under the baby's heartbeat, and instead of growing weaker musically the heart grows in volume, if slowing in tempo. It goes Bang BANG *BANG*! and death is a sudden cessation of that pulsing beat and we have only the baby's counterpoint sound to help over our intern until he walks into the corridor and starts for the street. The minute our intern walks out of the delivery room suddenly under the one drum we start almost an echo, a far-off sound. It is a slow time with a deliberate off-beat. It's a hot, crowded saloon with ten-cent gin. It's wanton, weary, bedeviled men and women. I feel, then, that we start one piano under the intern, that we start another piano as he walks out of the hospital. Now here the words create a symphonic pattern. The words themselves carry the meaning and tempo then. If the music attempts to narrate the city, to interpret it, then the music and the picture will overwhelm my dialogue.

. . . .

(Transcribed from *"Lorentz on Film,"* Program III.)

Appendix H

Bulletin from United Parents Associations, New York City, Inc.

The Motion Picture Commission calls your particular attention to:
Pare Lorentz's

The Fight for Life

This is a stirring and eloquent film produced with tremendous power and effectiveness depicting the fight of the medical profession to save mothers and unborn children from the disease-breeding filth of the slums.

The picture was produced and directed for the United States Film Service by Pare Lorentz who gave us *The Plow That Broke the Plains* and *The River.* Now he offers this powerful and provocative film which no parent can afford to miss. If you are interested in slum conditions, questions of health, and other basic social problems, then you *must* see this outstanding picture now playing.

Special group rates can be arranged in blocks of fifty tickets or more. Inquire at the office.

Print a notice of this film in your local publication.

A. M. Bush, *Chairman*
Motion Picture Commission

Appendix I

Proposals for an Inter-American Film Program submitted by George Gercke on August 16, 1939

United States Film Service

The considerations which led to the recommendation and adoption of an Inter-American film program last year remain equally valid this year. It would seem in fact to be even more desirable today that the unique opportunities for the interchange of ideas inherent in the motion picture medium be made available concurrently with the development and application of the Good Neighbor policies.

The proposals for a film program are thus re-submitted to the Committee for consideration without essential change in objectives or methods of achieving them. It may be noted, however, that an increase of $20,000 is proposed for certain production activities, resulting from studies developed during the year. This amount would cover the material already available in the various government agencies, and the acquisition of addi-

212

tional footage through purchase or other arrangements from producers in the United States and in the other Republics.

The proposals may thus be grouped as follows:

I. Production

    (a) Editing, titling, rescoring, recording, re-recording, etc., in English, Spanish and Portuguese versions, on the basis of six 3-reel pictures or their equivalents, from material already available or to be acquired $50,000.

    (b) Production of one new picture on the American Republics for circulation primarily in the United States   50,000.

    (c) Production of one new picture on the United States for circulation primarily in the other American Republics   50,000.

                  Total $150,000.

II. Distribution

    Development and maintenance of a film library and exchange for serving all the American Republics with films, still photos, study guides, exhibits, and other materials employed in visual education, including technical assistance; employment of the services of a head of the library and exchange, experienced in the motion picture field and able to formulate and direct policy and procedure under this program; and funds for travel, research, training, and other related requirements   30,000.

          Total cost of program $180,000.

The foregoing estimates are predicated upon the assumption that the United States Film Service, with an operating organization regularly engaged in motion picture activity in behalf of government agencies and the public, will administer this program as part of its general program.

The Film Service would appreciate the opportunity of presenting to the Committee at a later date proposals for the inauguration of preliminary studies and research prior to July 1, 1940, for the purpose of facilitating the introduction and operation of the general program on that date.

APPENDIX J

Essential data on the Films of Merit

The Plow That Broke the Plains (1936)

Production: Resettlement Administration Film Unit, Pare Lorentz in charge.

Direction, Script, and Editing: Pare Lorentz
Photography: Paul Strand, Ralph Steiner, Leo Hurwitz, Paul Ivano
Music: Virgil Thomson
Conductor: Alexander Smallens
Narrator: Thomas Chalmers
Editorial Assistant: Leo Zochling

The River (1937)

Production: Farm Security Administration Film Unit, Pare Lorentz in
    charge. (The project began under the Resettlement Administration but
    was transferred to the FSA when the RA became a part of it.)
Direction, Script, and Editing: Pare Lorentz
Photography: Floyd Crosby, Willard Van Dyke, Stacy Woodard
Music: Virgil Thomson
Conductor: Alexander Smallens
Narrator: Thomas Chalmers
Editorial Assistant: Lloyd Nosler and Leo Zochling

The Fight for Life (1940)

Production: United States Film Service
Direction, Script, and Editing: Pare Lorentz
Photography: Floyd Crosby
Music: Louis Gruenberg, Joe Sullivan
Conductor: Alexander Smallens
Editorial Assistant: Lloyd Nosler

Power and the Land (1940)

Production: United States Film Service
Direction: Joris Ivens
Script: Edwin Locke
Narration: Stephen Vincent Benét
Photography: Floyd Crosby, Arthur Ornitz
Music: Douglas Moore
Narrator: William P. Adams
Editor: Helen van Dongen

The Land (1941)

Production: United States Film Service, completed under the Agricultural
    Adjustment Administration
Direction and Script: Robert J. Flaherty

214

Photography: Irving Lerner, Douglas Baker, Floyd Crosby, Charles Herbert
Music: Richard Arnell
Narrator: Robert J. Flaherty
Editor: Helen van Dongen

SELECTED BIBLIOGRAPHY

Public Documents

U.S. Congress. *Department of Labor–Federal Security Agency Appropriations Bill, 1941*, 76 Cong., 3 sess., 1940, *Public Law 655*.

————. *Department of Labor–Federal Security Agency Bill, 1941*, 76 Cong., 3 sess., 1940, *Public Resolution 88*.

————. *Emergency Relief Appropriations Act, 1939*, 76 Cong., 1 sess., 1939, *Public Resolution 24*.

U.S. *Congressional Record*, 74 Cong., 2 sess., 1936, LXXX, Pt. 6; 76 Cong., 1 sess., 1939, LXXXIV, Pt. 7; 76 Cong., 3 sess., 1940, LXXXVI, Pt. 5.

U.S. Department of Agriculture. *Farmer's Bulletin 1825*, 1937.

————. *Little Waters*, 1935.

U.S. House of Representatives. *First Deficiency Appropriations Bill for 1937*, 75 Cong., 2 sess., 1936.

————. *Work Relief and Relief Appropriations Act, 1940*, 76 Cong., 1 sess., 1939. *Joint Resolution 326*.

————, Appropriations Subcommittee. *Department of Labor–Federal Security Agency Appropriations Bill, 1941*, 76 Cong., 3 sess., 1940, *House Report 1833*.

————. *Department of Labor–Federal Security Agency Appropriations Bill, 1941*, 76 Cong., 3 sess., 1940, *House Report 2186*.

————. *Hearings on Department of Labor–Federal Security Agency Appropriations Bill, 1941*, 76 Cong., 3 sess., 1940.

————. *Hearings on Work Relief and Relief Appropriations Act, 1940*, 76 Cong., 1 sess., 1939.

216

————. *Work Relief and Relief Appropriations Act, 1940*, 76 Cong., 1 sess., 1939, *House Report 833.*

U.S. National Emergency Council, U.S. Film Service. *Study Guide: The Plow That Broke the Plains.* n.d.

————. *Study Guide: The River.* n.d.

U.S. Senate, Appropriations Committee. *Hearings on Department of Labor–Federal Security Agency Appropriations Bill, 1941*, 76 Cong., 3 sess., 1940, *Report 1487.*

————. *Hearings on Work Relief and Public Works Appropriations Act, 1940*, 76 Cong., 1 sess., 1939.

Kansas State Board of Agriculture. *Soil Erosion by Wind.* Bulletin. Topeka, December, 1937.

Reports

Bennett, H. H. *Soils and Security.* Washington, U.S. Department of Agriculture, Soil Conservation Service, 1937.

U.S. Department of Agriculture. *Report of the Distribution of Department of Agriculture 16mm Motion Pictures for Fiscal 1961.* Washington, U.S. Department of Agriculture, 1962.

U.S. Public Works Administration. *Mississippi Valley Committee Report.* Washington, U.S. Government Printing Office, 1934.

Books

Adam, T. R. *Motion Pictures in Adult Education.* New York, American Association for Adult Education, 1940.

Agee, James, and Walker Evans. *Let Us Now Praise Famous Men.* Boston, Houghton Mifflin Co., 1960.

Albig, William. *Modern Public Opinion.* New York, McGraw-Hill Book Company, Inc., 1956.

Barzun, Jacques, and Henry F. Graff. *The Modern Researcher.* New York: Harcourt, Brace & Co., 1957.

Beard, Charles A., and Mary R. Beard. *America in Midpassage.* New York, The Macmillan Co., 1939.

217

Bluem, A. William. *Documentary in American Television.* New York, Hastings House, Publishers, 1965.

Bluestone, George. *Novels into Film.* Berkeley and Los Angeles, University of California Press, 1961.

de Kruif, Paul. *The Fight for Life.* New York, Harcourt, Brace & Co., 1938.

Devine, John. *Films as an Aid in Training Public Employees.* Chicago, Public Administration Service, 1937.

Ernst, Morris L., and Pare Lorentz. *Censored: The Private Life of the Movie.* New York: Jonathan Cape & Harrison Smith, 1930.

Film Council of America. *Sixty Years of 16mm Film, 1923–1983.* Evanston, Ill., Film Council of America, 1954.

Fulton, A. R. *Motion Pictures: The Development of an Art from Silent Films to the Age of Television.* Norman, University of Oklahoma Press, 1960.

Gassner, John, and Dudley Nichols. *Twenty Best Film Plays.* New York, Crown Publishers, 1943.

Gaus, John, and Leon Walcott. *Public Administration and the Department of Agriculture.* Chicago, Public Administration Service, 1940.

Griffith, Richard. *The World of Robert Flaherty.* New York, Duell, Sloan & Pierce, 1953.

Hardy, Forsyth (with American notes by Richard Griffith and Mary Losey). *Grierson on Documentary.* New York, Harcourt, Brace & Co., 1947.

Harley, John E. *World-wide Influences of the Cinema.* Los Angeles, University of Southern California Press, 1940.

Hoover, Kathleen, and John Cage. *Virgil Thomson, His Life and Music.* New York and London, Thomas Youseloff, 1957.

Jackson, John Henry, ed. "John Steinbeck's *The Grapes of Wrath,*" *The Grapes of Wrath.* New York, Limited Editions Club, 1940.

Jacobs, Lewis. *The Rise of the American Film.* New York, Harcourt, Brace & Co., 1939.

Knight, Arthur. *The Liveliest Art: A Panoramic History of the*

Movies. New York, The New American Library of World Literature, Inc., 1939.

Kracauer, Siegfried. *Theory of Film.* New York, Oxford University Press, 1960.

Lord, Russell, and Kate Lord. *Forever the Land.* New York, Harper & Brothers, 1950.

Lorentz, Pare. *The River.* New York: Stackpole Sons, 1938.

Manvell, Roger, and John Huntley. *The Technique of Film Music.* London, Focal Press, 1957; U.S. distributors: New York, Hastings House Publishers, 1957.

McCamy, James. *Government Publicity.* Chicago, University of Chicago Press, 1939.

Moley, Raymond. *The Hays Office.* New York, The Bobbs-Merrill Co., 1945.

Reisz, Karel. *The Technique of Film Editing.* London, Focal Press, 1961; U.S. distributors: New York, Hastings House Publishers, 1961.

Rotha, Paul. *Documentary Film.* 3d ed. rev. and enl. London, Faber & Faber Ltd., 1956; U.S. distributors: New York, Hastings House Publishers, 1956.

————, and Richard Griffith. *The Film till Now.* 3d ed. rev. and enl. New York, Twayne Publishers, Inc., 1960.

Stefferud, Alfred, ed. *After a Hundred Years: The Yearbook of Agriculture, 1962.* Washington, U.S. Government Printing Office, 1962.

Taylor, Deems. *A Pictorial History of the Movies.* Rev. and enl. New York, Simon & Schuster, 1950.

Thorp, Margaret Farrand. *America at the Movies.* London, Faber & Faber Limited, 1946.

Tugwell, Rexford G. *The Democratic Roosevelt.* Garden City, Doubleday & Co., Inc., 1957.

Vidor, King. *A Tree Is a Tree.* New York, Harcourt, Brace & Co., 1953.

Waldron, Gloria. *The Information Film.* New York, Columbia University Press, 1949.

Periodical and Newspaper Articles

Note: Many of the periodical and newspaper sources referred to in this book were found in the personal files of Pare Lorentz and in the files of the Museum of Modern Art.

Barnes, Howard. "The River," *New York Herald Tribune*, February 6, 1938.

Black, C. M. "He Serves Up America," *Collier's*, August 3, 1940, 22.

Boehnel, William. "Best Films," *New York World-Telegram*, December 28, 1940.

———. "The Fight for Life," *New York World-Telegram*, March 7, 1940.

———. "New Film Tells Story of Floods," *New York World-Telegram*, January 29, 1938.

Bowen, George Rothwell. "Poor Eat Garbage in Film," *New York Journal American*, March 22, 1940.

Bromley, Dorothy Dunbar. *New York Post*, March 15, 1940.

Calverton, V. F. "Cultural Barometer," *Current History*, April, 1938, 55.

Churchill, Douglas. "Caught on the Wing in Hollywood," *New York Times*, April 24, 1938.

Crowther, Bosley. "Grim Reality Note," *New York Times*, April 7, 1940.

———. "Lorentz Experiments," *New York Times*, March 10, 1940.

———. *New York Times*, May 5, 1940.

Defoe, Allen Roy. "Your Baby," *New York Journal American*, April 30, 1940.

———. "Your Baby," *New York Journal American*, May 1, 1940.

De Voto, Bernard. "The River," *Saturday Review of Literature*, April 9, 1938.

"Documented Dust," *Time*, May 25, 1936, 47–48.

"Dust Storm Film," *Literary Digest*, May 16, 1936, 22.

Ellis, Peter. "The Plow That Broke the Plains," *New Theatre*, July, 1936.

Englander, Rose A. " 'Fight for Life' Fails to Scare Women," *New York World-Telegram*, March 22, 1940.

Evans, Raymond. "USDA Motion Picture Service, 1908–1943," *Business Screen*, Vol. V, No. 1 (1943).

"Federal Film Hit," *Business Week*, February 19, 1938, 35.

"Federal Movie Furor," *Business Week*, July 11, 1936, 14.

"The Fight for Life" (reviews), *Life*, March 18, 1940; *Look*, March 12, 1940; *Magazine of Art*, April, 1940, 323–24; *National Board of Review Magazine*, March, 1940, 1; *Scholastic*, April 1, 1940, 34; *Time*, March 25, 1940, 92; *Variety*, March 6, 1940.

Folliard, Edward T. "Tugwell's Farmer's Lot Is Sad Compared to Soviet Film Idyll," *Washington Post*, May 11, 1936.

Franklin, Jay [John Franklin Carter], "We the People" [syndicated column], October 29, 1937.

Grenfell, Joyce. "Broadcasting," *London Sunday Observer*, August 21, 1938.

Griffith, Richard. "A Big Year for Fact Films," *New York Times*. September 17, 1939.

Gross, Ben. "Listening In," *New York Daily News*, May 22, 1938.

Hartung, Philip T. "Power and the Land," *Commonweal*, December 20, 1940, 232.

Haythorne, Reed N. "Uncle Sam Busy Lenser," *American Cinematographer*, September, 1937, 398.

Hearon, Fanning. "Interior's Division of Motion Pictures," *School Life*, September, 1937, 6–7.

Hoellering, Franz. "Films," *The Nation*, March 16, 1940, 372.

Howe, Hartley. "U.S. Film Service Presents," *U.S. Camera*, June–July, 1940.

Hughes, Spike. "There's Another Job to Be Done," *London Daily Herald*, August 17, 1938.

Jenkins, C. A. "Progress on the Thames," *New York Times*, June 19, 1938.

"Job to be Done," *World Film News*, September, 1938, 219.

Le Jeune, C. A. "Films of the Week," *London Observer*, June 5, 1938.

Levin, Meyer. "The Candid Cameraman," *Esquire*, January, 1938, 177.

Lord, Russell. "Flaherty Rediscovers America," *Land*, Vol. I, No. 1 (1941), 67.

Lorentz, Pare. "The Plow That Broke the Plains," *McCall's*, July, 1936.

Lorentz, Pare. "The River," *McCall's*, May, 1937.

McEvoy, J. P. "Young Man with a Camera," *Reader's Digest*, August, 1940, 73–76.

Mercey, Arch. "Films by American Governments," *Films*, Summer, 1940.

"The Movie No One Will See," *Christian Century*, June 3, 1936, 788–89.

Nugent, Frank. "One Down, Two Doubled," *New York Times*, February 13, 1938.

————. "Pare Lorentz Again Goes to Fact for His Drama in His New Film, 'The Fight for Life' at the Belmont," *New York Times*, March 7, 1940.

————. "Raw Deal for the New Deal," *New York Times*, May 24, 1936.

————. "The River," *New York Times*, February 5, 1938.

Oliver, W. E. " 'Fight for Life' Music Ingenious," *Los Angeles Herald Express*, June 26, 1940.

Pearson, Drew. "Washington Merry-Go-Round," *Worcester Gazette and Post*, April 13, 1940.

Platt, David. " 'The River' Indicts Private Power Utilities," *Daily Worker*, February 7, 1938.

Player, William O., Jr. "Cut," *New York Post*, May 23, 1940.

"The Plow That Broke the Plains" (reviews), *National Board of Review Magazine*, June, 1936; *Variety*, May 12, 1936.

"Power and the Land" (reviews), *Magazine of Art*, January, 1941, 43; *New York Post*, December 11, 1940; *Time*, October 14, 1940, 114; *Variety*, October 2, 1940.

Pryor, Thomas M. "Uncle Sam: Film Producer," *New York Times*, July 12, 1936.

"The River," *National Board of Review Magazine*, November, 1937.

Rotha, Paul. "The Outlook for American Documentary Films," *New York Times*, May 1, 1938.

Seldes, Gilbert. "The River," *Scribner's*, January, 1938, 67.

Sher, Jack. "The River," *Detroit Free Press*, June 30, 1940.

Sterling, Philip. "Following 'The River,'" *New York Times*, October 15, 1939.

Strauss, Theodore. "The Giant Shimmies down the Beanstalk," *New York Times*, October 12, 1941.

Tazelaar, Margaret. "On the Screen," *New York Herald Tribune*, May 26, 1936.

Time, May 6, 1940, 15.

Tucker, Ray. "News behind the News," *New London Day*, March 23, 1940.

White, William L. "Pare Lorentz," *Scribner's*, January, 1939.

Woolfert, Ira. "Talk of Hollywood," *Baltimore Evening Sun*, October 29, 1940.

"WPA: Pathé Wins Film Contract as 'New Deal Goes Hollywood,'" *Newsweek*, August 15, 1937, 18.

223

INDEX

227

The text for *Pare Lorentz and the Documentary Film* has been set on the Linotype in 12-point Bodoni. Designed by Giambattista Bodoni at the beginning of the nineteenth century, Bodoni was the first and most successful attempt to break completely with the old-style tradition and create a new and different face.

The paper on which the book is printed bears the watermark of the University of Oklahoma Press and is designed for an effective life of at least three hundred years.